Gray's Wild Game & Fish Cookbook
A MENU COOKBOOK

Gray's Wild Game & Fish Cookbook

A MENU COOKBOOK

By Rebecca Gray with Cintra Reeve

DOWN EAST BOOKS

Camden, Maine

Text copyright © 1983, 1986, 1995 by Rebecca C. Gray.
All rights reserved.
Cover illustration © 1995 by Chris Van Dusen
ISBN 0-89272-354-8
Library of Congress Catalog Card Number 94-80008
Color separation: Four Colour Imports, Louisville, Ky.
Printing: Capital City Press, Inc., Montpelier, Vt.

5   4   3   2   1

Down East Books / Camden, Maine

Contents

Preface

S everal years ago, Ed and I took our children to live with another American family in a chateau in the Loire Valley of France. It was for only a couple of weeks, but it was the first time I had the opportunity to live in France, and rural France at that. We quickly fell into a very French routine of one of us rising early to go purchase the day's fresh-made bread, returning to eat croissants and drink cappuccino, and to linger over breakfast discussing what to look for at market and what we would eat that day. We never planned or bought food for more than one day at a time, and we spent nearly 80 percent of our day either preparing for or eating a meal. And it was wonderful. I believe we fell easily into this routine because the French philosophy of weaving food into the pattern of one's daily life is not conceptually foreign to us. Indeed, it should not be foreign to anyone who hunts and fishes, for in its most ancient and simplistic application that is what hunting and fishing is all about—a day devoted to the procurement of dinner.

When I wrote *Gray's Wild Game Cookbook* in 1983 and *Gray's Fish Cookbook* in 1986 I tried to impart a bit of my lifestyle into each book—a philosophy of life that emphasized entwining hunting, fishing, and food together in order to produce great wild cuisine. In the game cookbook I tried to show why cooking wild can be exhilarating, while acknowledging that at times it can be intimidating, too. As I say in the preface, "A chicken's life and diet is highly predictable and rather boring; so is eating or cooking a chicken. . . . Wild is what the game animal's life is; a partridge may have feasted on wild grapes, a Canada goose summered in the clean air of Labrador, and the ducks nibbled on Minnesota's wild rice. The duck may also have nearly starved to death on the Ipswich mud flats and been forced to eat a meager diet of crustaceans. All of these elements affect flavor and, for the most part, remain a mystery to the chef and the guests until the tasting reveals it." The "surprise" element is what makes it exhilarating when you make it work and intimidating when you don't. It also is what leads a good cook to experimentation, flexibility, and creativity—good attributes to have in life, not just in cooking.

In the fish cookbook I explained in the preface that, "To become engrossed in the fun of experimentation, enjoy familiarity with the fish, to respect him is to also learn how to focus and concentrate on fishing. . . . Cooking is not different than fishing in this respect. . . . Taking the time, having the patience, caring about the preparation of the fish is what makes the difference. I believe you very literally taste the difference in a meal when a cook has been thoughtful and focused on the food." If you learn to experiment, learn to respect the fish, and can totally focus while fishing and while cooking the fish, then you will have the greatest fun and cook the best meal. I am not particularly a great cooker of fish, but rather a proficient blender of good days of fishing with good fish meals.

Each of my previous books divulged some of my convictions about fishing and hunting and food. And now this new book adds one more piece to the ethic. As more and more of our trips seem to encourage the pursuit of both hunting and fishing at the same time, it seems only natural that there should be a combined volume of both books.

When asked why I wanted to "write" this book, I must respond as Ed Gray always did when asked why he started *Gray's Sporting Journal*, "Because I wanted to read it." I wanted this book, a single book that had all of the necessary parts of the two hardback books but added a new element. This book combines lifestyle components, and then some. I wanted a book that was easy to use, easy to take on a trip, easy to give away to a worthy host, easy to take afield. So did many of my readers, and, of course, that is the best reason to produce any book. So here it is. Dedicated to all the wonderful people who faithfully read my columns in *Gray's Sporting Journal* and now continue to read me elsewhere.

Venison

A number of years ago, our well-known writer friend, Charley Waterman, came to visit us. So knowledgeable, so lucid, so funny, he was the ideal for the role of hunter/writer's mentor. Not that I was either a hunter or a writer, but at that point I sure aspired to be. I could easily have spent every waking moment beside Charley listening to his stories and never tired of it. Driving through the wilds of the Boston city streets, I picked his brain on everything from the anti-hunters and the rationale for killing to how a husband goes about teaching a wife to enjoy hunting. Wishing to savor the subject and perhaps take notes, I had saved my favorite topic for last: cooking game. What was Charley's favorite recipe, how long did he and Debie cook a duck, how long did they hang their venison? It all came spewing forth to get the simple reply, "We don't do much of anything to our game, just cook it."

Penny Reneson had exemplified for me much about how to be the wife of a habitual hunter: when to consider calling the forest ranger if he's over-due; when to assert your own desires to hunt; when to stay at home with the children—all those moments of quandary. Penny seemed instinctively to know how to deal with all of them, and I admired her for the ability. We rode to a Ducks Unlimited dinner and I questioned her on the subject I thought would be explosive: game cooking. "We don't do much of anything to our game, just cook it."

Of course, when pressed, both Charley and Penny had some quite definite ideas about game cooking, but nonetheless there was a message to be had: The best result is when you don't do anything but cook it. And, however incongruous a statement that might seem in a cookbook such as this, it is true. It is also why we have tried to keep our recipes and menus simple. Our accent in this book is on the ingredients, not on the complexity of the recipes. But in the acquisition of ingredients, we have neither sought simplicity nor spared the reader's time or money.

The 1982 hunting season was the first in many years that we were forced to hunt ducks without a dog. Our five-year-old golden retriever had died suddenly and mysteriously of a kidney ailment during the summer months, leaving us without a trained dog for duck fetching. Quite cleverly, I simultaneously became pregnant with our third child and too fat to wear waders. Ed was left to face duck season by himself. One morning, he arrived home later than usual—one black duck in hand and slightly chagrined. He explained that he had had to strip on the marsh and dive into the icy water in order to retrieve the beyond-wader-reach bird. We do go to great lengths. Cold and wet and fatigue and time and life and death are forever part of it.

It is important for the cook to remember what has gone before. To become cavalier is at best tactless. Ordering up the good green olive oil in advance, making the veal stock from scratch, watering the sage plant every week, spending the extra dollars on liqueurs—all that is our part of it.

And if it seems at times to be too much for too little, just be happy you don't have to jump naked into icy water during October to swim for the duck.

In the olden days (as in the era of Robin Hood), the word *venison* referred to any game, not just deer. We have not been that liberal with the word, but we do use it here in its broader sense to cover all members of the deer family: caribou, moose, elk, antelope, white-tail, and mule deer. (This is a cook's taxonomy, not a biologist's.) So all of the venison recipes in this chapter are applicable to these animals. Some slight adjustments in quantities of accompanying ingredients and cooking times should be made to accommodate a larger-size (e.g., moose, elk) cut of venison.

Venison Burgers with Chateaubriand Butter
Fried Bread
Vegetable Salad
Fresh Fruit

Serves four

Venison burgers not only are delightful to eat but often your best alternative for tougher cuts or those damaged in the field. If the outfitter has not butchered the deer for you and you fancy doing it yourself, you may find it difficult getting the meat ground into burger. If you are a city-dweller and hunting refers to what shoppers do at Bloomingdale's or Macy's rather than something that goes on in the woods, chances are you will not find a butcher willing to grind the meat for you. Even the *la-di-da* butchers who have gouged you for years and theoretically owe you a favor are bound by the state sanitary codes and don't like to risk any infringement of the law. Rural butchers are likelier to be able to handle your request to grind the meat and add the pork fat necessary to create burger. If you are going to try to grind it yourself, here are two suggestions: (1) Try to select meat that is free of any fat or sinew. (2) A food processor works better than a hand-crank meat grinder. I once spent a tearful evening trying to jam big chunks of deer leg meat through a meat grinder. It simply did not work. In general, grinding meat at home is tedious and better done in small batches or left to the butcher or outfitter. (For more on grinding, see page 283.)

VENISON BURGERS WITH CHATEAUBRIAND BUTTER

                1 cup white wine
                3 shallots, minced
                1 handful fresh parsley, chopped
                1 tsp. chervil
                1 tsp. tarragon
                1 cup veal stock (see page 27)
                1 cup (2 sticks) unsalted butter
                  Salt and pepper
                2 lbs. chopped or ground venison

In a small saucepan, combine the wine, shallots, parsley, chervil, and tarragon and bring to a boil. Reduce heat and simmer very, very slowly until the liquid has been reduced by half. Add the stock and continue to reduce until ½ cup liquid remains. Allow to cool. Whip the butter till soft and add the cooled wine-and-stock mixture. Season with salt and pepper and wrap in plastic wrap. Shape into a log and freeze 1 hour or overnight. Form the meat into patties and cook over a charcoal grill. Slice several pats of the butter for each burger and serve on top. (The remainder of the butter can be used in soup or as a nice sandwich spread. Keeps 1 month in the freezer.)

FRIED BREAD (see page 132)

VEGETABLE SALAD

                1 14-oz. can artichoke hearts
                ½ lb. fava beans (can be purchased
                    fresh from specialty produce
                    stores)
                ½ lb. fresh peas
                ½ lb. new potatoes

Drain, rinse, and quarter the artichoke hearts. Shell, peel, and blanch the fava beans. Plunge into cold water. Shell and blanch the peas. Plunge into cold water. When both fava beans and peas are cool, combine with the artichokes. Cook the little potatoes in enough salted boiling water to just cover them for 20 minutes. Let cool and then quarter them. Add the potatoes to the other vegetables and then toss with an herb vinaigrette.

Saddle of Venison
Potatoes and Porcini
Braised Fennel
Clafoutis

Serves four

It took me years to find out what was meant by a "saddle of venison." I had heard of a rack or a haunch, but never a saddle. A saddle of venison is the equivalent of a standing rib roast in beef. It is the middle section of chops left intact to make the premier of roasts. At the point of butchering, the saddle can cause the very worst consternation. Whether 'tis nobler to wade through a series of delicious meals of venison chops or to go for the glut of an incredible roast. . . . If you go for the glut, we suggest the following recipe:

SADDLE OF VENISON

¼ cup olive oil
1 tbsp. lemon juice
5 to 6 lbs. saddle of venison
      Enough pork lard to cover the
        saddle
1 tsp. salt
1 tbsp. crushed juniper berries
1 onion, sliced
5 tbsp. unsalted butter
¼ cup red wine vinegar
      Sprinkle of flour
1 lemon

Combine the oil and lemon juice and rub over the meat. Let it sit for a couple of hours. Lard with 2-inch strips of pork lard in even rows. Mix the salt and crushed juniper berries together and rub all over the meat. Sauté the onion in 1 tablespoon of the butter and spread on the bottom of a roasting pan. Place the meat on top. Add the vinegar to the pan. Melt the remaining butter and baste the meat with it. Roast in a preheated oven at 350° about 1 hour. Then sprinkle the lard with flour and baste with pan drippings. Bake until the lard is crispy.

Julienne the lemon rind and blanch 5 minutes in boiling water. Combine rind with the juices from the roasting pan and serve on top of the sliced meat.

POTATOES AND PORCINI

  2 oz. dried wild mushrooms
       (dried porcini from a
       gourmet shop is usually
       used, but fresh morels are
       best, if available)
  ½ cup heavy cream
  1 small garlic clove, minced
  3 tbsp. unsalted butter
      Salt and pepper
  2 lbs. boiling potatoes

Rinse the dried mushrooms quickly in cold water, using a strainer so any grit will be removed. Chop coarsely and put in a saucepan with the heavy cream. Simmer very slowly until the cream is reduced to ¼ cup and aromatic with the mushrooms. Sauté the garlic in 1 tablespoon of the butter for a moment and add it to the mushroom/cream mixture. Season with salt and pepper and set aside.

Peel the potatoes and cut them into ¼-inch slices. Rinse them twice in cold water, letting them sit 10 to 15 minutes each time. Strain and dry potatoes. Butter a shallow earthenware casserole. Put in one layer of potatoes and then one layer of mushroom mixture. Make the last layer potatoes and dot with remaining 2 tablespoons of butter. Season with salt and pepper and bake 20 minutes in a 425° oven.

BRAISED FENNEL

  4 heads fennel
  4 tbsp. unsalted butter
  1 cup veal stock (see page 27)
      Salt and pepper
  ½ lb. Gruyère cheese, grated

Trim, core, and halve the fennel heads. Butter a baking dish and arrange the fennel in it. Add the stock and salt and pepper and cover with buttered wax paper. Bake in a preheated oven at 400° for 30 minutes. Remove the wax paper and continue cooking for 10 minutes. The stock should have reduced some. Now add the grated cheese and bake until it is melted and brown.

CLAFOUTIS

½ cup flour
¾ cup milk
1 tsp. vanilla extract (or grated
 lemon or orange rind)
 Pinch of salt
2 eggs
¼ cup granulated sugar
1 lb. cherries, pitted (or use any
 good fruit)
 Confectioners' sugar

Combine the flour, milk, vanilla or rind, salt, eggs, and 2 tablespoons of the granulated sugar. Preheat the oven to 375°. Butter an ovenproof serving dish and pour a third of the batter in it. Bake that for 10 minutes. Remove from the oven, add the fruit, and sprinkle with the remaining granulated sugar. Pour in the rest of the batter and continue baking for 30 minutes. Sprinkle with confectioners' sugar and cut into pie-shaped wedges.

Venison Strip Steaks
Fried Potato Skins
Grilled Red Pepper Salad
Strawberry Ice Cream

Serves four

One of the disadvantages of writing a cookbook so strongly stressing technique rather than concoction is that occasionally words simply are not descriptive enough. Such is the case when trying to communicate "doneness" of meat. Cooking time is always approximate in cookbooks, especially where game is concerned, so it should not be regarded as gospel. Try pressing the meat to see if it has a springy texture; then it's done. Wiggle a leg to see if it's loose; then it's done. Or cut into it if you're uncertain (better a slice in it than to serve it too rare or overcooked). Enviable is Cintra's (cooking teacher and co-author) ability to smell doneness. As much as I hate to admit it, experience and using your senses are more reliable guides to determining whether dinner is ready than what is printed in these pages. We have included cooking times only as a general guide for how to gauge the cocktail hour. But always check for doneness.

VENISON STRIP STEAKS

4 thin strip steaks (about ½ lb. each)
2 tbsp. oil
¼ cup cognac
½ cup veal stock (see page 27)
4 tbsp. unsalted butter
16 capers, large ones, packed loosely in brine
Salt and pepper

Pan-fry the steaks in oil a minute or two on each side and remove to a plate. Deglaze the pan with cognac and add the stock. Reduce the liquid to ¼ cup and whisk in the butter. Rinse the capers well and add them to the sauce. Slice the steak, pour the juices into the sauce, and season with salt and pepper. Pour the sauce over the meat.

FRIED POTATO SKINS

    5 potatoes (Idaho or russet)
    3 tbsp. unsalted butter
    ½ tsp. chopped garlic (optional)
       Salt and pepper
    1 tsp. finely chopped parsley

Remove the skin from the potatoes with a potato peeler—or a knife if you wish to retain more of the potato. Fry in the hot butter and garlic until crisp. Sprinkle with salt and the chopped parsley. Season with salt and pepper.

GRILLED RED PEPPER SALAD

2 or 3 red peppers
     1 cup good green olive oil
     2 cloves garlic, peeled

Prepare one day ahead.
Halve the red peppers and remove the seeds. Place them cut-side down on a piece of foil in the broiler and broil 2 to 3 minutes till they are black. (They can also be grilled whole, turning once.) Remove and let cool. Peel off the black skin, remove any seeds, and slice the peppers. Put in a jar with the olive oil and garlic cloves and let stand at least overnight. Toss with lettuce and your favorite vinaigrette. They are good in sandwiches and will last a week.

STRAWBERRY ICE CREAM

    4 egg yolks
    ½ cup granulated sugar
       Pinch of salt
   1½ cups medium cream
    2 tsp. *framboise* liqueur or vanilla extract
    6 cups berries (The ice cream will taste only as
          good as the berries used.)
       Enough ice and salt for the ice cream machine
       Extra berries for garnish

Beat together the egg yolks, sugar, and salt till they are smooth but do not ribbon. Add 1 cup of the cream and mix well. Cook over medium heat, stirring constantly, until the custard thickens. Remove from the heat, strain, and whisk till cool. Add *framboise* or vanilla and chill. Purée the strawberries. Blend with the custard and add the remaining ½ cup of cream.
Churn in ice cream machine according to the manufacturer's directions. Serve with fresh strawberries on top.

Venison Stew
Homemade Pasta
Orange Tart

Serves four

One of the common bonds between those who cook and those who hunt is that both avocations lead to the accumulation of equipment. It is so convenient to have exactly the right little tool to accomplish the task either in the field or in the kitchen. It also could send you to the poorhouse. It is very helpful indeed to own an electric pasta machine, but it is not necessary for making very good homemade pasta. It is very nice to own a choice of three deer rifles, but you can only hunt with one at a time. Use what you already own and upgrade when you know your passions.

VENISON STEW

2	cups red wine
½	cup vinegar
1	onion, sliced
1	carrot, sliced
	Few parsley stems
8	juniper berries
1	tbsp. salt
1	bay leaf
2	crushed cloves
4	sprigs tarragon
3 to 4	lbs. venison stew meat
¼	lb. pancetta, diced
4	tbsp. unsalted butter
1½	cups veal or chicken stock (approximately)
1	tbsp. cornstarch
	Salt and pepper

Make a marinade out of the wine, vinegar, onion, carrot, parsley stems, juniper berries, salt, bay leaf, cloves, and tarragon sprigs, and let the cubed venison sit in it at least overnight.

Drain the marinade from the meat and reserve it. Dry the meat and brown it with the pancetta in butter. Cover about two-thirds with the marinade and stock.

Cover first with foil pressed close to the meat and brought over the sides of the pot, then add a lid and simmer about 1 hour. Test for doneness with a skewer.

Strain the sauce from the meat, discard the bay leaf, and thicken the sauce with cornstarch. Season with salt and pepper and reheat with the meat.

HOMEMADE PASTA

> 2 cups semolina flour
> ½ tsp. salt
> 1½ cups all-purpose flour,
>   for kneading and
>   dusting
> 2 eggs
> 1 tbsp. water
> 1 tbsp. olive oil

Make a mountain of the semolina flour (not the all-purpose) on the countertop, sprinkle the salt on the flour and then make a crater in the mountain. Lightly beat the eggs, water, and oil together and pour into the crater. With a fork, blend the flour into the egg mixture slowly until all the flour is moist, then knead into a small ball. Continue to knead 10 to 20 minutes until the ball, when sliced through the middle, has almost *no* air bubbles. Then place in a plastic bag and put into the refrigerator for at least 1 hour. Cut the ball into six sections. Take one of the sections and knead it for a few minutes. Flatten with a rolling pin and crank through a pasta machine on the widest setting. Fold the pasta and crank it through again. Repeat this five more times. Now put the pasta through each setting on the machine without folding it. Finally, cut the pasta and place on a plate and toss with ½ cup all-purpose flour. Repeat the procedure for the remaining sections of dough.

The pasta may now be left to dry. Of course, dried pasta can be stored, or, after an hour or so, cooked.

ORANGE TART

For pastry:
1 cup flour
1 tsp. salt
½ cup unsalted butter
1 egg yolk
2 tbsp. water

For filling and glaze:
4 to 6 navel oranges (4 if large, 6 if small)
1 cup red currant jelly
2 tsp. grated orange rind

Serve with:
1 cup heavy cream, whipped
2 tsp. Grand Marnier
2 tsp. confectioners' sugar

To make the pastry, combine the flour and salt, add butter in pieces. Blend by pressing butter pieces between thumb and forefingers until in small pieces and incorporating with the flour. With a fork or whisk, mix together the egg yolk and water and add this to the flour mixture. Stir until a dough begins to form. Shape into a ball with your hands and wrap in plastic wrap. Chill until firm (about an hour).

To make the filling, stand each orange on end and, with a sharp knife, cut off the peel and the pith. Then remove each section of orange from remaining membranes with your knife. Drain the sections on a piece of paper towel while you make the tart shell and glaze.

Heat the currant jelly and rind together for 15 minutes then strain out the rind (you may have to reheat the glaze gently before using).

Preheat the oven to 350°. Butter a 10-inch tart pan and roll out the dough and press into the pan. Chill for 15 minutes and then prick with a fork. Line the tart with aluminum foil and fill with beans or pastry weights to prevent the pastry from puffing too much while cooking. Cook 18 to 20 minutes and then remove the foil and beans. With a pastry brush, paint the tart shell with a little of the glaze. Return the tart to the oven until done (about another 10 minutes). Remove the tart shell from the oven and let cool, then carefully slip it out of the pan onto a serving plate. Now arrange the drained orange sections on the tart shell in an overlapping pattern with a rosette in the center. Paint the orange sections with glaze. Whip together the cream, Grand Marnier, and confectioners' sugar and serve with the tart.

Venison Stew with Artichoke Hearts and Sun-Dried Tomatoes
Basil Bread
Green Salad
Custard Oranges

Serves four

One year we received a gift of 50 pounds of butchered venison, already wrapped and frozen. We didn't know the hunters or the outfitter or the butcher or even the source of the the deer. It was the first time I realized how valuable it is to be able to listen to the long, drawn-out tales of how the buck got bagged and dragged before you have to go in the kitchen and cook it. Prior to that, I had always had the privilege of staring glassy-eyed at the hunter while my subconscious soaked up the pertinent details of how big and old the deer was, how clean the shot was, and what type of terrain the deer inhabited. I had been rather mechanical in applying that knowledge to my choice of recipes for the meat (see page 273, "Game Care"). I learned my lesson; I certainly had a hard time figuring out what to do with those 50 pounds of meat to make them tasty. If you can't be there yourself, at least ask a lot of questions.

The following is a recipe I would use for good-quality stew meat, either a neck roast from a large deer or the shank roast from a smaller deer, cut up.

VENISON STEW WITH ARTICHOKE HEARTS AND SUN-DRIED TOMATOES

1½ lbs. venison stew meat	2 14-oz. cans (or 2 boxes frozen) artichoke hearts
4 tbsp. oil	
1 small onion, chopped	1 tbsp. cornstarch
1 small carrot, chopped	6 tbsp. unsalted butter
1 cup veal or chicken stock	Salt and pepper
3 cups good red wine	1 tbsp. chopped parsley
Bouquet garni	1 small garlic clove, finely chopped
½ cup sun-dried tomatoes	
	1 tbsp. grated lemon rind

Brown the meat in the oil and remove from the pot. In the same pot, sauté the onion and carrot. Return the meat to the pot and add the stock and wine. Bring to a boil and add the bouquet garni and sun-dried tomatoes. Soak the canned artichoke hearts for a while in cold water to remove the salty taste (this is unnecessary if they are frozen) and then add them to the pot.

Cover the pan with foil, pressing down so there is no space between the foil and the liquid. Add a lid and simmer about 20 minutes, or until a skewer comes out easily and cleanly from a piece of the meat.

When done, drain the juices into a large skillet and thicken with cornstarch over low heat. Whisk in the butter and season with salt and pepper. Add the meat to the skillet and add the parsley, garlic, and lemon rind. Check for seasoning and serve.

BASIL BREAD (see page 95)

CUSTARD ORANGES

4 large navel oranges
3 egg yolks
⅓ cup granulated sugar
1½ oz. Cointreau
1⅓ cups heavy cream
Cocoa for garnish

Cut off the top of each orange and scoop out the inside. Rinse shells and allow to drain. Beat the egg yolks and sugar together, then add the Cointreau. Now whip 1 cup of the cream until it is stiff. Mix one-third of the whipped cream into the egg yolk mixture, then fold in the remaining whipped cream. Fill each orange shell with the egg-cream mixture and set on a plate in the refrigerator for at least 2 hours. When ready to serve, whip the remaining ⅓ cup cream and put a dollop on each orange top. Dust with cocoa.

Venison with Port
Roast Potatoes
Sautéed Watercress
Peach and Pear Ice with Crystallized Violets

Serves four

VENISON WITH PORT

4 to 5 lbs. saddle of venison
    Pork lard (enough to cover the
      saddle in 2-inch strips)
4 finely chopped carrots
4 finely chopped onions
    A few parsley stems
⅔ cup unsalted butter
2 cups port wine
½ tsp. cinnamon
½ tsp. powdered cloves
    Salt and pepper to taste

Preheat the oven to 500°. Lard the saddle and tie with string to hold in place. Sauté the carrots, onions, and parsley stems in 6 tablespoons of the butter. Spread the vegetables on the bottom of a roasting pan and put the venison on top. Pour the port over it and bake about 10 minutes at 500°. Lower the heat to 400° and continue to roast for another half hour or so, basting with pan juices every 10 minutes.

Remove the meat to a platter, skim off any fat, and, on top of the stove, reduce the liquid to about ½ cup. Add the cinnamon and cloves and whisk in the remaining butter and any juices that might have exuded from the sliced meat. Add salt and pepper to taste and serve the sauce over slices of the meat.

SAUTÉED WATERCRESS

3 bunches watercress
3 to 4 tbsp. unsalted butter
Salt and pepper

Cut each bunch of watercress into 2-inch lengths (the bunches should be cut approximately into thirds). Sauté the watercress in the hot unsalted butter uncovered for a second or two, then cover for 2 minutes. Remove the lid, season with salt, pepper, and a little more butter, and serve.

PEACH AND PEAR ICES WITH CRYSTALLIZED VIOLETS

1½ 12-oz. jars peach jam
2 lbs. ripe peaches
2 pinches of salt
Lemon juice to taste
1½ 12-oz. jars pear jam
2 lbs. ripe pears
Crystallized violets for garnish

Make each ice separately.

Heat the peach jam slowly until it melts. Skin each peach and remove the stone. Slice the peaches and purée in a blender or food processor. Now add the melted jam and purée. Add a pinch of salt and season with lemon juice to taste. Strain into cake tins and cover with plastic wrap. Make sure the wrap is flush with the ice, then cover with foil. Freeze for several hours.

Repeat the process for the pear ice.

They should be served together, quite soft, and garnished with crystallized violets. (Crystallized violets are available in gourmet shops.)

Venison Scallops
Persillade Potatoes
Green Beans
Tarte Tatin

Serves four

VENISON SCALLOPS

3 or 4 hazelnuts (enough for 2 tbsp.
    chopped)
  3 tbsp. oil
    Rind from ¼ orange
8 to 10 venison scallops (Slice ½-inch
    pieces of meat from a good
    cut of roast, such as the eye
    of the round, making sure to
    cut across the grain.)
  ¼ cup Armagnac
  1 cup veal stock (see page 27)
  ¼ cup plus 1 tbsp. unsalted butter
    Salt and pepper

Toast the whole nuts in the oven till they are light brown. Wrap them in a tea towel for 10 minutes to create steam and loosen the skins from the nuts. Rub off the skin and chop fine (or use packaged chopped hazelnuts). Sauté the nuts in 1 tablespoon of the oil.

Remove the orange rind (making sure to avoid the pith) from the orange with a potato peeler and julienne into slivers. Blanch 5 minutes in boiling water. Rinse, drain, and reserve.

Pan-fry the scalloped venison in 2 tablespoons of the oil for 1 or 2 minutes on each side. Remove from the pan and set aside. Deglaze the pan with Armagnac and then add the stock. Reduce the liquid to ½ cup. Whisk in the butter and season with salt and pepper. Add the nuts and orange slivers and serve over the venison scallops.

PERSILLADE POTATOES

½ bunch parsley
2 garlic cloves
2 large potatoes
2 tbsp. bacon fat or butter
  Salt and pepper

Chop the parsley and garlic fine and mix together. Peel and slice the potatoes thin, then sauté them in bacon fat, covered, over medium heat for 5 minutes. Remove the lid and add the parsley and garlic mixture. Cook a few more minutes. Season with salt and pepper and serve.

TARTE TATIN

6 hard Golden Delicious apples
½ cup water
¾ cup granulated sugar, plus a
    few sprinkles
2 tbsp. unsalted butter
  Sprinkle of cinnamon
1 sheet Pepperidge Farm puff
    pastry (or your own)
  Lightly whipped cream

Peel and slice the apples thinly.

Caramelize the sugar by cooking the water and ¾ cup sugar in a skillet until it is light brown. Remove immediately from the heat, as it will continue to cook.

Spread the caramelized sugar over the bottom of a cake tin and layer the apple slices in concentric circles on top. Only the first layer will show, so be sure to make that your best. Dot each layer with butter and sprinkle with sugar and cinnamon.

Once the cake tin is full, roll out the puff pastry and cover the apples with it. Cut a few tiny holes in the pastry to let the steam escape. Bake in the middle of a preheated oven (450°) 20 minutes. Then reduce the heat to 350° and continue to bake 30 to 40 minutes.

Remove and let cool for a few minutes, then invert onto a serving plate. If it has hardened too much, put the cake tin on the stovetop and remelt the caramel, then invert. Be careful of the extra juice that may run out. This juice can be cooked down, cooled, and added to the whipped cream.

Venison Chops with Pine Nuts and Red Peppers
Pepperoni Bread
Green Salad
Stuffed Oranges

Serves four

As a child, I lost my appetite at the taste of unsalted butter; it simply did not seem right. As an adult, I never use salted butter. Historically, salt was added to butter to mask rancidity, and from what I can tell, the only reason for adding it to butter now is to satisfy some lurking childhood biases in consumers. Unsalted butter is more expensive, but it can be justified by regarding it as a healthier alternative. (Who needs more salt in his or her diet?)

VENISON CHOPS WITH PINE NUTS AND RED PEPPERS

> 1 sweet red pepper
> 2 tbsp. unsalted butter
> ¼ cup pine nuts
> ¼ cup walnut oil
> 4 venison chops
> Salt and pepper

Cut the red pepper and remove the seeds. Slice into thin strips and sauté in the butter. Sauté the pine nuts separately in 2 tablespoons of the walnut oil. Toss the peppers and nuts together and set aside.

Sauté the chops in the remaining walnut oil for 1 or 2 minutes on each side. Place on plates and top each chop with the pepper and nut mixture. Season with salt and pepper to taste.

PEPPERONI BREAD (see page 113)

STUFFED ORANGES (see page 57).

**Venison Chops with Mustard Butter
Roast Potatoes with Rosemary
Green Beans and Beet Salad
Coffee Granita**

Serves four

In many of the recipes, we have listed veal stock as an ingredient. To our knowledge, veal stock is not something that can be bought; it can only be made. And even though it is expensive and time-consuming, it is not difficult, and it is very, very worth doing. Cintra has made it a once-a-month ritual. The 12-hour simmer can even take place while you sleep. And after it has become a part of your life, it will be like hunting: You forget the extra time and effort and remember only how good it is.

VENISON CHOPS WITH MUSTARD BUTTER

4 venison chops
1 tbsp. oil
¼ cup cognac
¼ cup veal stock (see page 27)
½ cup heavy cream
1 tbsp. prepared grainy mustard
Salt and pepper

Pan-fry the chops in oil and set aside. Deglaze the pan with cognac and add the veal stock and cream. Reduce to half the quantity, remove from heat, and whisk in any juices that have oozed from the resting chops. Add the mustard. Season the sauce to taste with salt and pepper and serve over the chops.

ROAST POTATOES WITH ROSEMARY

16 small red potatoes
4 tbsp. melted unsalted butter
Rosemary (dried or fresh)
Salt and pepper

Paint the potatoes with the melted butter and sprinkle liberally with rosemary. Place on a cookie sheet and bake about 35 minutes at 350°, or until they are tender. Season with salt and pepper.

GREEN BEANS AND BEET SALAD

    1 lb. fresh green beans
    8 medium-size beets
    1 tbsp. vinegar
    1 tsp. prepared mustard
    ½ cup olive or walnut oil
       Splash of soy sauce
       Salt and pepper to taste
       Lettuce
       Mint

Blanch the beans in salted boiling water until they are just tender. Plunge them into ice water to stop the cooking and preserve the color. Drain them and let dry. Steam the beets until they are tender and can be pierced with a fork (about ½ hour). Let them cool, then peel and julienne them.

Make a vinaigrette by combining in a blender the vinegar, mustard, oil, soy sauce, salt, and pepper. Pour half the vinaigrette on the beets and half on the beans. Toss each separately, as the beets will bleed if you toss them too much together. Then toss the two vegetables together gently and serve on a bed of lettuce. Garnish each plate with a sprig of mint.

COFFEE GRANITA

    1½ cups strong espresso
     2 tbsp. granulated sugar
        Heavy cream or whipped cream

If the coffee is not strong enough, let it infuse for ½ hour or so. Strain. Dissolve the sugar in the coffee and chill. Then freeze in ice trays or a brownie tin, stirring every 15 minutes or so for about 3 hours. Serve immediately with cream or whipped cream.

Coffee granita is not meant to be a solid ice: it should have a melt-in-your-mouth texture.

Venison Steaks with Wild Mushrooms
Blue Cheese Polenta
Spinach and Bibb Lettuce Salad
Strawberry Ice

Serves four

In all the years of working on the food photography for *Gray's Sporting Journal*, I was continually impressed with the value of attractive food presentation. What the eye perceives as being luscious becomes so to the taste buds, too. It is an art, and although photos are created by professional artists, I have seen equal creativity in the practiced cook. Game, of course, can present its own unique problems for pleasant presentation at the table. But the extra moments spent pulling every feather from the duck legs or taking a pair of tweezers to the venison to remove the last hair does more toward ensuring a tasty meal than any exotic recipe.

VENISON STEAKS WITH WILD MUSHROOMS

1 oz. dried wild mushrooms
1 cup heavy cream
2 lbs. venison steak
1 tbsp. oil
¼ cup cognac or Armagnac
⅓ cup veal stock (see page 27)
Salt and pepper

Rinse the mushrooms in cold water quickly and put into a pot with the cream. Bring to a boil and reduce the heat to a slow simmer. Continue to simmer until the cream is reduced by half and the mushrooms are soft.

Pan-fry the steak in the oil and remove to a plate to let rest. Deglaze the pan with cognac or Armagnac and add the veal stock. Bring to a boil and let reduce by half. Add the cream and mushroom mixture and any juices that have exuded from the resting steak and simmer a few minutes. Season with salt and pepper and serve the sauce over the sliced meat.

24

BLUE CHEESE POLENTA

      1 small onion chopped fine
            (optional)
      6 tbsp. unsalted butter
      2 cups milk
      ¾ cup cornmeal
      5 oz. blue cheese, diced
      ½ tsp. nutmeg
 2 to 3 tsp. kosher salt
      ½ cup heavy cream
         Pepper

If you are using the onion, sauté it in the butter until translucent. Then, in a small saucepan, bring the onion, butter, and milk to a boil. Add the cornmeal slowly, stirring constantly till thick and the spoon can stand up in it. Be careful as the polenta will spit at you. Remove from the heat and add the cheese, nutmeg, salt, cream, and pepper and mix well. Turn immediately into buttered muffin tins and let rest approximately half an hour till set. Remove from the tins and put in a heavy ovenproof pan and bake at 400° for 15 minutes. (If you like, you can add a little more cheese to the tops of the polenta muffins before putting them in the oven.) Makes eight muffins.

STRAWBERRY ICE

      6 cups strawberries
            (approximately)
      ½ cup water
      1 cup granulated sugar
         Pinch of salt
         Fresh lemon juice to taste
            (optional)
      1 tbsp. kirsch
         Enough ice and salt for
            your ice cream freezer

Wash and hull the strawberries. Purée in the blender. You should have about 1 quart of purée. Boil the water, add the sugar, and cook 5 minutes. Let cool. Add the sugar syrup to the purée to please your taste. Add salt and lemon juice to help the taste if need be, then pour in the kirsch. Chill the mixture in the canister from your ice cream maker. Then freeze according to the ice cream machine's directions.

Venison Steaks, Marinated
Grilled Red Pepper Salad
Mashed Potatoes with Fresh Basil
Vanilla Ice Cream with Homemade Butterscotch Sauce

Serves four

When we were going through the editing process for the first edition of this book, Cintra wrote all over the manuscript in several places and in big bold letters, "remove the bay leaf." Of course, this is an instruction given in every cookbook, and I wondered why Cintra was so concerned that it be repeated religiously here. When questioned, she said that bay leaves are not digestible, and their sharp edges can even perforate the stomach wall. This piece of information made it easier to remember always to put the instruction in the recipes—and take the bay leaf out!

VENISON STEAKS, MARINATED

2	lbs. venison steak
25 to 30	juniper berries, lightly toasted and crushed
	Juice from 2 lemons (about ⅓ cup), plus the finely grated rind
1	tsp. celery salt
10	peppercorns, crushed
2	tbsp. ground coriander seed
1	bay leaf, crumbled
2½	cups olive oil
2	tbsp. unsalted butter
¼	cup cognac
⅔	cup veal stock (see page 27)
½	cup heavy cream
	Salt and pepper
2	tsp. sour cream

Marinate steak for 4 days in the following mixture: In a blender, or with a mortar and pestle, blend the juniper berries, lemon rind, celery salt, peppercorns, coriander seed, and bay leaf. Add this to the oil and lemon juice. Add the venison to the marinate.

Wipe the steak dry and pan-fry it in butter. Remove the meat and let rest. Deglaze the pan with cognac and then add the veal stock. Bring to a boil and reduce the liquid by one-fourth. Add the heavy cream and continue to let it boil and reduce. Add any juices that have exuded from the steak while it has been resting and after it has been carved. Remove the sauce from the heat and whisk in salt, pepper, and sour cream. Serve over the steak.

VEAL STOCK

6	lbs. veal shank
3	lbs. veal trimmings
4	large onions, unpeeled, with a clove stuck in one
3 or 4	carrots, peeled
3	lbs. veal bones
3	cups white wine
2	tsp. salt
	Peppercorns
2	tsp. thyme
1	bay leaf
	Handful of parsley stems

In a 350° oven and in several batches, brown the meat. It is best to do this in a large roasting pan. Don't let the bottom burn. As you go along, add a little water if necessary.

Put all meat in a large stock pot. Add the onions, carrots, and bones.

To the roasting pan where the meat was browned, add the wine and enough water to cover the dried meat juices. Bring this to a boil on top of the stove, scraping sides and bottom with a whisk. When the juice is just a ½-inch layer on the bottom of the pan, add it to the stock pot.

Fill the stock pot with water to cover the meat and vegetables. Bring to a boil and then reduce to a simmer. Add 2 teaspoons of salt, several peppercorns, thyme, bay leaf, and parsley stems.

Simmer 12 hours, adding boiling water as necessary to maintain the stock level. Strain through a colander lined with a wet piece of cheesecloth. Skim off the fat and reduce to one-third. Cool to room temperature. Freeze in ice cube trays. Once frozen, remove the cubes with a knife and store in plastic bags.

Do not let the stock sit long at room temperature or it will sour. And never let it sit at room temperature with the bones in; always strain them out, even if you have to stop the cooking in the middle and restart later. Meat stock is fertile ground for bacteria.

GRILLED RED PEPPER SALAD

            2 or 3 red peppers
                 1 cup good green olive oil
                 2 cloves garlic, peeled

Prepare one day ahead.

Halve the red peppers and remove the seeds. Place them cut-side down on a piece of foil in the broiler and broil 2 to 3 minutes till they are black. (They can also be grilled whole, turning once.) Remove and let cool. Peel off the black skin, remove any seeds, and slice the peppers. Put in a jar with the olive oil and garlic cloves and let stand at least overnight. Toss with lettuce and your favorite vinaigrette. They are good in sandwiches and will last a week.

MASHED POTATOES WITH FRESH BASIL

            5 potatoes (Idaho or russet)
            ½ cup (1 stick) unsalted butter
                  cut into pats
            ½ cup heavy cream
               Fresh basil to taste
               Salt and pepper to taste

Wash, peel, and quarter the potatoes. Put them in cold, salted water and bring to a boil. Cook till they are soft when you insert a fork, about 20 minutes. Remove potatoes from water and push through a sieve or potato ricer into a bowl. Add butter and cream and whisk till fluffy. Chop the basil and add it with the salt and pepper to the potatoes.

If you are trying to hold the potatoes, put them in a double boiler, uncovered, and reserve half of the butter and cream to add at the last minute.

HOMEMADE BUTTERSCOTCH SAUCE

            ¾ cup water
            2 cups granulated sugar
               Pinch of salt
          2½ cups hot cream
            4 tbsp. unsalted butter, softened
                  (optional)

Make a sugar syrup with the water, sugar, and salt. Cook till light brown. Remove from heat and add the heated cream, stirring all the time. For a richer sauce, add the softened butter. Serve over vanilla ice cream.

Charcoal-Grilled Venison Steaks with Rosemary Butter
Bibb Lettuce and Tomato Salad
White Bean Purée
Coffee Ice Cream with Frangelico

Serves four

In beef, the cut identifies for us the quality of the meat. Unfortunately, what we have learned is that a great cut of beef is not necessarily paralleled in venison. Venison steaks, for example, are quite often the less desirable cut of meat; the chops are the best. Nonetheless, you can't go wrong with a charcoal-grilled steak.

CHARCOAL-GRILLED VENISON STEAKS WITH ROSEMARY BUTTER

- 2 tsp. dried rosemary
- ½ tsp. garlic, chopped
- ½ cup (1 stick) unsalted butter
  Salt and pepper
- 2 lbs. venison steak

Chop the rosemary and the garlic very fine. Whip the butter and add the rosemary, garlic, salt, and pepper to taste. Wrap the butter in plastic wrap and shape into a log. Place in the freezer while you start the charcoal. Once the coals are burnt down, but still quite hot, cook the steak quickly. Serve slices of the butter on top of each portion.

WHITE-BEAN PURÉE

- 1 lb. white beans, soaked 1 hour
- 2½ cups water
- 2½ cups chicken stock
- 1 onion
- 2 cloves
- 1 bay leaf
  Pinch of thyme
  A few parsley stems
  Salt and pepper to taste
- ½ cup (1 stick) unsalted butter, softened
- ¾ cup heavy cream

Drain the soaking beans, then add the water and stock. (If you don't have chicken stock, you can make it with chicken bouillon cubes.) Peel the onion and insert the cloves in it. Add the onion, bay leaf, thyme, parsley stems, salt, and pepper to the bean pot and bring to a boil. Simmer until the beans are tender (½ hour to 1 hour). Remove bay leaf.

In small batches, churn up the bean mixture in a food processor. Zip it for just a second—not to purée, just to break the skins of the beans. Push beans through a strainer back into the pot and mix in the butter and cream. Reheat gently and season with salt and pepper.

Grilled Venison Chops with Blue Cheese and Caraway
Sweet Potato Gratin
Braised Fennel
Fresh Figs

Serves four

GRILLED VENISON CHOPS WITH BLUE CHEESE AND CARAWAY

- ½ cup (1 stick) unsalted butter
- 1 tbsp. blue cheese, crumbled
- ½ tsp. crushed caraway seeds
- Few drops of Worcestershire sauce
- Salt and pepper
- 4 venison chops
- 2½ tbsp. oil

Whip the butter till it is soft. Add the cheese, caraway, Worcestershire, salt, and pepper and mix well. Roll up in plastic wrap and shape into a log. Freeze for at least 1 hour, or preferably overnight. Pan-fry the chops in oil, 2 to 3 minutes a side (depending on thickness) and place on plates. Put two or three pats of the cheese butter on each chop, allowing the butter to melt over the meat.

SWEET POTATO GRATIN

- 3 white potatoes
- 3 sweet potatoes (or yams)
- Butter (for greasing the dish)
- 2½ cups heavy or medium cream
- ½ tsp. cognac
- ¼ tsp. powdered cloves
- ¼ tsp. nutmeg
- A pinch of thyme
- Salt and pepper

Peel and cut the potatoes into ⅛-inch slices. Layer in a buttered baking dish. Combine and add the cream, cognac, clove, nutmeg, thyme, salt, and pepper. Bake at 325° for 1½ hours.

BRAISED FENNEL (see page 8)

31

Venison Steak with Red Wine
Bittergreens and Cheese Salad
Garlic Toasts
Rhubarb Tart

Serves four

All game, because of its high protein content, continues to cook after it has come off the stove. But for some reason I have found it more so with venison than with other types of game. It is a fact worth remembering—you can always cook something more but not less. Also, not only does game continue to cook, it also loses heat very quickly and becomes cold. We make an extra effort to serve game on warmed plates or platters so it is still warm when it gets to the table.

VENISON STEAK WITH RED WINE

2 lbs. venison steak
2 tbsp. oil
6 tbsp. unsalted butter
2 tbsp. finely chopped shallots
⅔ cup good red wine (the better
    the wine, the better the sauce)
½ cup veal stock (see page 27)
  Salt and pepper

Pan-fry the steak in oil until done. Remove to a platter. In the pan, put 1 tablespoon of the butter and the shallots. Sauté over medium heat until the shallots are barely soft. Add the wine and bring to a boil. Continue boiling until you have one-third left. Add the veal stock and simmer till half of that is left. There should be about ½ cup liquid in all now. Slice the meat against the grain. Whisk the remaining butter into the sauce and add any juices from the steak on the platter. Season the sauce with salt and pepper and serve over the steak.

BITTERGREENS AND CHEESE SALAD (see page 97)

GARLIC TOASTS

1 loaf French bread
8 heads of firm garlic
5 tbsp. good green olive oil
Salt and pepper

Cut the French bread into ½-inch slices and toast on a cookie sheet at 300°, making sure both sides are lightly browned.

Separate all the garlic cloves, peel, and remove any green sprouts. Place garlic cloves in cold, salted water. Bring to a boil and simmer for 5 minutes. Drain and repeat the boiling process three more times. The garlic cloves should be easily pierced with a fork. Purée the cloves with the olive oil in a food processor or blender, or mash with a fork. Add salt and pepper to taste. Spread the garlic purée on the toast slices and run under the broiler to glaze. Serve immediately.

RHUBARB TART

½ lb. pastry (yours or store bought)
3 lbs. rhubarb (preferably young stalks)
¾ cup granulated sugar
Grated rind of 1 lemon
Splash of vanilla extract or sherry

⅔ cup crème fraîche, or a mixture of sour cream and heavy cream
2 tbsp. confectioners' sugar
½ tsp. ground cloves
½ lb. pastry

Roll out the pastry into a buttered 9-inch tart or pastry dish and refrigerate 1 hour.

With a knife, peel the thin outer layer from each rhubarb stalk and slice stalks very thinly. Put in a heavy saucepan with the granulated sugar. Cover and cook 15 minutes over medium-low heat. Then remove the lid and increase the heat to evaporate all juices. Stir constantly to keep it from sticking and burning. When it has the consistency of jam, remove and let cool. Add the lemon rind and a few drops of the vanilla or sherry.

Preheat the oven to 425°. Prick the bottom of the refrigerated pastry shell with a fork and place foil tightly over the pastry. Fill with pie weights or dry beans and bake 8 minutes on the lower shelf of the oven. Remove the foil and weights, prick the crust again, sprinkle with a little granulated sugar, and return it to the oven for 5 more minutes, or until the crust is caramelized. Remove it from the oven and carefully slide the crust onto a cake rack to cool.

Whip the crème fraîche (or the cream and sour cream) together with the confectioners' sugar and ground cloves. When it's thick, spread it over the bottom of the pastry shell. Then spread the rhubarb over the whipped-cream mixture and serve within 30 minutes, otherwise the crust becomes soggy.

Venison Calzone
Sliced Tomatoes with Basil
Fried Sage Leaves
Poached Pears

Serves four

Deer are everywhere, it seems. I was particularly impressed with that fact after visiting friends in Connecticut. Ed was on a deer hunt and I had ventured off unescorted to a Ducks Unlimited dinner. Rather than make the trip back to Massachusetts the same evening, I stayed with friends. In the morning, they suggested a quick pass through their back woods in search of deer. It tickled my fancy to think about potentially shooting a deer in Connecticut during a morning stroll while Ed was spending a week in the Maine woods trying to get his deer. Dressed improperly in the cocktail attire of the previous evening, and allowing only an hour for the hunt, I was amazed to glimpse some 20 good-size deer in that time. And we would have had our venison had it not been for some nearsighted shooting on the part of my companion. But since some 122,816,330 pounds of deer meat are brought to the table in America annually, variety in recipes is mandatory. This recipe offers a good change of pace from venison loaf or burgers.

VENISON CALZONE

3 cups all-purpose flour
1 pkg. dry yeast
1 tsp. salt
2 tbsp. dried oregano
1 cup ground venison, sautéed in
    bacon fat with a little onion
    and garlic
1 cup eggplant, chopped and
    sautéed
½ cup grated or slivered Gruyère
    cheese
¼ cup chopped parsley
    Black ground pepper

In a medium-size bowl, mix 1 cup of the flour with the yeast and add enough warm water (not hot water) to make a moist and cohesive ball. Fill the bowl with warm water to cover the ball. Let sit 5 to 15 minutes until the ball pops to the surface.

Meanwhile, take the remaining amount of flour (this can be all white flour or a mixture such as ⅔ white and ⅓ whole wheat) and put it on top of the counter. Make a trench in the middle of the pile and add the salt. Reconstitute the oregano in a little hot water, then add it to the flour trench. You will need to add more water, fluffing it into the flour with your fingers. The mixture should be slightly cohesive but not wet, as the yeast/flour ball will be quite wet.

When the yeast ball has risen to the surface of the water, scoop it out and set in the middle of your pile of flour. Knead the ball and the flour together and continue to knead 8 minutes or so. Put the dough in an oiled or floured bowl, cover it with a towel, and place it in a warm spot to rise 2 hours or until doubled in bulk.

Punch down and roll out into a 3-inch-by-12-inch rectangle. In the center of the dough, layer the sautéed burger, eggplant, and grated cheese and sprinkle with parsley and pepper. Then pull the sides of the dough up over the meat mixture and wrap tightly, pinching the seams. Flip it over so the seam is on the bottom. Let it rise again (till puffy looking, about 45 minutes) and bake in a preheated oven at 425° till done (about 35 to 40 minutes).

FRIED SAGE LEAVES

½ cup large sage leaves
2 tbsp. unsalted butter

Fry the sage leaves in butter until they are stiff. Remove with wooden tongs and season with salt. Use as a garnish on or around meat or as an hors d'oeuvre.

POACHED PEARS

4 ripe pears
Several drops of lemon juice
2 cups water
1⅓ cups granulated sugar
1 vanilla bean, split lengthwise

Peel the pears with a vegetable peeler and core from the bottom with a melon baller. Rub the peeled pears with lemon juice. In a saucepan, combine water, a few drops of lemon juice, and sugar and bring to a boil. Add the split vanilla bean and reduce heat. Simmer 5 minutes. Then add pears and continue to simmer about 10 minutes, or until the fruit is tender. Remove pears from syrup and stand them upright on a plate in the refrigerator. The chilled pears can be served topped with crème anglaise, whipped cream, chocolate shavings, or a liqueur.

Venison Chops with Basil Cream
Homemade Pasta with Parsley
Salad with Hazelnut Dressing
Brandied Apricots with Crème Anglaise

Serves four

VENISON CHOPS WITH BASIL CREAM

1 pt. heavy cream
½ tbsp. dry or 1 tbsp. fresh
        chopped basil
4 venison chops
1 tbsp. oil
1 tbsp. unsalted butter
    Small amount of stock (veal
        or chicken) or water
    Salt and pepper

Pour the cream into a skillet, bring to a slow boil, and add the basil. Simmer until thick and reduced one-half. If it gets too thick, add a little water and stir. Set aside.

Meanwhile, brush away any bone chips left from butchering the chops and remove all fat from the venison. In a skillet, sauté the chops very quickly in the oil and butter, 2 or 3 minutes per side. Remember that venison continues to cook long after it comes off the heat. The chops should be pink. To the pan, add a little stock or water and deglaze; then add the basil cream. Stir the sauce, season with salt and pepper, and serve with the chops.

HOMEMADE PASTA WITH PARSLEY
(see below and page 13)

For this menu cook the homemade pasta in a large quantity of boiling water for a minute or two. Rinse in cold water then return it to the pan and add 2 tablespoons unsalted butter and 2 tablespoons finely chopped parsley. Toss and season with salt and pepper.

SALAD WITH HAZELNUT DRESSING

    1 head Boston lettuce
    ½ cup hazelnuts
    ¾ cup hazelnut oil
    3 tbsp. vinegar
    1 shallot clove, chopped fine
    1 tsp. prepared mustard
       Salt and pepper to taste

Wash and spin-dry the lettuce. Toast the hazelnuts until golden brown in 350° oven. Remove and cover with a tea towel to create steam and loosen the skins. Rub off the skins and chop nuts fine. Sprinkle over the lettuce.

Combine the remaining ingredients in the blender and run on high for a few seconds. Pour over the salad and toss.

BRANDIED APRICOTS WITH CRÈME ANGLAISE

    1 lb. fresh apricots
    3 cups brandy (or enough
       to cover)

Place the apricots in a jar and cover with brandy. Seal and let stand at least 48 hours. Serve with crème anglaise (see page 130).

Upland Birds

The first time I ever went hunting, it was for upland birds. On a very hot September day in Virginia, we waited under a tree on the edge of a cornfield for dove to fly. It was like all hunting and fishing is—filled with parts that were unique only to that hunt and filled with other parts that were like many hunts—past and future.

We parked the cars and walked a short dirt road that led to the cornfield. Our host, a kind gentleman and father of a friend of ours, with great exuberance raced twenty or so paces ahead of us in obvious excitement over the beginning of his hunting season. A starling fluttered overhead and in an instant the man had raised his gun and pulled the trigger. I remember his wife crying out her husband's name as the little bird fell to the ground and the ring of the shot lingered in the air. For several minutes the novice in me prevented my comprehending what had transpired. And then, with a tremendous flood of horror, I realized what had happened. The wrong bird had been shot. A bird that was not a game bird and never, unless starvation was staring you in the face, to be eaten lay uselessly dead. It was a mistake by a nice man with a puppy dog–like attitude and eyesight that was not what it had once been. But it was a mistake that scratched at my conscience and stayed on my mind.

I realized that purpose had a lot to do with my own willingness to hunt. For me, killing an abundant quantity, or for the sport, or just for the sake of a bad mistake, had no purpose. But hunting becomes a joy for me when it provides sustenance and requires ability in the field and kitchen.

On the other hand, while I do hope for proficiency in my hunting and cooking, I also don't want any prowess to become pretentiousness.

Ed and I used to hunt a particularly great covert in Dorset, Vermont. As time went on, we noticed that the great covert often had a certain Jeep parked at its edge. We asked a local friend about the Jeep and got as a reply a grin and the name of a well-known and highly successful partridge hunter. A year or so later, there was an article in *Sports Illustrated* about this same famous hunter and a game of one-upmanship that was played among the Dorset great grousers: To ask a large group of friends over for a big grouse feed and to offer seconds to everybody. That game's not for me—not only because I'm not that good a hunter but because I'm not that good an eater. Two grouse is too much for me to eat, too much for most people to eat. Game, or any precious food, should be like a good sexual experience: It should be just enough to satisfy but not totally satiate the desire for more.

These are, of course, my own opinions, and I state them here so the cook and reader of these menus has a better idea about the design of each menu and the kind of portion and quality control I've laced throughout them. Or, in short, if the slob in you is screaming to be released, you'll need to double these recipes and move to Belgium where starling is served in the best of restaurants.

Quail for the Campfire
Grilled Red Onion
Charcoal-Grilled Bread
Almond Cake

Serves four

These recipes are designed for you to use the first night of an *ooh-la-la* camping trip. But of course they can be done right at home either in an oven or on your outdoor grill.

Good, extra-virgin olive oil is important to many of the recipes in this book, but particularly to this bread. I recommend ordering some from a catalog if you can't get any at a local gourmet shop.

QUAIL FOR THE CAMPFIRE

4 quail
    Salt and pepper
    Fresh rosemary and thyme leaves
        (a bunch) *or* 1 tbsp. each dried
        rosemary and thyme per bird
4 bacon strips

Salt and pepper the cavity of each bird and stuff with the fresh herbs or sprinkle dried herbs into the cavity. Truss and wrap first with a strip of bacon and then with buttered parchment paper or foil (several layers of parchment paper—two of the foil). Place in hot cinders for 35 minutes. Be sure to turn the birds every so often and renew the foil/paper if necessary.

GRILLED RED ONION

        2 red onions
        2 tbsp. unsalted butter
           Salt and pepper

Slice the onions ¼-inch thick and charcoal grill or broil them lightly for 2 to 3 minutes per side. Now sauté them quickly in the butter over a medium heat and season with salt and pepper.

Or you can dribble green olive oil over them and serve hot or cold.

CHARCOAL-GRILLED BREAD

        1 loaf of French bread
        1 garlic clove
           About ½ cup good
              green olive oil

Slice the bread into ½-inch pieces and rub each side with the garlic. Grill over a medium-low fire and then pour a little of the olive oil on each piece.

ALMOND CAKE

        ¾ cup whole almonds
        6 tbsp. unsalted butter
        3 eggs
        ⅔ cup granulated sugar
        ½ cup sifted all-purpose flour
        3 tbsp. brandy
           Dusting of confectioners' sugar

Toast the almonds on a cookie sheet in a 300° oven for about 20 minutes or until they are golden tan. Be sure to shake the nuts often while cooking so they do not get overdone. Chop the almonds very fine. This can be done in a food processor.

Melt the butter and allow to cool. Stir in the eggs and sugar. Then add the flour, almonds, and brandy.

Butter and flour an 8-inch square pan and pour the batter into it. Bake at 325° for 20 minutes or until a skewer pulls out clean when you stick it in the center of the cake. Let cool in the pan, then cut into squares and dust with the confectioners' sugar.

Green Grape Quail
Wild Rice with Walnuts
Sliced Tomatoes with Fresh Basil
Crème Brûlée

Serves four

This menu you might think about using early on in the quail season when the fresh basil and tomatoes are still easily obtainable from a garden or vegetable stand. Nothing is worse in my mind than having to serve those pale orange, hard balls packaged in plastic baskets and cellophane. Don't be scared off by the use of grape leaves in this recipe. They are very often found in chain supermarkets or you can substitute by using foil, although this is, obviously, not as much fun.

The cooking method for the wild rice—that of covering the rice with 3 inches of water and boiling it all without a lid until the water has evaporated—is one that I discovered from an enclosure in a package of the wild grain. It works with any amount of wild rice. It also is a method that ensures doneness and doesn't involve all that ridiculous soaking that is so often recommended.

The crème brûlée suggested here is a more liquid one than is sometimes served. If you like your crème brûlée to resemble the consistency of week-old refrigerated Jell-O, you will need to cook this recipe at least twice as long.

GREEN GRAPE QUAIL

  4 quail
  4 bacon strips
  8 grape leaves
    Butter
  1 lb. seedless green grapes

Wrap each quail first in bacon and then in grape leaves. Put wrapped quail in a buttered pan and cut a piece of wax paper to fit over the top of the birds. Butter the side of the wax paper which touches the birds. Cover birds with wax paper and a lid and cook at 425° for 15 minutes. Add the grapes and baste the birds with the juices. Cook for 10 minutes more.

WILD RICE WITH WALNUTS

⅓ cup walnuts, chopped
½ cup wild rice
   Salt and pepper
1 tbsp. unsalted butter

Toast the chopped walnuts till brown at 350° while you cook the wild rice. Cook the rice by putting it in a saucepan with enough water so it is covered by 3 inches. Bring it to a boil and then simmer it uncovered until all the water has evaporated, about ½ to ¾ hour. Add the salt and pepper and butter. Gently stir in the toasted walnuts and serve.

CRÈME BRÛLÉE

6 eggs
5 tbsp. granulated sugar
3 cups heavy cream (or 1½
     cups heavy cream and 1½
     cups whipping cream)
1 tbsp. vanilla
½ to ⅔ cup light brown sugar

Separate the eggs and combine the yolks well with the white sugar and cream. Heat the mixture until very warm over a medium heat stirring constantly. Remove from the flame and add the vanilla. Pour through a strainer into a baking dish. Put the dish into a roasting pan and surround it with an inch or so of boiling water. Bake it in a preheated oven at 300° for 25 minutes or until the custard is just setting around the edges but is still soft in the middle. Remove from the oven and let it sit in the water bath while it cools. Then refrigerate the custard for at least two hours or overnight. Just before serving, sprinkle the custard with the brown sugar and put under a very hot broiler for a few seconds. If you cannot get your broiler hot enough to do the job in just a few seconds, put the dish in cracked ice so the custard won't overcook while the brown sugar forms a nice hard crust. Serve immediately or chill again and serve.

Grouse Pancetta
Julienned Celery and Zucchini
Fried Polenta
Poached Prunes and Apricots with Cognac and Cream

Serves four

If you are unfamiliar with pancetta, I recommend it most highly. It is essentially Italian-cured bacon and ranges in quality depending on where you buy it. It is available in almost any supermarket delicatessen or Italian market.

Polenta is a starch and an excellent alternative to the ones you get so tired of serving. A form of polenta was used as a staple by the Roman soldiers when they fought against Hannibal, which says nothing about its taste but does date its use. Listed in almost all the general cookbooks (*Joy of Cooking, New York Times Cookbook*) I find it interesting that it seems never to get served. So try it; you will like it.

GROUSE PANCETTA

Pancetta (approximately 1 lb.)
1 garlic clove, peeled
  Fresh sage leaves (a bunch)
  Salt and pepper
4 grouse

Dice about half the pancetta into ⅛-inch pieces. Crush the garlic and add it to the pancetta along with a few sage leaves and salt and pepper to taste. Stuff each bird with the mixture and truss. Cover with sage leaves and then whole slices of pancetta. Wrap each bird in foil or preferably in the cooking type of brown paper bag painted with oil. Roast at 350° for 40 minutes. Open it up at the table; the aroma is splendid!

JULIENNED CELERY AND ZUCCHINI

    6 stalks celery
    1 zucchini
    2 tbsp. unsalted butter
      Salt and pepper

Scrape the outside of each celery stalk (except for the young tender ones) with a vegetable peeler and cut into 2-inch lengths. Now julienne into ⅛-inch-diameter sticks. Cut the zucchini into 2-inch chunks and then julienne into ⅛-inch-diameter sticks. Sauté the celery and zucchini together in butter till they are hot but still crisp. Season with salt and pepper.

FRIED POLENTA

    1 onion
    ½ cup (1 stick) unsalted butter
    3 cups milk
    1 cup cornmeal
    1 cup water
    ½ tsp. nutmeg
      Salt and pepper
      Fat for frying (bacon, pancetta,
        or butter)

Chop the onion very fine and sauté it in the butter till translucent. Add the milk and bring it to a boil. Combine the cornmeal and water, stir with a fork, and then add it to the boiling milk and onion mixture. Stir continuously until the mixture is so thick the spoon stands up in it. Remove it from the heat and add the nutmeg and season with salt and pepper. Grease a cookie sheet and spread the polenta ½ to ¼ inch thick on it. Let stand until cool and slightly hardened. Now cut with cookie cutters and fry the shapes in the fat till they are brown. Serve.

POACHED PRUNES AND APRICOTS WITH COGNAC AND CREAM (see page 125)

Spitted Woodcock
Green Beans with Wild Mushrooms
Baked Goat Cheese
Peach and Pear Ices with Crystallized Violets

Serves four

The grape leaves are found in most supermarkets or can be left out of this recipe entirely if you can't get any.

Don't feel that you must instantly become a wild mushroom expert and run into the woods with your basket in order to follow this menu. True wild-mushroom experts are hard to come by. I don't know if this is because fool-proof wild-mushroom identification is so hard it requires an I.Q. level not common to most of us or because wild mushroom "experts" die young. But most of us who eat wild mushrooms seem to have two methods of obtaining them: Learn one or possibly two types of absolutely distinct, non-harmful mushrooms, like puffballs or chicken-of-the-woods, and never pick anything else. Or, buy them dried, which you can do more and more easily as people tire of the bland taste from the cultivated mushrooms.

SPITTED WOODCOCK

8 woodcock
8 bacon strips
8 grape leaves
    French bread slices (10 or so
        depending on the way the
        birds are spitted).
4 tbsp. Armagnac or cognac
1⅓ cups veal or chicken stock
4 oz. unsalted butter (1 stick)
        at room temperature and
        cut into bits to blend better
Salt and pepper

Truss each bird and wrap first in a strip of bacon and then in a grape leaf. Spit the birds placing a buttered piece of French bread on either side of each bird. Lay the skewered birds and bread in a roasting pan and cook in the oven for 450° for 20 minutes. After cooking, place the birds and bread on heated plates. In the roasting pan add the cognac. Scraping the bottom of the pan with a wire whisk add the stock and, over a high flame, cook until the liquid is reduced to about ¾ cup. Now whisk in the butter and season with salt and pepper. Spoon over birds. This is meant to be just a moistener for the birds, not a real sauce.

GREEN BEANS WITH WILD MUSHROOMS

1 lb. green beans
1 oz. dried wild mushrooms
2 tbsp. unsalted butter
Salt and pepper

Blanch the green beans and then chill them immediately in ice water. Reconstitute the mushrooms in a little warm water. Rinse the mushrooms in cool water saving the reconstituted juice. Reduce the juice in a sauté pan (be sure not to get any of the mushrooms' grit in the pan) until it is just a glaze on the bottom of the pan. Melt the butter with the glaze and add the mushrooms and beans. Sauté, then season with salt and pepper.

BAKED GOAT CHEESE

4 ½-inch slices of goat cheese
   (or an amount that looks
   appropriate for four
   individual servings)
½ cup olive oil
   Sprig of fresh thyme
⅔ cup fine-sifted bread crumbs
1 tsp. dried thyme
   Lettuce leaves (Bibb or Boston
      mixed with bittergreens is good)
      tossed with a tasty vinaigrette

Marinate the slices of cheese in the olive oil and thyme sprig for a day or more.

Mix the bread crumbs with the dried thyme and dredge the slices of marinated cheese in the dry mixture making sure to cover the slices well.

Bake in a preheated oven at 400° for about 5 minutes till the cheese just starts to bubble. Place the lettuce on individual salad plates and, with a spatula, lay the cheese on top. Serve immediately.

PEACH AND PEAR ICES WITH CRYSTALLIZED
VIOLETS (see page 18)

Dove Salad
Cornsticks
Tangerine Sorbet

Serves four

I know, I know. It is a terrible pain in the neck to pluck and roast these little tiny birdies, particularly as you throw out the skin later. But it is worth it. And remember—there has been some trouble and expense gone to getting them in the first place.

Walnut oil is expensive and does go rancid more readily than most cooking oils but it is a great addition to this and many recipes and worth ordering from or buying in a gourmet shop.

Sorbets and ices, I have found, are very dependent on the liqueur that is added, and I think it wise, particularly with this sorbet, to try and use the Mandarin Napoleon recommended. It truly adds to the flavor.

DOVE SALAD

6 roasted dove
2 bacon strips
1 cup white wine
1 tbsp. vinegar
⅛ tsp. salt
 Pepper
¼ tsp. prepared mustard
¼ cup walnut oil
1 head chicory or escarole
1 head Bibb lettuce
½ cup walnuts
2 tbsp. unsalted butter
 Salt and pepper
 Lemon juice

Wrap the dove in bacon strips, truss, and place in a small roasting pan. Pour white wine over them and cook at 400° for 20 minutes. Let cool and then remove the meat from the bones. Discard the skin and chop the meat into small pieces. Now in the roasting pan where the dove cooked combine the vinegar, salt, a few pepper grinds, the mustard, and the walnut oil. Whisk this together over a low flame.

Wash the chicory and Bibb lettuce. Sauté the walnuts in butter and chop. Now toss the dove, lettuce, and walnuts together in a bowl with the vinegar mixture. Add salt and pepper or lemon juice to taste.

49

CORNSTICKS

1½ cups cornmeal
2 tsp. baking powder
1 tsp. salt
2 tbsp. sugar
¼ cup flour
2 eggs
1 cup buttermilk
3 tbsp. bacon drippings

Sift together the cornmeal, baking powder, salt, sugar, and flour. Beat the eggs, then add the buttermilk and bacon drippings and combine with the dry ingredients. Bake in a 425° oven for 15 to 25 minutes. (Exact baking time depends on whether you cook them in cornstick molds or muffin tins.)

TANGERINE SORBET

10 to 12 tangerines
½ cup water
1 cup granulated sugar
Pinch of salt
Splash of lemon juice
1 tbsp. Mandarin Napoleon liqueur
(tangerine liqueur)
Enough ice and salt for your ice
cream freezer

Squeeze enough tangerines so you have 1 quart of juice. Boil ½ cup of water and add the sugar and cook for 5 minutes. Let cool. Add the sugar syrup to the fruit juice to taste. Add the salt and lemon juice to help the taste, then pour in the liqueur. Chill the mixture in the canister from your ice cream maker. Then freeze according to the ice cream machine's directions.

Fried Dove
Zucchini with Tomato
Gorgonzola Polenta
Tollhouse Cookies

Serves four

In a cookbook I was reading once, polenta was described as "hardtack." Perhaps because plain polenta, like most starches, has a blandness similar to the hard biscuits used by soldiers. Polenta's taste depends strongly on how it is cooked and what can be added to its taste. This, of course, is one of the great virtues of any starch; particularly so with polenta. Cheese is a great addition to polenta.

Tollhouse cookies seem a little silly to put into a cookbook. But clearly they are a most favorite cookie and should be baked more often. In this one exception to my rule of always using unsalted butter, I think chocolate-chip cookies come out better using salted butter (see page 272).

FRIED DOVE

½   cup flour
¼   tsp. dried thyme
     Salt and pepper
2   eggs
2   tsp. oil
2   tsp. water
10   dove, breasted out
1½   cups fine bread crumbs (strained)
½   cup (1 stick) clarified unsalted butter

Combine the flour, thyme, and a dash of salt and pepper. Combine the eggs, oil, and water and mix well. Dip the breasts first in the flour mixture, then in the egg mixture and finally in the crumbs, making sure to coat the breasts thoroughly with each dip. The breasts can rest on a cake rack for 20 minutes or so. Heat enough clarified butter over a medium flame to cover the pan bottom by ⅛ inch. Cook the breasts 3 to 4 minutes per side till they are lightly brown and done to the touch.

ZUCCHINI WITH TOMATO

6 small zucchini
4 small tomatoes
Unsalted butter
Basil
Salt and pepper

Make four deep cuts into each zucchini, slicing almost to the base and creating a fan out of each zucchini. Slice the tomatoes and slip them into the zucchini cuts. Arrange carefully in a buttered baking dish and sprinkle with basil. Dot with butter and bake in a 350° oven for 20 minutes or until tender. Place in a serving dish with a spatula and season with salt and pepper.

GORGONZOLA POLENTA

1 small onion chopped fine (optional)
6 tbsp. unsalted butter
2 cups milk
¾ cup cornmeal
5 oz. Gorgonzola, diced
½ tsp. nutmeg
2 to 3 tsp. kosher salt
½ cup heavy cream
Pepper

If you are using the onion, sauté it in the butter until translucent. Then, in a small saucepan, bring the onion, butter, and milk to a boil. Add the cornmeal slowly, stirring constantly till thick and the spoon can stand up in it. Be careful as the polenta will spit at you. Remove from the heat and add the cheese, nutmeg, salt, cream, and pepper and mix well. Turn immediately into buttered muffin tins and let rest approximately half an hour till set. Remove from the tins and put in a heavy ovenproof pan and bake at 400° for 15 minutes. (If you like, you can add a little more cheese to the tops of the polenta muffins before putting them in the oven.) Makes eight muffins.

Preserved Woodcock with Olives
Basil Pasta
Sun-Dried Tomato Bread
Cantaloupe Ice

Serves four

The concept of cooking and eating an undrawn bird comes from Europe where it is quite common, and anyone who has spent time there can't understand having a game cookbook without recipes for birds in the round. This, however, does not mean you have to try it. I have not, although my husband has and says it is quite good.

Sun-dried tomatoes, listed in the bread recipe, are no longer very difficult to find. Most often found in Italian grocery stores or in gourmet shops in canisters like any other dried fruit, they also are available packed in oil at a higher cost. They are wonderful and worth whatever price you are asked to pay. If you cannot find them, this recipe will work without them.

The cantaloupe ice is very dependent on using a ripe, maybe even an over-ripe cantaloupe. It is not worth the trouble without one, and raspberry or peach should be substituted.

PRESERVED WOODCOCK WITH OLIVES

     4 woodcock, undrawn
     8 oz. black, pitted Niçoise olives
     8 oz. salt pork, cut into sticks
            1 inch by ¼ inch
        Salt and pepper
     4 garlic cloves, peeled and crushed
     2 large sprigs (or 3 tsp. dried) thyme
     ½ tsp. rosemary
    20 peppercorns
     8 juniper berries
     5 tbsp. olive oil
     3 tbsp. cognac

Pluck the woodcock and leave them in the round (undrawn).

In a saucepan put the olives, salt pork, and 1 quart water. Bring the water to a boil and then simmer for 5 minutes. Drain in a strainer and then rinse the olives/salt pork in cold water.

In a tureen arrange the woodcock and sprinkle them with salt and pepper, the crushed garlic, thyme, rosemary, peppercorns, juniper berries, and the olive/salt pork combination. Combine the olive oil, cognac, and a little water, and paint each bird with it. Cover the tureen with a tight-fitting lid and cook in a preheated oven at 250° for 4 hours. The meat should be so soft it could be spread.

BASIL PASTA (see page 93)

SUN-DRIED TOMATO BREAD

     3 cups all-purpose flour
     1 pkg. dry yeast
     1 tsp. salt
     ½ cup sun-dried tomatoes
     ¼ cup olive oil
     ¼ cup wine
     1 sprig thyme
     2 cloves garlic
     ⅓ cup pitted black olives

In a medium-size bowl, mix 1 cup of the flour with the yeast and add enough warm water (not hot water) to make a wet spongy ball. Try not to work the ball too much when forming it. Fill the bowl with warm water so the ball is on the bottom. Let sit 5 to 15 minutes until the ball pops to the surface. Meanwhile take the remaining amount of flour (this can be all white flour or a mixture such as ⅔ white and ⅓ whole wheat) and put it on top of the counter. Make a trench in the middle of the pile and add the salt. Reconstitute the tomatoes by cooking them in the oil, wine, thyme, and garlic over a medium-low heat until they are soft. Let them cool and then chop them coarsely. Add the olives, the reconstituted tomatoes, and some of the oil and wine mixture to the flour trench. You may also need to add a couple tablespoons of water. Fluff the flour with your fingers so the other ingredients get worked through. The mixture should be slightly cohesive but not wet, as the yeast/flour ball will be quite wet. When the ball has risen to the surface of the water, scoop it out and set in the middle of your pile of flour. Knead the ball and the flour together and continue to knead for 8 minutes or so. Put the dough in a buttered bowl with a towel over it and place in a warm spot to rise two hours. Punch down and let rise again or shape and bake in a preheated oven at 425° till done (about 35 to 40 minutes). Remember it can rise and be punched down four times, after that the yeast dies. Also, after the first rising it can be punched down and left to rise slowly overnight in the refrigerator.

CANTALOUPE ICE

      2 very ripe cantaloupes
    ¾ cup confectioners' sugar
         Pinch of salt
         Lemon juice to taste
      1 tbsp. white rum
         Enough ice and salt for your
              ice cream machine

Halve the cantaloupes and scoop out the seeds. Now scoop out the fruit and make sure you have about 1 quart. Purée the cantaloupe in a blender and then add the sugar, salt, and lemon juice sparingly until the mixture tastes right. Now add the rum and make any adjustments for taste. Place the cantaloupe mixture in the canister of your ice cream machine and place in the refrigerator for a couple of hours. Then freeze it in the machine according to the manufacturer's directions. For a nice effect you can pack the ice cream back into the cantaloupe shells.

Minted Dove
Leg of Lamb
White Bean Purée
Green Salad
Stuffed Oranges

Serves four

Mint saves the reputation of many a black-thumbed gardener, and chances are if you have a source you have an abundant source. So use it lavishly in this recipe.

We've recommended soaking the white beans for only an hour. That overnight business is passé and a leftover from the trading post days.

If you don't have a favorite way to cook a leg of lamb, here is a method we recommend:

Remove all the fat from a 6- to 8-pound leg of lamb. Stick slivers of garlic and leaves of rosemary randomly into it at an angle and brush with olive oil. Let sit in the refrigerator for 1 to 2 days. Cook in a preheated oven at 400° for 12 minutes per pound.

MINTED DOVE

5	tbsp. unsalted butter
⅛	tsp. garlic, chopped fine
¼	tsp. basil reconstituted in hot water
	Salt
	Several peppercorns, crushed with the blade of a large knife
2	small shallots, chopped fine
8 to 10	dove, skinned, the breasts removed, and the carcasses saved
2	tbsp. cognac
	Pepper
6	oz. very lean salted pork
60	mint leaves
1	cup wine
1	bay leaf
	Sprigs of rosemary and thyme (or dried)

Whip 4 tablespoons of butter until it is fluffy and soft. Add the garlic and basil and mix thoroughly. Season with salt and crushed peppercorns to taste and chill. When the butter is cold enough make 32 balls with a small melon baller. They should be about the size of a peanut. Set on wax paper and freeze. Now sauté the shallots in 1 tablespoon of butter for a few seconds. Cover and wilt but do not let brown. Grind the dove breasts in a food processor and mix together with the shallot and the cognac. Salt and pepper to taste. Sauté a tiny amount at a time of the meat mixture with the salted pork and check for seasoning, adjust, then sauté remaining meat.

Remove the frozen balls of compound butter from the freezer. Dip your fingers in cognac and cover butter ball with several tablespoons of the dove mixture and then wrap with 1 or 2 mint leaves. Set the wrapped dove on a steamer rack in the refrigerator. Cut or crush up the dove carcasses. Brown in the oven and set in the bottom of the steamer. Cover the carcasses with wine and water and bring to a boil. Add the bay leaf and sprigs of rosemary and thyme. Reduce to a simmer and cook for 30 minutes to make a fragrant broth. Now place the rack with the mint/dove bundles on it into the steamer making sure the rack does not touch the broth. Cover tightly with a lid and steam gently for 5 minutes. Serve as an hors d'oeuvre or a first course.

WHITE BEAN PURÉE (see page 30)

STUFFED ORANGES

4 large navel oranges
1 qt. orange ice or sherbet
   Sprigs of mint

Cut off the top of each orange and scoop out the orange and pith. Rinse the shells and allow to drain. Soften the sherbet or ice and then fill each orange shell. Refreeze. Decorate with mint sprigs.

**Quail Soup
Pasta with Chestnuts and Pine Nuts
Olive Oil and Salt Bread
Custard Oranges**

Serves four

The olive oil and salt bread will be a flop if you don't use a good green olive oil and a coarse kosher salt. Also, making the ¼-inch holes is difficult, and the utmost care should be taken. It is terrific bread and worth the trouble.

Whenever you make a custard dessert, flavoring (as in this case the Cointreau) is essential. If the liquor cabinet cannot provide it, vanilla is a good substitute.

QUAIL SOUP

    10 quail, skinned
     3 tbsp. unsalted butter
     1 large carrot, chopped fine
     2 shallots or onions, chopped fine
   1½ qts. chicken stock
        Bouquet garni
2 or 3 juniper berries
     4 tbsp. rice
     4 slices French bread cut into
        ½-inch cubes
     2 cups heavy cream
        Salt and pepper
     3 tbsp. sour cream

Remove the breasts from the quail and set aside. Crush and break up the remaining carcasses and brown them in the butter. Add the carrot and shallots, toss, then cover the pan and cook over a low flame for 15 minutes. Add the stock and bring to a boil. Add the bouquet garni, juniper berries, and rice. Reduce the flame and simmer for 2 hours.

Cube the French bread and fry. Set aside.

Slice the quail breasts on the diagonal and sauté quickly (about 30 seconds) in sizzling butter. Set aside.

Bring cream to a boil in a large frying pan and reduce to simmer. Stir every now and then until it is halved in quantity and thickens. Set aside.

Once the carcasses have simmered for two hours remove and, along with the vegetables, grind up in a food processor or meat grinder. Then grind again in a blender. Push the purée through a strainer, scraping the bottom, and then return it to the broth, discarding the bones, etc. Bring it to a boil and stir in the reduced cream. Check taste for salt and pepper. Remove from the heat and blend in the sour cream. Add the pieces of breast meat and the croutons just before serving.

PASTA WITH CHESTNUTS AND PINE NUTS

½ lb. chestnuts
¼ cup pine nuts
4 tbsp. unsalted butter
1 cup heavy cream
1 tsp. sage
½ lb. prepared pasta
Salt and pepper

Make an **X** on the "tail" end of each chestnut with a knife. Roast the "scored" chestnuts under the broiler till their shells are slightly black and cracked. Let them cool, then peel and slice them so you have about ½ cup of chestnuts. Sauté the pine nuts in butter till light brown then add the chestnuts and sauté a bit more. Reduce the cream by letting it boil slowly in a frying pan till it is halved in quantity then add the sage. Cook the pasta, drain and wash, and return it to the cooking pan and toss with the cream. Add the pine nuts and chestnuts and check for seasoning.

OLIVE OIL AND SALT BREAD

3 cups all-purpose flour
1 pkg. dry yeast
1 tsp. salt
2 tbsp. thyme
¼ cup good green olive oil
1 tbsp. kosher salt

In a medium-size bowl, mix 1 cup of the flour with the yeast and add enough warm water (not hot water) to make a moist and cohesive ball. Try not to work the ball too much when forming it. Fill the bowl with warm water so the ball is on the bottom. Let sit 5 to 15 minutes until the ball pops to the surface.

Meanwhile take the remaining amount of flour (this can be all white flour or a mixture such as ⅔ white and ⅓ whole wheat) and put it on top of the counter. Make a trench in the middle of the pile and add the salt. Reconstitute the thyme by pouring a little hot water in with it first and then add it to the flour trench. You may also need to add a couple tablespoons of water. Fluff the flour with your fingers so the other ingredients get worked through. The mixture should be slightly cohesive but not wet as the yeast/flour ball will be quite wet.

When the ball has risen to the surface of the water, scoop it out and set in the middle of your pile of flour. Knead the ball and the flour together and continue to knead for 8 minutes or so. Put the dough in a buttered bowl with a towel over it and place in a warm spot and let rise two hours. Punch down and shape into a round, flat pancake about 8 to 12 inches wide. Let rise again and very carefully poke ¼-inch holes all around the top of the bread with the end of a wooden spoon. Fill the holes with the olive oil (or you can use walnut oil) and sprinkle with the kosher salt. Bake in a pre-heated oven at 425° till done (about 35 to 40 minutes). Remember it can rise and be punched down four times; after that the yeast dies. Also, after the first rising it can be punched down and left to rise slowly overnight in the refrigerator.

CUSTARD ORANGES (see page 16)

60

Pheasant Sandwich
Ruffed-Grouse Sandwich with Hazelnut Butter
Cold Wild Rice Salad
Assorted Cheeses (Brie, Goat, Saga)
Olives
Fresh Fruit
Cookies and Cheese

Serves four

Ruffed grouse are my favorite upland bird to eat. Unfortunately, they have also proven to be nearly impossible for me to shoot; making them into sandwich meat is almost more than I can bear. Fortunately, I've had the pleasure of hunting with the most charming and successful of grouse hunters, Richard Montague. Mr. Montague not only makes his own beer, speaks several dead languages, has owned both a series of well-mannered Brittanies and a pretty little bicycle shop in remote Vershire, Vermont, but he manages to fill his freezer with 30 to 40 grouse each season. It is to characters such as Richard that this recipe is dedicated.

For some reason the upland birds are more difficult to pluck than the water fowl. The skin tears more readily, and, particularly in the case of pheasant, the feathers are more difficult to pull out. Consequently, I suggest using this recipe on leftover pheasant so you get two meals for the work of one plucking. Another alternative to plucking for sandwich meat is to save this recipe for the times the hunter visits his happy pheasant preserve. Most private pheasant preserve owners ask their hunters if they would prefer to take home the specific birds shot that day or ones already plucked and cleaned. Certainly for a sandwich-meat bird, pride of ownership can be foregone.

PHEASANT SANDWICH

  1 cup (2 sticks) unsalted butter
½ tbsp. basil
  1 finely chopped shallot
¼ tsp. grated lemon rind
     French bread or any good bread
     Leftover pheasant or roast
       pheasant sliced thin
     Watercress
     Salt and pepper

Whip the butter until it is fluffy. Reconstitute the basil in a little hot water and add it to the butter along with the shallot and lemon rind. Spread French bread thickly with the compound butter and lay on the pheasant and watercress. Season with salt and pepper.

RUFFED GROUSE SANDWICH WITH HAZELNUT BUTTER

½ cup hazelnuts
1 cup (2 sticks) unsalted butter
1 tbsp. finely chopped parsley
Salt and pepper
Whole-wheat bread
2 grouse, roasted and cooled

Toast the hazelnuts on a cookie sheet in a 350° oven till they are brown. Be careful not to burn them. Remove the nuts from the oven and cover with a tea towel for 15 minutes or so to create steam, then rub off the skins with the tea towel. Chop fine. Whip the butter and add the nuts, chopped parsley, salt, and pepper to taste. Spread whole-wheat bread thickly with the compound butter and lay thin slices of grouse on top.

COLD WILD RICE SALAD

½ cup wild rice
4 or 5 radishes
1 cup seedless green grapes
2 tbsp. vinegar
½ cup olive oil
1 tsp. prepared mustard
1 shallot, chopped
1 tsp. tarragon

Place the rice in a pot with 3 inches of water covering it. Bring to a boil and then turn the heat down and let simmer, uncovered, until all the water is gone (about 30 minutes). Slice the radishes very thin. Cut the grapes in half. Toss the radishes and grapes in with the rice. Combine the remaining ingredients in the blender and zip on high for a few seconds. Check for seasoning. Pour the vinaigrette over the rice mixture and check again for seasoning.

Roast Wild Turkey
Fontina Polenta
Fava Beans, Peas, and Pancetta
Green Salad
Rhubarb Tart

Serves four

Although many states now offer a fall turkey hunt, this menu is specifically designed for a spring turkey hunt. Neither rhubarb nor the fava beans are available fresh except in the spring.

ROAST WILD TURKEY

½ cup (1 stick) unsalted butter
1 tbsp. dried thyme
  Salt and pepper
  Lemon juice
1 wild turkey
  Sprigs of fresh thyme
    (a bunch)
10 or so bacon strips

Make a compound butter by whipping the unsalted butter. Reconstitute the dried thyme by soaking it in a little hot water and then add it in to the butter. Whip the butter and add salt, pepper, and lemon juice to taste. Refrigerate for 1 hour or overnight. Spread the butter between the skin of the turkey and the meat trying not to tear the skin. Salt and pepper the cavity and stuff with the sprigs of fresh thyme. Truss the turkey and lay the bacon strips over it. Soak a covering of cheesecloth first in water, wring it out, then soak in butter, and cover the whole bird with it. Roast at 325° for 10 minutes per pound. Baste the turkey with its own juices every ½ hour. If the bird has not browned nicely ½ hour before he is supposed to be done, remove the cheesecloth.

FONTINA POLENTA

    1 small onion chopped fine
          (optional)
    6 tbsp. unsalted butter
    2 cups milk
    ¾ cup cornmeal
    5 oz. fontina, diced
    ½ tsp. nutmeg
2 to 3 tsp. kosher salt
    ½ cup heavy cream
       Pepper

If you are using the onion, sauté it in the butter until translucent. Then, in a small saucepan, bring the onion, butter, and milk to a boil. Add the cornmeal slowly, stirring constantly till thick and the spoon can stand up in it. Be careful as the polenta will spit at you. Remove from the heat and add the cheese, nutmeg, salt, cream, and pepper and mix well. Turn immediately into buttered muffin tins and let rest approximately half an hour till set. Remove from the tins and put in a heavy ovenproof pan and bake at 400° for 15 minutes. (If you like, you can add a little more cheese to the tops of the polenta muffins before putting them in the oven.) Makes eight muffins.

FAVA BEANS, PEAS, AND PANCETTA

    1 lb. fava beans
    4 oz. pancetta
    1 box frozen peas, defrosted
          (Birds Eye Tiny Tender Peas
          are better than most fresh
          unless from your own garden)
       Salt and pepper
       Butter to taste

Remove the fava beans from their pods. Peel the outer skin from each bean. This is very tedious and boring but important and worth doing. Steam the beans till barely done, about 5 minutes. Then dip in ice water. Dice the pancetta into ⅛-inch pieces and sauté over a low heat until it is not quite crispy. Remove it from the pan. Rinse the defrosted peas in cool water and drain well. Put the peas and the fava beans into the pan with the pancetta fat and, over a medium flame, heat through. Put into a serving dish, add salt, pepper, pancetta, and a little butter and toss.

RHUBARB TART (see page 33)

Pheasant in Wine
Fiddleheads
Baked Grits
Strawberry Tart

Serves four

Fiddleheads are spring-time ferns which have not unfolded and look like wheels on the end of a stalk. They can be collected in the woods or, I've noticed, more and more grocery stores are selling them. There is one advantage to buying the store bought ones; the chaff which we refer to in the recipe has at least been partially removed. Lest you be too cavalier with this notion I impart the following tale:

Set on always trying to obtain wild food and wanting my children to understand the bounty of the woods, the family set out on an excursion to gather fiddleheads and came home quite successfully with a large basket full. I tried everything I could think of to get the chaff off—from soaking to picking and finally in desperation I called my friends, the Renesons, who I knew to be fanciers of the vegetable. Unfortunately, Chet answered the phone. When I queried him as to how to get the moldy stuff off the fiddleheads he suggested the following: In the bow of your Grand Laker canoe place your spouse and the basket of fiddleheads. In the stern, seated at the throttle of the 50-horse Johnson, place yourself dressed in black sou'wester and hat. Once untied from the dock, speed boat at full throttle the length of a 10-mile lake with spouse holding up each individual fiddlehead and you dodging the flying chaff which is, hopefully, flying back at you.

Besides finding this method impractical from my city dwelling, Chet's deadpan delivery of the method did not convince me of reliability. However, in the years that have ensued I have been more and more tempted to try. The chaff is very, very difficult to get off, and I suggest leaving all but the cleanest of fiddleheads (collected early in the day and early in the spring) to cover the forest floor.

PHEASANT IN WINE

2 pheasants, cut up
  Bacon fat
1 carrot
1 onion
½ celery stalk
4 tbsp. unsalted butter
1 cup white wine
1 cup chicken stock
3 tsp. basil
1½ tsp. cornstarch

First brown the pheasant pieces in a little bacon fat. Remove the pheasant from the pan. Dice the carrot, onion, and ½ celery stick into ⅛-inch dice and sauté them in the pan with the butter. Return all the pheasant pieces but the breasts to the pan, set on top of the vegetables. Add the wine and stock so the pieces are not quite covered. Bring to a simmer and add the basil. Press aluminum foil down on top of the birds so that there is no space between the liquid and the foil and then cover the pan with a lid. Cook about 20 minutes. Add the breasts and cook for an additional 5 minutes.

Put the pheasant pieces onto a warmed platter. Thicken the juices with cornstarch and pour the sauce over the birds just before serving.

FIDDLEHEADS (see page 123)

BAKED GRITS

1½ tsp. salt
¾ cup grits
3 cups boiling water
2 eggs
⅛ tsp. cayenne
½ lb. grated sharp cheddar cheese
4 tbsp. unsalted butter, sliced
  into thin pats

Add the salt and grits to the boiling water and cook until done or the consistency of bubbling oatmeal. Remove from the heat and let cool slightly then add the eggs, cayenne, butter and cheese. Check the seasoning and then place in a buttered baking dish and cook in a preheated oven at 350° for 1 hour.

STRAWBERRY TART

1 sheet Pepperidge Farm puff
   pastry, or your own
1 tbsp. butter
2 tbsp. granulated sugar
½ pt. heavy cream
½ tbsp. Grand Marnier
3 tbsp. sour cream
2 pts. strawberries
2 tbsp. currant jam

Preheat the oven at 425° for at least 20 minutes.

Roll out the pastry and fit into a porcelain tart or quiche dish heavily buttered. Roll the rolling pin over the top to cut the extra pastry off the edges. Let rest in the refrigerator for 1 hour. Prick the pastry with a fork and then flatten a piece of foil over it. Put dry beans, peas, or pastry weights on top of the foil. Cook in the lower part of the hot oven for 7 minutes, then carefully open the oven and remove the foil and weights. Sprinkle with sugar and continue cooking for at least 5 minutes until the crust is a light brown with a shiny, caramelized surface. Then remove from the oven and let cool 1 minute. Slide the pastry out of the dish onto a cake rack to cool completely. Whip the cream. About halfway through whipping add the Grand Marnier (*framboise* is good, too) and the sour cream. Spread over the bottom of the pastry shell. Arrange the strawberries on top of the cream attractively (raspberries, blueberries, or any fruit are good also). Melt the currant jam over a low flame. Remove and let cool slightly. Add a dash of the liqueur you used in the cream to the jam. Now, with a 2-inch pastry brush, paint the strawberries with the jam mixture. Serve immediately as it will become soggy if you try to hold it more than one hour.

Grilled Quail
Grilled Mushrooms
Purée of Peas
Pear Cake

Serves four

Peas are one of the few vegetables that are just as good from a frozen package as fresh. Unless you have grown them yourself and picked them yourself and they are young and tiny, then, of course, there is no comparison. But then you shouldn't be wasting them on a purée like this recipe, either.

GRILLED QUAIL

¼ lb. pancetta
12 crushed juniper berries
4 cloves garlic, peeled and crushed
4 shallots, peeled and crushed
2 bay leaves
1 cup white wine
4 quail, butterflied (see page 285)
2 tbsp. oil
1 tbsp. unsalted butter
Salt and pepper

Dice the pancetta and sauté. When it is about halfway cooked add the juniper berries, garlic cloves, shallots, bay leaves, and wine. Stir together and then pour over the quail. Cover and refrigerate overnight turning the birds two or three times. Remove from the refrigerator about 1 hour before cooking.

Grill the birds in a little oil and butter bone-side first as always. Cook about 3 minutes per side and baste with the marinade. Add salt and pepper to taste.

GRILLED MUSHROOMS

1 lb. large mushrooms (whole or
    halved)
3 tbsp. unsalted butter
Salt and pepper

Grill the mushrooms for 3 to 4 minutes and then sauté them in the butter. Season with salt and pepper.

PURÉE OF PEAS

2 1-lb. bags of frozen peas
4 tbsp. unsalted butter, cut into
    pats
½ cup cream
Salt and pepper

Cook the peas in 2 cups of water, covered, till they are tender, about 10 minutes. Drain the peas and push through a strainer. Discard the skins and return the purée to the pan with the butter and cream. Whisk over a low flame for a few seconds until warm. Add salt and pepper to taste.

PEAR CAKE

3 large Cornice pears
2 tbsp. pear brandy
½ cup unsalted butter at
    room temperature
½ cup granulated sugar
    (plus some to
    sprinkle in pan)
2 large eggs
2 tsp. vanilla
¾ cup flour

    Preheat the oven to 325° and butter a 10-inch cake pan; sprinkle it with sugar. Peel, core, and cut the pears into 12 pieces and arrange the pieces in the pan in an overlapping circle making a rosette in the center with the remaining slices. Sprinkle with some of the brandy. In a medium-size bowl cream the butter until it is fluffy. Add the sugar and beat again till fluffy. Add eggs, one at a time, incorporating them well. Now add the vanilla and gently mix in the flour. Add the remaining brandy and mix. Spoon or pour the batter over the arranged pears in the cake pan, making sure they are all covered. Bake about 45 minutes or until the edges of the cake come away from the side of the pan. Remove from the oven, let cool and then unmold. Serve with whipped cream.

Quick Charcoal Quail
Sautéed Watercress
Cauliflower and Mayonnaise
Chocolate Cake

Serves four

Sautéed watercress is wonderful and should be used often.

Using homemade mayonnaise really makes a tremendous difference to the cauliflower, and using fancy chocolate versus Baker's makes less of a difference to the cake even though we say it does. If short on time don't drive to the gourmet shop for the chocolate; make the mayonnaise instead.

QUICK CHARCOAL QUAIL

      Several juniper berries per bird
4   quail
4   strips of bacon

Insert several juniper berries into each bird and truss. Wrap the bird in a strip of bacon and slide onto a spit. Charcoal on the grill, or if the rain begins to douse the fire, roast in the oven at 350° for 20 minutes.

SAUTÉED WATERCRESS

      3   bunches watercress
3 to 4   tbsp. unsalted butter
      Salt and pepper

Cut each bunch of watercress into 2-inch lengths (the bunches should be cut approximately into thirds). Sauté the watercress in the hot unsalted butter uncovered for a second or two, then cover for 2 minutes. Remove the lid, season with salt, pepper, and a little more butter, and serve.

CAULIFLOWER WITH MAYONNAISE

1 head cauliflower
1 cup thin mayonnaise (preferably
    homemade; see page 282). If not
    homemade thin with a little
    heavy cream.
½ tsp. prepared mustard
    Salt and pepper
    Chives

Take the leaves off the cauliflower and separate into florets leaving ½- to 1-inch stems on them. Bring several quarts of water to boil and drop the cauliflower in by handfuls. When the cauliflower is just tender remove from the boiling water and plunge into an iced bath. After it is cooled, drain. Season the mayonnaise with mustard, salt, pepper, and chives and pour over the cauliflower. Toss and serve.

CHOCOLATE CAKE

½ lb. (2 sticks) unsalted butter,
    plus extra for buttering pan
½ lb. unsweetened chocolate (the
    better the chocolate, the
    better the cake)
1 tbsp. vanilla
1 tbsp. lemon juice
2 tbsp. orange liqueur (Cointreau)
10 eggs, separated
1½ cups granulated sugar
    Pinch of salt
    Flour for dusting pan
    Sprinkle of confectioners' sugar

Combine the butter and chocolate in a saucepan and melt them over a low flame. Add the vanilla, lemon juice, and liqueur. Remove from the heat. Beat together the egg yolks, sugar, and a pinch of salt until they ribbon lightly and then combine with the chocolate mixture. Beat the egg whites until they support a whole raw egg without sinking and then stir one-third of the whites into the chocolate mixture. Fold in the remaining whites.

Butter and flour a 10-inch springform pan. Cut a 10-inch round of wax paper and butter and flour that, placing it on the bottom of the springform pan. Pour the cake batter into the pan and bake in a preheated oven of 250° for 2½ hours. Let cool completely and remove it from the pan. Sprinkle with confectioners' sugar.

Pheasant Salad
Soup in a Pumpkin
Basil Bread
Figs in Rum

Serves four

PHEASANT SALAD

2 or 3 pheasants
2 tbsp. butter
1 cup heavy cream
1 tsp. basil
Salt and pepper
1 can (14 oz.) artichoke hearts
(in brine)
½ cup olive oil
1 tsp. mustard
2 tbsp. vinegar
½ garlic clove, finely chopped

Breast out the pheasant and oven poach the breast meat by doing the following: Quickly toss the breasts in the melted butter until they are just becoming white on the outside and then place them in a buttered baking dish. Cut a piece of wax paper to fit the top, butter it, and press it over the pheasant. Bake for 5 minutes at 450° or until the meat is just springy to the touch. Remember that all meat, but especially the high-in-protein game, continues to cook, often as much as by a third more, after it has been removed from the heat. Now remove the breasts from the pan, skim off any fat in the juice, and set the juice aside.

Meanwhile reduce the cream: Over a high heat bring the cream to a boil. Reduce to a simmer. Add basil, salt, and pepper and stir every now and then so it doesn't stick to the pan. Cook until it is halved in quantity and thick. Mix in the juices left over from cooking the pheasant and let cool. Slice the pheasant breasts on the diagonal.

Drain the artichoke hearts and soak them in cold water. Change the water 2 or 3 times to remove the metallic taste from the artichokes that they got from being in the can. Cut into quarters.

Combine the remaining ingredients in the blender for 30 seconds or so to make a vinaigrette. Mix the vinaigrette with the reduced cream and pheasant juices and pour over the artichokes and pheasant pieces. Toss and check for salt and pepper. Serve on lettuce with French bread.

SOUP IN A PUMPKIN

1 perfect little pumpkin that
    will fit in your oven and
    weighs about 6 lbs.
½ cup (1 stick) unsalted butter
1 onion, chopped
5 cups chicken stock
  Bay leaf
  Pinch of thyme
  Several parsley stems
  Salt and pepper
½ cup cream
  Croutons
  Chopped parsley

Scoop out the pumpkin. Discard the seeds and string and save the flesh. Be sure not to scoop too close to the skin. Cut the pumpkin flesh into small chunks and sauté it in the butter along with the onion until the pumpkin is soft. Add the stock, herbs, and parsley stems. Season with salt and pepper and let cook until the mixture is quite soft. Remove bay leaf. Purée in the blender or a food processor and then strain. Add the cream and check for seasoning. Return the pumpkin soup to the pumpkin shell and cook in the oven for 40 minutes at 350°. Garnish with the croutons and chopped parsley and serve, scraping the pumpkin shell sides as you ladle the soup into the bowls.

BASIL BREAD (see page 95)

FIGS IN RUM

2 lbs. fresh figs
1 cup water
1 cup granulated sugar
1 vanilla bean
4 tbsp. rum
  Pinch of dried thyme or a sprig
    of fresh thyme
1 cup heavy cream

Wash and drain the figs. Simmer the water and sugar together for 5 minutes then add the figs and vanilla bean. Cook slowly over a low heat for 1 hour. Remove from the heat and let cool. Add the rum and thyme sprigs and cover the fruit tightly. Let it all sit in the refrigerator for 2 days. Whip the cream and serve on top of the figs.

Pheasant and Cabbage
Cooked Apples
Cheese

Serves four

Cintra and I are very lucky to live near a wonderful apple farm that maintains some 30 or 40 different types of apple trees. The farmer lovingly lists on paper for his customers each type of apple, its unique characteristics, history, and how the apple should be used. It would be nice to refer you to a specific type of cooking apple for this recipe but impractical and very provincial. I do recommend making inquires to local grocers or orchard owners as to what are the best cooking (versus eating) apples in your area to buy.

PHEASANT AND CABBAGE

2 whole pheasants, plucked and
      ready for roasting
   Bunch of fresh, or dried, herbs
      of your choice (thyme, basil,
      sage, rosemary, are all good)
4 thin slices of pancetta
½ head of red cabbage
½ head of green cabbage
2 tbsp. unsalted butter
   Salt and pepper
   Caraway

To prepare the pheasants, stuff the cavity of each bird with the fresh herbs and truss. Wrap each pheasant in pancetta or regular bacon and roast at 350° for 30 minutes. Remove the bacon and cook for an additional 15 or 20 minutes till the birds are brown. While the birds are cooking prepare the cabbage. Halve and then quarter each cabbage and cut off the stiff core. Slice thinly as if for cole slaw. Sauté the cabbage, each color separately, quickly in butter till cooked but still crunchy. Season with salt, pepper, and a light dose of caraway. Place the birds on a warmed platter and arrange the cabbage in rings around the birds.

COOKED APPLES

3 tbsp. unsalted butter
4 apples
1 tbsp. Calvados
¼ cup cream
  Salt and pepper

Make noisette butter by melting the butter over a medium-high heat in a frying pan until the butter has turned a light brown (remember it continues to darken after it is taken from the heat). Meanwhile peel and dice the apples. Cook them in the butter until just tender on a medium heat. Turn the heat to high, add the Calvados and let the heat evaporate it. Pour in the cream and cook a few minutes until the cream has thickened. Season with salt and pepper.

Woodcock Armagnac
Fennel and Peas
Roast Potatoes
Garlic Toasts
Tarte Tatin

Serves four

Woodcock are perhaps my least favorite upland bird. This may be because every time I've shot one I've had such bad luck in finding the downed bird that I have a bad taste in my mouth about them before they even make it to the kitchen. More likely my distaste comes from the knowledge that they feed on worms. Ed says they are the only carnivorous upland bird; he loves them. They are many people's favorite bird, and I include them here with a good shot of Armagnac, which makes everything all right by me.

When we do not include a specific recipe for something listed in the menu—as in this case with the roast potatocs—it is because we assume you know how to cook it and have a favorite method of doing so, or because it requires no cooking at all.

WOODCOCK ARMAGNAC

8 woodcock
2 tbsp. hot unsalted butter
3 tbsp. Armagnac
½ cup heavy cream
   Salt and pepper
   Lemon juice or mustard

Breast out the woodcock. Sauté the breasts in the hot butter very fast (about 1 minute per side) and then remove them from the pan. Add the Armagnac to the juices left in the pan and stir with a wire whisk, making sure to scrape the bottom. Now add the cream and cook on a high heat till thick and reduced to about half the original quantity. Season with salt and pepper and a few drops of lemon juice or a little mustard if you need more tartness. Serve over the breasts.

FENNEL AND PEAS

2 heads fennel, halved and cored
2 tbsp. unsalted butter
1 box frozen peas, defrosted
    (Birds Eye Tiny Tender Peas
    are the best)
   Salt and pepper

Peel the outer stalks of the fennel with a potato peeler. Julienne all the stalks into ⅛-inch pieces cutting against the grain of the fennel. Sauté the fennel in butter for several minutes till it is tender but not limp. Now add the defrosted peas and heat through. Add salt and pepper to taste.

GARLIC TOASTS (see page 33)

TARTE TATIN (see page 20)

Chukar Stuffed with Hazelnuts
Grated Zucchini
Sautéed Cherry Tomatoes
Cheese and Thyme Toast
Fresh Fruit

Serves four

CHUKAR STUFFED WITH HAZELNUTS

⅓ cup toasted and finely chopped
    hazelnuts
¼ cup bread crumbs, sifted fine
1 tbsp. parsley, chopped fine
   Salt and pepper
   Pinch of thyme
2 tbsp. cream (for moistening)
4 chukars, skinned
3 tbsp. unsalted butter

Toast the hazelnuts on a cookie sheet in a 350° oven till they are brown. Be careful not to burn them. Remove the nuts from the oven and cover with a tea towel for 15 minutes or so to create steam, then rub off the skins with the tea towel. To chop them fine, you can use a food processor. Combine the hazelnuts with the bread crumbs, 1 teaspoon of the parsley, salt, pepper, a pinch of thyme, and some cream to moisten it all. Cut the breasts off the bone. Make a slice on the keel-bone edge of each breast and stuff with the nut mixture. Oven-poach the breasts by doing the following: Quickly toss the breasts in 2 tablespoons of melted butter. When the breasts are just turning white remove them and put into a buttered baking dish. Cut a piece of wax paper to fit the top, butter it, and press it over the chukar breasts. Bake for 5 minutes at 400° or until the meat is just springy to the touch. Slice the breast on the diagonal in three pieces and arrange attractively on a platter. Lightly brown the remaining butter in a small pan and add any juices from the poaching pan. Dribble this over the top of the breasts and sprinkle with the remaining parsley, chopped fine. Season with salt and pepper.

GRATED ZUCCHINI

6 medium zucchini
Salt and pepper
1 lb. spinach
1 shallot, chopped
2 tbsp. unsalted butter

Grate the zucchini coarsely. Put it in a strainer and sprinkle with salt. Let stand and drain for 20 minutes. Meanwhile, wash spinach and shake dry, barely wilt over a medium-low flame with the lid on for a second. Drain the spinach and let it cool, then chop. Squeeze the water out of the zucchini. Sauté the shallot in butter over a medium-low heat, then add the zucchini. Add the spinach. Stirring continuously, heat the vegetables over medium heat until hot to the touch. Add salt and pepper to taste and serve.

SAUTÉED CHERRY TOMATOES

24 cherry tomatoes
2 tbsp. unsalted butter
Several sprigs of fresh basil
(or any other fresh herb
you may have; dried herbs
work, too)
Salt and pepper

Prick each cherry tomato with a pin to prevent the tomato skins from bursting, and remove the green tops. Sauté in the butter till hot and sprinkle with the chopped herb, salt, and pepper. Serve.

CHEESE AND THYME TOAST

1 loaf French bread
¼ cup olive oil
½ lb. Gruyère cheese
Sprinkles of dried thyme
Salt
Hot pepper flakes

Slice the bread and grill it. Brush each piece with oil and lay a piece of cheese on top. Sprinkle the thyme, salt and pepper flakes on top and broil till the cheese just bubbles.

Water Fowl

M ost game cookbooks list duck recipes by species. We have not done that here. It took me a long time to learn that although there is tremendous difference when hunting a duck, what species he is makes very little difference once he is in the kitchen. This does not mean there is not any difference between ducks; quite the contrary. But the differences come from what his diet is, his age, what kind of weather he's been enduring, how he has been treated in the field and overall size—not specifically from what type of duck he is. In general, an older, larger duck is tougher than a young, small duck. In general, a late-season duck who has already endured a time of compromising diet and hard weather will have a poorer taste. And of course, whether he has been cleanly shot and carefully dressed will affect the taste. (See the chapter on "Game Care" for more details.) What a game cook needs to develop is a knowledge of how to cook the bird according to how it looks rather than how to cook him because he is a mallard or a black duck. A fleshy, pale-skinned duck with no tears in the skin and all blood and fat deposits removed properly will simply taste better.

In order to impress this fact on the reader, I've removed the species names from each recipe in the hope that you will consider the condition of the duck you are about to cook first and what species he is second. The recipe should be chosen on the basis of what needs to happen to the duck more than because he is a pintail or a widgeon.

There are two broad differences that I have tried to note with each recipe. First, I've indicated when the recipe should be used for the sea ducks and second, what general size of duck the recipe calls for. The suggested sea duck recipes are based on how much you might want to cover some of the fish taste that often goes along with their flavor. The indication on size is to give you some idea of how the temperature and allotted time were determined for cooking the duck. Any of the recipes are applicable to any species of duck—just take into account what was in mind when the recipe was being designed.

Duck with Ginger and Scallions
Sautéed Watercress
Cheese and Thyme Toast
Chocolate Cake

Serves four

DUCK WITH GINGER AND SCALLIONS

4 ducks, breasted out
4 tbsp. hot unsalted butter
1 bunch of scallions
1 2-inch piece of ginger root
¼ cup sesame oil
1 cup veal or chicken stock

Slice the duck breasts horizontally in half and sauté in 1 tablespoon of the butter for 3 to 4 minutes per side or until springy to the touch.

Chop the green part of the scallions into ¼-inch pieces. Peel and julienne the ginger into pieces ⅛ by 1 inch in size and put into a little cup with some sesame oil.

Put the cooked duck breasts onto a heated platter. Add the stock to the pan that the ducks were cooked in and cook over a high heat scraping the bottom with a wire whisk. Cook until the liquid has been reduced to ¼ cup. Whisk in the remaining 3 tablespoons of butter. Now add the ginger/oil and scallions. Arrange the ducks attractively on the warmed platter and pour the sauce over them. Serve.

SAUTÉED WATERCRESS (see page 18)

CHEESE AND THYME TOAST

1 loaf French bread
¼ cup olive oil
½ lb. Gruyère cheese
  Sprinkles of dried thyme
  Salt
  Hot pepper flakes

Slice the bread and grill it. Brush each piece with oil and lay a piece of cheese on top. Sprinkle the thyme, salt, and pepper flakes on top and broil till the cheese just bubbles.

CHOCOLATE CAKE (see page 72)

Ducks with Rosemary and Sage
Fontina Polenta
Zucchini with Tomatoes
Coffee Ice Cream with Frangelico

Serves four

Throughout this book we recommend using fresh herbs. Often this was the type of ingredient that I secretly dreaded seeing in a recipe and either ignored by using dried instead or decided the cookbook wasn't any good. Please don't make hasty judgments. Cintra taught me early on that fresh herbs make a tremendous difference, particularly when not much else is happening in the recipe. However, we do not expect you to be a gourmet cook and a green-thumb gardener. How can one body have time for both? We suggest buying little thyme plants or whatever, using them mercilessly throughout hunting season, and throwing them out when the leaves have all been used or you forget to water it. Don't worry about trying to preserve the plant for some magnificent herb garden. Use it, throw it out, and buy more. But do use it.

This recipe would be good for mallards, pintails, or black ducks.

The state where we used to live (Massachusetts) has more ice cream parlors than any other in the country. Consequently, it was always easy for us to slip down to the local parlor and buy their freshly made ice cream. If you live where they have more gas stations than any other state you'll find this is still a fine and easy dessert. Unlike some flavors, coffee ice cream seems to be generally good from any source, and the hazelnut liqueur makes it *ooh-la-la.*

DUCKS WITH ROSEMARY AND SAGE

- 2 tbsp. rosemary
- 3 tbsp. sage
- 2 tbsp. salt
- 2 tbsp. pepper
- 1 small onion
- 1 cup duck and chicken livers
  chopped fine
- 2 roasting ducks
- 4 strips bacon
- 4 cups veal or chicken stock
- 2 tbsp. cognac
- 3 tbsp. unsalted butter

Hopefully the rosemary and sage are fresh; if so, chop fine. Add to the salt and pepper. Chop the onion fine and add to the chopped livers. Take half the herb mixture and add it to the onions and livers. Stuff the onion, liver, and herbs into the cavity of each duck and truss. Rub the remaining half of the herb mixture over the skin and add two strips of bacon on to each bird. Roast at 350° for 40 minutes. Remove the bacon and brown for 10 more minutes. Place the ducks onto a heated platter.

Reduce the stock to two cups.

Deglaze a pan with cognac and add the reduced stock. Now remove the livers from the ducks and add it to the stock. Whisk in the butter while heating the liver mixture over low heat. Carve the ducks and pour a little of the sauce over the meat.

FONTINA POLENTA (see page 64)

ZUCCHINI WITH TOMATO

- 6 small zucchini
- 4 small tomatoes
  Unsalted butter
  Basil
  Salt and pepper

Make four deep cuts into each zucchini, slicing almost to the base and creating a fan out of each zucchini. Slice the tomatoes and slip them into the zucchini cuts. Arrange carefully in a buttered baking dish and sprinkle with basil. Dot with butter and bake in a 350° oven for 20 minutes or until tender. Place in a serving dish with a spatula and season with salt and pepper.

Grilled Sea Ducks
Grilled Vegetables
Garlic Cheese Bread
Poached Pears

Serves four

GRILLED SEA DUCKS

1 loaf of day-old French bread
3 cloves of garlic
½ cup (1 stick) unsalted butter
     or 2 to 3 tbsp. bacon or
     pancetta fat
4 sea ducks, breasted out
   Salt and pepper

Slice the French bread and rub each side of the slices with the garlic. Sauté the bread in butter or bacon fat and let cool. Crumble the bread and set aside.

Grill the breasts over a medium-hot wood fire for 3 to 4 minutes per side. Sprinkle the breasts with the bread crumbs and season with salt and pepper.

GRILLED VEGETABLES

　2　red peppers
　1　eggplant
　　Salt and pepper
　1　zucchini
　1　yellow squash
　2　tbsp. unsalted butter

Roast the red peppers on the grill, turning them till each side gets black. Remove and let cool. Peel off the black skin. Remove the seeds and cut peppers into 1-inch slivers.

Slice the eggplant into ¼-inch-thick pieces. Sprinkle both sides of each piece with salt and let stand and drain for 30 minutes. Grill till the grill marks show on each side.

Cut the zucchini and yellow squash into ¼-inch slices and grill until the marks show.

Toss the four vegetables together and sauté in hot butter over a medium heat. Add salt and pepper to taste.

GARLIC CHEESE BREAD

　　French bread
　1　garlic clove
　3　oz. fontina
　3　oz. mozzarella
　　Salt and pepper

Slice the French bread and rub each piece with the peeled garlic clove. Toast under the broiler. Sliver the fontina and the mozzarella and sprinkle on top of the toast. Run them under the broiler for a minute or two and then season with salt and pepper.

POACHED PEARS (see page 36)

Grilled Breast of Mallard
Gorgonzola Polenta
Cucumber and Radishes
Fresh Fruit

Serves four

This recipe is very much designed for a mallard, particularly a mallard who's been spending his time away from the ocean. I've always been a staunch supporter of the blacks and mallards that live by the sea and honestly believe there is very little difference in taste from those that feast on corn each day. But there is one thing that makes an inland mallard special—the skin. For some reason these ducks have especially good skin. It does seem unfortunate to go to the trouble of plucking a duck just to breast him out, but the skin sautéed separately is delicious.

This recipe might also be recommended for use on a duck-hunting camping trip.

GRILLED BREAST OF MALLARD

4 mallards
2 to 3 tbsp. pancetta or bacon fat

After the ducks have been plucked, skin them and cut the breasts out. Save the skin and pound the breasts to ¼-inch thickness and paint with melted bacon fat.

Cut the skin into strips and sauté in the fat till crispy (about 20 minutes). Chop and set aside.

Grill the breasts over a medium-hot wood fire, about 3 minutes a side. Sprinkle the pieces of skin over the breasts and serve.

GORGONZOLA POLENTA (see page 52)

CUCUMBERS AND RADISHES

1 bunch radishes
2 cucumbers
2 tbsp. unsalted butter
   Salt and pepper
   Mint or dill

Clean and slice thickly (⅛-inch thick) the radishes. Peel the cucumbers then cut them in half the long way. Scoop out the seeds and then slice each half into ⅛-inch pieces. Sauté the cucumbers and radishes in the butter. Season with salt, pepper, and a little mint or dill.

Stuffed Duck Breasts
Green Beans and Wild Mushrooms
Bibb and Radish Salad
Grapefruit Sabayon

Serves four

My preference in general is to pluck and roast a duck. This is not always desirable, however, if he is quite shot up or the skin has torn for some other reason. This recipe is for just such a dilapidated duck.

Dried wild mushrooms can be purchased in nice little plastic bags now. There certainly is no need to risk life and psyche by trying to collect them if you are unfamiliar with the varieties.

STUFFED DUCK BREASTS

 1 lb. spinach
 ¼ cup currants, soaked in a
      little Armagnac
 ¼ cup veal or chicken stock
 1 egg
 ¾ cup bread crumbs
 1 tsp. tarragon
 1 tbsp. fresh, chopped basil
    Salt and pepper
 4 ducks, breasted out
 5 tbsp. unsalted butter

Wash the spinach and put it in a pan with a tight lid over a medium heat for a few minutes until the spinach is just barely limp. Let cool and then chop. Combine the spinach with the currants and their juices, the stock, the egg, the bread crumbs, the tarragon, the basil, salt, and pepper to taste. Cut a pocket in each duck breast and stuff the spinach mixture into the breast. Oven-poach the breasts by sautéing them in the butter for just a few minutes. Place in a buttered baking dish and cut a round of wax paper to fit over the top of the dish and butter it. Press the wax paper over the breasts. Cook for 5 minutes at 400° or until the meat is springy to the touch.

Make a noisette butter by heating the remaining amounts of butter until it turns a hazelnut brown. Pour over the breasts. Season with salt and pepper.

GREEN BEANS WITH WILD MUSHROOMS

    1 lb. green beans
    1 oz. dried wild mushrooms
    2 tbsp. unsalted butter
       Salt and pepper

Blanch the green beans and then chill them immediately in ice water. Reconstitute the mushrooms in a little warm water. Rinse the mushrooms in cool water saving the reconstituted juice. Reduce the juice in a sauté pan (be sure not to get any of the mushrooms' grit in the pan) until it is just a glaze on the bottom of the pan. Melt the butter with the glaze and add the mushrooms and beans. Sauté, then season with salt and pepper.

GRAPEFRUIT SABAYON

    2 pink grapefruit
    2 white grapefruit
    3 egg yolks
    ½ cup granulated sugar
    ½ cup wine or rum
       Pinch of salt
    1 tbsp. Grand Marnier
          liqueur or lemon juice

Cut the peel off of the grapefruit, making sure to remove all of the white pith. Then slice into rounds and core and seed each round. Arrange attractively in an ovenproof dish.

Make the sabayon by first beating the egg yolks and sugar together until it lightly ribbons. Add the wine and a pinch of salt. Over medium-low heat (the pan should never get too hot on the bottom to touch), whisk constantly to incorporate air into the egg, sugar, and wine mixture. Once it's thickened, blend in the liqueur or lemon juice and pour the sabayon over the grapefruit. Run the dessert under the broiler for a few minutes to just brown the surface.

Duck Salad
Basil Pasta
Cantaloupe Ice

Serves four

Sun-dried tomatoes, listed in the next recipe, are no longer very difficult to find. Most often found in Italian grocery stores or in gourmet shops in canisters like any other dried fruit, they also are available packed in oil at a higher cost. They are wonderful and worth whatever price you are asked to pay. If you cannot find them, this recipe will work without them.

When making a vinaigrette it's nice to know that a mistake of too much vinegar or lemon can be corrected by adding a little more salt.

Mallard would be a good duck for this recipe.

Homemade pasta is wonderful, although tedious to make (see page 13) and definitely would be wasted in this recipe. The imported boxed pasta is suited to heavy sauces and vinaigrettes and can be purchased in delightful shapes.

Try to use a very ripe cantaloupe for the ice recipe.

DUCK SALAD

- 4 ducks, roasted
- 2 apples
- 8 slices bacon
- ¾ cup sun-dried tomatoes
- 2 cloves garlic
  Bouquet garni (bay leaf, parsley
    stems, thyme)
  A few peppercorns
- 1 tsp. fennel seeds
- ⅓ cup olive oil
- ⅓ cup white wine
- ½ lb. snow peas
- 2 scallions
- ½ tbsp. vinegar
- ¼ tsp. prepared mustard
  Salt and pepper

Roast the four ducks by stuffing each with half an apple and then trussing it. Lay two strips of bacon on each duck and roast in a 350° oven for 50 minutes. Let the ducks cool and then remove the meat from the bones.

Next reconstitute the sun-dried tomatoes. In a small pot combine the peeled garlic cloves, tomatoes, bouquet garni, peppercorns, a few crushed fennel seeds, the olive oil, and white wine. Simmer over a low heat until the tomatoes are soft (about 15 minutes). Let cool and dice. Be sure to save the oil and white wine mixture for making the dressing. Add the tomatoes to the pieces of duck meat.

Blanch the snow peas in a large quantity of salted, boiling water for about 30 seconds. Remove from the water and plunge into ice water to maintain the green color. Drain and dry and add to the duck and tomatoes.

Chop the green part of the scallions and add it to the salad with the crushed fennel seeds.

Make a dressing by putting into the blender the juice from the reconstituted tomatoes, the vinegar, and the mustard. Blend on high for 10 seconds. Taste for seasoning and correct. Pour over the duck combination and toss.

BASIL PASTA

1 cup olive oil
2 large cloves garlic
1 bay leaf
⅓ cup vinegar
  Touch of lemon juice
1 tbsp. prepared mustard
  Salt and pepper
1 large bunch fresh basil
1 lb. pasta
  Hot pepper flakes
6 oz. goat cheese

In the cup of olive oil cook the peeled garlic cloves over a medium low heat for about 20 minutes or until the garlic is soft but still holds its shape. Add the bay leaf while the oil is still hot and let sit overnight.

Make a little vinaigrette with the vinegar, lemon juice, mustard, salt, and pepper. Pour the vinaigrette into a blender and add the basil with the stems removed and the olive-oil garlic (less the bay leaf). Blend till smooth. Check for seasoning.

Cook the pasta particularly al dente (it will absorb the moisture from the basil mixture and become mushy if cooked till soft). Let cool somewhat or it will discolor the beautiful green of the basil. Drain the pasta and toss with the basil vinaigrette. Sprinkle with red pepper flakes and crumbled goat cheese. Decorate with any extra little basil leaves.

CANTALOUPE ICE

2 very ripe cantaloupes
¾ cup confectioners' sugar
  Pinch of salt
  Lemon juice to taste
1 tbsp. white rum
  Enough ice and salt for your
    ice cream machine

Halve the cantaloupes and scoop out the seeds. Now scoop out the fruit and make sure you have about 1 quart. Purée the cantaloupe in a blender and then add the sugar, salt, and lemon juice sparingly until the mixture tastes right. Now add the rum and make any adjustments for taste. Place the cantaloupe mixture in the canister of your ice cream machine and place in the refrigerator for a couple of hours. Then freeze it in the machine according to the manufacturer's directions. For a nice effect you can pack the ice cream back into the cantaloupe shells.

Grilled Marinated Ducks
Grilled Red Onion
Grilled Mushrooms
Basil Bread
Crème Brûlée

Serves four

In all of the bread recipes listed in this book a flour and yeast ball is made first. The purpose of this is to test the yeast and ensure that it can make the bread rise. If, however, you are already a bread-maker and set in your ways, don't hesitate to use your own basic bread recipe and add the reconstituted basil to the milk or water in the recipe.

This is not a heavy, jelly-like crème brûlée. Expect it to be a true custard.

This is a good recipe for widgeon.

GRILLED MARINATED DUCKS

  3 onions
  4 carrots
  2 tbsp. unsalted butter
  1 bottle red wine
  2 ducks, butterflied (see page 285)
     Parsley stems
     Fresh thyme sprigs
  2 lemon slices
  1 bay leaf
 20 crushed peppercorns
  2 tsp. salt

Chop the onion and carrots and sauté in the butter till the onions are translucent. Add the red wine and bring to a simmer. Add the remaining ingredients and pour over the ducks. Let marinate for one to two days, turning the breasts every so often.

Dry roast the duck in a preheated oven for 20 minutes at 450°.

Grill over a medium-low fire, starting skin-side down on the grill for 15 minutes. Turn over and grill 4 more minutes. Take off grill and rest 5 minutes. Cut in portions to serve.

GRILLED RED ONION

2 red onions
2 tbsp. unsalted butter
Salt and pepper

Slice the onions ¼-inch thick and charcoal grill or broil them lightly for 2 to 3 minutes per side. Now sauté them quickly in the butter over a medium heat and season with salt and pepper.

Or you can dribble green olive oil over them and serve hot or cold.

GRILLED MUSHROOMS (see page 69)

BASIL BREAD

3 cups all-purpose flour
1 pkg. dry yeast
1 tsp. salt
2 tbsp. basil

In a medium-size bowl, mix 1 cup of the flour with the yeast and add enough warm water (not hot water) to make a moist and cohesive ball. Fill the bowl with warm water so the ball is covered. Let sit 5 to 15 minutes until the ball pops to the surface. Meanwhile take the remaining amount of flour (this can be all white flour or a mixture such as ⅔ white and ⅓ whole wheat) and put it on top of the counter. Make a trench in the middle of the pile and add the salt. Reconstitute the basil by pouring a little hot water in with it first and stirring then add it to the flour trench. You will need to add more water, a few tablespoons at a time, fluffing it into the flour with your fingers. The mixture should be slightly cohesive but not wet as the yeast/flour ball will be quite wet. When the ball has risen to the surface of the water, scoop it out and set in the middle of your pile of flour. Knead the ball and the flour together and continue to knead for 8 minutes or so. Put the dough in an oiled or floured bowl with a towel over it and place in a warm spot to rise several hours or until double in bulk. Punch down and let rise again or shape and bake in a preheated oven at 425° till done (about 35 to 40 minutes). Remember it can rise and be punched down four times, after that the yeast dies. Also, after the first rising it can be punched down and left to rise slowly overnight in the refrigerator.

CRÈME BRÛLÉE (see page 44)

Roasted Duck
Potatoes Steamed with Sage
Bittergreens and Cheese Salad
Tangerine Sorbet

Serves four

A very controversial issue in game cooking is the length of cooking time for ducks. Some people prefer their ducks cooked for 10 or 15 minutes, some for hours. Of course the preference also determines the results. Some like blood-red meat, some like leather-brown meat. We go with the middle-of-the-road system. We prefer to cook our blacks and mallards at 350° for 50 minutes so that they are pink inside but share no risk of being either bloody or leathery. It is, of course, purely a matter of taste not only specifically with ducks but with any meat. If you are uncertain how you prefer your ducks and don't have a large quantity to experiment with, try it my way. This recipe is good for blacks, mallards, and pintails.

Be sure to use the liqueur suggested in the sorbet; it makes a difference.

ROASTED DUCK

2	carrots	8	strips of bacon
1	celery stick	2	cups white wine
2	onions	4	cloves garlic, peeled
6	parsley stems		and crushed
2	tbsp. bacon fat	1	bay leaf
4	ducks		Salt and pepper
8	sprigs of thyme	4	tbsp. unsalted butter

Chop the carrots, celery, onion, and parsley stems fine and sauté in fat in the roasting pan. Set ducks on this bed of vegetables. Place two sprigs of thyme and two strips of bacon on each duck. Add the white wine and bring to a simmer. Now add the garlic, bay leaf, salt, and pepper. Roast in a pre-heated oven at 350° for 40 minutes, discard the bacon and continue cooking for 10 minutes more to brown them. Remove the ducks and place on a heated platter. Purée the vegetables and juices in the blender, first removing the bay leaf. Strain the purée and return it to the stove, whisking in the butter. Season with salt and pepper.

Carve the ducks and pour a little of the sauce over each serving.

POTATOES STEAMED WITH SAGE

12 little red potatoes (or what seems
    the right number for four folks)
1 tbsp. crumbled dried sage
4 tbsp. unsalted butter
¼ cup freshly grated Parmesan cheese
    Salt and pepper

Wash and cut the potatoes in half (if they are big). Place the potatoes on a vegetable steaming rack and sprinkle with sage. Put the rack into a saucepan with just half an inch of boiling water. Steam covered for 5 minutes or until tender. Put the potatoes into a serving dish and pat with butter. Sprinkle with Parmesan cheese, salt, and pepper to taste. Toss and serve.

BITTERGREENS AND CHEESE SALAD

    Bibb lettuce
    Escarole, chicory, and arugula
    French bread for croutons
    Garlic clove
5 tbsp. unsalted butter
4 strips of bacon
3 oz. blue cheese
    Vinaigrette
    Salt and pepper

Wash and dry the greens and break into bite-size pieces. Slice the bread into 1-inch square pieces, rub with garlic, dry in a 300° oven, and then fry in butter. Set aside. Cut the bacon into 1-inch pieces and fry till medium done, not quite crisp. Cut the cheese into small cubes. Combine the lettuce, bacon, and cheese and toss with the vinaigrette. Add the croutons and check for seasoning. Serve.

TANGERINE SORBET (see page 50)

Minted Roast Duck with Potatoes, Carrots, and Turnips
Green Salad
Plum Cake

Serves four

Wild creatures tend to have very little fat. And what fat they do have is not marbled throughout the meat but stored in certain specific locations. It also is fat which, if cooked with the bird, will harm the taste (see page 276). Theoretically the fat has all been cleaned out of the bird, and in order to cook it so it isn't dried out you must add good-tasting fat—or a liquid—to the bird while cooking. This recipe suggests a nice technique for doing that and is particularly good for black ducks.

You know how to make the salad.

MINTED ROAST DUCK WITH POTATOES, CARROTS, AND TURNIPS

½ cup (1 stick) unsalted butter	2 ducks for roasting
1½ tbsp. dried mint, reconstituted in a little hot water	4 potatoes
	4 carrots
Salt, pepper, and a pinch of cayenne	4 large turnips (2 to 3 lbs.)
	2 tbsp. bacon fat

Whip the butter. Add the mint, salt, pepper, and cayenne to taste and whip again. Carefully pull the skin of the duck slightly away from the meat and slip the butter between the breasts and the skin, covering as much surface as possible.

Peel and quarter the potatoes. Peel the carrots and cut into 2-inch chunks. Peel and halve the turnips. Sauté all three vegetables in the bacon fat. Place the sautéed vegetables in a roasting pan with the ducks and cook at 450° for 10 minutes. Turn the oven down to 325° and finish cooking, about 35 minutes more.

PLUM CAKE

15 to 20   prune plums
2   tbsp. plum brandy
½   cup unsalted butter at room temperature
½   cup granulated sugar (plus some to sprinkle in pan)
2   large eggs
2   tsp. vanilla
¾   cup flour

Preheat the oven to 325° and butter a 10-inch cake pan; sprinkle it with sugar. Cut plums in half and remove pits. Arrange the halves in the pan in an attractive pattern. Sprinkle with some of the brandy. In a medium-size bowl cream the butter until it is fluffy. Add the sugar and beat again till fluffy. Add eggs, one at a time, incorporating them well. Now add the vanilla and gently mix in the flour. Add the remaining brandy and mix. Spoon or pour the batter over the arranged plums in the cake pan, making sure they are all covered. Bake about 45 minutes or until the edges of the cake come away from the side of the pan. Remove from the oven, let cool and then unmold. Serve with whipped cream.

Duck Roasted with Red Pepper Butter
Persillade Potatoes
Sautéed Green Beans and Cherry Tomatoes
Almond Cake

Serves four

Sweet roasted red peppers come in nasty little jars from the supermarket. And they do not taste very good. When you roast them yourself they take on a nice charcoal taste and aren't watery from sitting in a jar. Not only are they delicious in the butter as suggested here, but they are great in salads. They also can be kept in the refrigerator with a little olive oil for instant salad and sandwich use.

The Sautéed Green Beans and Cherry Tomatoes is something you know how to do. Blanch the beans and prick the tomatoes with a pin before sautéing for best results.

DUCK ROASTED WITH RED PEPPER BUTTER

½ cup roasted and peeled red pepper
1 cup (2 sticks) unsalted butter, softened
1 garlic clove, chopped fine
½ tsp. fresh ground pepper
  Salt
4 duck breasts, butterflied (see page 285)

Preheat the broiler. On a cookie sheet place 2 or 3 red peppers as close as possible to the heat, turning them till charred on all sides. Let cool. While the peppers cool remove all charred black skin. Whip the butter till soft and light. Chop the peppers fine and add them, the garlic, pepper, and salt to the butter. Whip together and then let sit in the freezer for several hours. Remove the butter from the freezer an hour or so before serving. Grill the butterflied breasts and put several slices of compound butter on the meat. Serve.

PERSILLADE POTATOES (see page 20)

ALMOND CAKE (see page 42)

Sea Duck Fricassee
Fennel, Mint, Cucumber, Radish Salad
Fried Polenta
Fresh Fruit

Serves four

One problem with duck hunting if you live by an ocean is that the most plentiful ducks are sometimes not the best tasting. The sea ducks that feed on fish and shellfish are a continual challenge to the gourmet cook. How do you prepare them so the fish taste is masked but the good game-duck taste comes through? In addition to recipes such as these, which are heavy on the masking, there are a few home techniques of exorcising the fish taste from the duck meat. One such technique that I can vouch for is to breast out the bird and cook the pieces in near-boiling milk for a few minutes and then sauté in butter and serve as an hors d'oeuvre. But for a full main course you might try the following:

SEA DUCK FRICASSEE

2 onions, chopped fine
1 leek, chopped fine
4 carrots, sliced
2 cups veal or chicken stock
4 ducks, breasted out
2 tsp. thyme
4 tbsp. unsalted butter
2 large tomatoes, skinned,
       seeded, and chopped
   Salt and pepper

Sauté the onions, leeks, and carrots till the onions are translucent. Add the stock and bring to a boil. Let bubble on medium-low heat until the liquid has been reduced by half. Add the duck breasts and thyme and reduce the heat, cover with a piece of foil pressed down to touch the surface of the meat. Simmer over a low heat for 10 minutes or when the breasts feel springy to the touch. Remove the breasts and purée the vegetables with the liquid in a blender or food processor. Return the purée to the heat and reduce it to thicken if necessary. Whisk in the butter, add the tomatoes and duck breasts, and heat for a few seconds. Season to taste and serve immediately.

FENNEL, MINT, CUCUMBER, RADISH SALAD

1 head fennel
2 cucumbers
1 bunch radishes
Several sprigs of mint
1 garlic clove
¼ cup olive oil
Salt and pepper

Trim, core, and cut the fennel. Wash and slice the cucumbers and radishes. Chop the mint and garlic fine and add to the vegetables. Pour the olive oil over it all and season with salt and pepper. Toss and serve.

FRIED POLENTA

1 onion
½ cup (1 stick) unsalted butter
3 cups milk
1 cup cornmeal
1 cup water
½ tsp. nutmeg
Salt and pepper
Fat for frying (bacon, pancetta, or butter)

Chop the onion very fine and sauté it in the butter till translucent. Add the milk and bring it to a boil. Combine the cornmeal and water, stir with a fork, and then add it to the boiling milk and onion mixture. Stir continuously until the mixture is so thick the spoon stands up in it. Remove it from the heat and add the nutmeg and season with salt and pepper. Grease a cookie sheet and spread the polenta ½ to ¼ inch thick on it. Let stand until cool and slightly hardened. Now cut with cookie cutters and fry the shapes in the fat till they are brown. Serve.

Sea Duck with Pancetta and Prosciutto
Roast Potatoes with Rosemary
Fresh Green Peas
Kiwi Ice

Serves four

Fresh green peas are, of course, a springtime item, so this menu is intended for that lone duck saved in the freezer from last fall's hunt. Otherwise Birds Eye Tiny Tender Peas are okay.

SEA DUCK WITH PANCETTA AND PROSCIUTTO

4 oz. pancetta
4 skinned duck breasts, sliced
    into two flat pieces as if
    for scallopini
4 slices prosciutto
2 tbsp. parsley, chopped fine
  Salt and pepper

Dice the pancetta into ⅛-inch pieces and then sauté till almost crisp. Remove from pan with a slotted spoon and set aside. Sauté the duck breasts in the hot fat and remove when just barely done (remember they'll keep cooking after they've been removed from the pan). Let the breasts cool slightly and slice the pieces on the diagonal. While the duck is cooking julienne the prosciutto and sauté it quickly for a few minutes. Add the cooked pancetta, duck meat, and parsley and toss. Season with salt and pepper and serve.

ROAST POTATOES WITH ROSEMARY

       16 small red potatoes
        4 tbsp. melted unsalted butter
           Rosemary (dried or fresh)
           Salt and pepper

Paint the potatoes with the melted butter and sprinkle liberally with rosemary. Place on a cookie sheet and bake about 35 minutes at 350°, or until they are tender. Season with salt and pepper.

KIWI ICE

       24 kiwi (approximately)
        ½ cup hot water
        1 cup granulated sugar
           Pinch of salt
        1 tbsp. vodka
           Lemon juice (optional)
           Enough ice and salt for
               your ice cream freezer

Scoop out the insides of the kiwi and purée in the blender. You should have about 1 quart of purée. Boil ½ cup of water and add the sugar and cook for 5 minutes. Let cool. Add the sugar syrup to the fruit juice as needed to please your taste. Add salt and lemon juice to help the taste if need be and then pour in the vodka. Chill the mixture in the canister from your ice cream maker. Then freeze according to the ice cream machine's directions.

Sea Duck with Anchovy Butter
Olive Oil and Salt Bread
Soup in a Pumpkin
Figs in Rum

Serves four

There is another home remedy for fishy tasting ducks that I have heard about several times but have never tried myself. By soaking the duck meat in 1 teaspoon salt and 1 teaspoon baking soda to 2 cups water for about an hour, the fishiness is gone. It may be a method to attempt before trying this recipe.

SEA DUCK WITH ANCHOVY BUTTER

- 1 onion, sliced
- 1 tbsp. olive oil
- ⅓ cup parsley stems
- ¼ cup red wine
- ¼ cup plus 1 tbsp. brandy
- 4 skinned duck breasts
- ½ cup (1 stick) unsalted butter
- 2 anchovies, rinsed in cold water
- ⅓ cup Niçoise olives, pitted and
        chopped fine
     Salt and pepper

Sauté the onion in the oil until translucent. Remove from heat and add parsley stems and ¼ cup each of wine and brandy. Whisk and place in a container with the breasts to marinate overnight.

Make a compound butter by whipping the butter till soft, add the anchovies, olives, a tablespoon of brandy, and a little fresh ground pepper. Chill for at least 1 hour and taste for seasoning.

Grill the breasts and serve with a dollop of butter.

OLIVE OIL AND SALT BREAD (see page 60)

SOUP IN A PUMPKIN (see page 74)

FIGS IN RUM (see page 74)

Marinated Duck Breasts
Plain Roast Potatoes
Julienned Celery and Zucchini
Strawberry Tart

Serves four

When I first started to hunt and to cook wild game it seemed almost sacrilegious to skin ducks and marinate them. I have since learned that those of us who are fortunate to do a lot of hunting and who hunt hard throughout the season don't always end up with the finest specimen of bird. There are, upon occasion, edible ducks that need some help either because they are badly shot up or have endured a harsh winter. This recipe is for just such a duck.

There are also some ducks that are simply inedible no matter what you do to them. There was a friend of ours who had come to visit from Alaska. John has since become quite a good friend, but at the time we were new to each other and new to our mutual hunting ethics. I knew him to be quite a proficient hunter and outdoorsman. And I assumed that anyone from Alaska must be a subsistence hunter inclined to saving and using everything, from beaks to feet. We sat in our Boston apartment after a long day's hunt, cleaning ducks. John pulled at the feathers of the last duck and after several pulls revealed green skin on the poor little black duck. I was horrified when I saw it, not so much from the sight of it but at the thought that this backwoodsman would probably want to cook and eat him anyway. Pleased I definitely was when I saw John's plucking slow to a stop and the little carcass drop into the garbage can. "We throw those out in Alaska," was all he said. We throw them out in Boston, too. And when in doubt, I'd throw any duck out rather than risk the memory of a bad taste or worse.

MARINATED DUCK BREASTS

  8 toasted and crushed juniper
       berries
10 peppercorns, crushed
  1 tbsp. rosemary
  4 oz. cognac
  4 skinned duck breasts
  4 oz. pine nuts
  3 tbsp. unsalted butter

Combine the juniper berries, peppercorns, rosemary, and cognac in a bowl and place the skinned breasts in it to marinate 24 hours. Be sure to turn them in the marinade every so often.

Sauté the pine nuts in a tablespoon of the butter until light brown and remove from the pan. Now add the remaining two tablespoons of butter and sauté the duck until done. Serve with the pine nuts sprinkled on top.

JULIENNED CELERY AND ZUCCHINI

6 stalks celery
1 zucchini
2 tbsp. unsalted butter
   Salt and pepper

Scrape the outside of each celery stalk (except for the young tender ones) with a vegetable peeler and cut into 2-inch lengths. Now julienne into ⅛-inch-diameter sticks. Cut the zucchini into 2-inch chunks and then julienne into ⅛-inch-diameter sticks. Sauté the celery and zucchini together in butter till they are hot but still crisp. Season with salt and pepper.

STRAWBERRY TART (see page 67)

Grilled Lemon Duck
Grated Zucchini
Sautéed Cherry Tomatoes
Charcoal-Grilled Bread
Pear Cake

Serves four

The ducks in this recipe must be butterflied (see page 285). This is not some unusual bird/animal act but rather a method of preparing the duck so it will cook completely evenly. By flattening the bird out to bake he is less likely to dry out in the legs and breast. Butterflying can be done to any duck (and upland birds, too) but is particularly good for the smaller ducks. Teal or wood ducks are suggested for this recipe.

GRILLED LEMON DUCK

1 sweet red onion
4 ducks
   Salt and pepper
   Oregano
6 lemons, sliced
   very thin
   Olive oil

Peel and slice the onion and lay it on the bottom of a large roasting pan. Butterfly (see page 285) and flatten the breasts of the ducks, and season with salt, pepper, and oregano. Set the breasts skin-side up on top of the onions and completely cover with the lemon slices. Paint with olive oil, cover, and refrigerate overnight.

One hour before cooking, remove the ducks from the refrigerator. Take the lemon slices off and reserve (also reserve the onion slices). Baste the ducks again with the oil. Grill the breasts, bone side first, quickly on both sides and return to the roasting pan with the onions. Replace the lemon slices and baste again with olive oil. Roast at 350° for 35 minutes. (Make any necessary adjustments for time and temperature depending on size of the bird.) Season with salt and pepper.

GRATED ZUCCHINI

  6 medium zucchini
     Salt and pepper
  1 lb. spinach
  1 shallot, chopped
  2 tbsp. unsalted butter

Grate the zucchini coarsely. Put it in a strainer and sprinkle with salt. Let stand and drain for 20 minutes. Meanwhile, wash spinach and shake dry, barely wilt over a medium-low flame with the lid on for a second. Drain the spinach and let it cool, then chop. Squeeze the water out of the zucchini. Sauté the shallot in butter over a medium-low heat, then add the zucchini. Add the spinach. Stirring continuously, heat the vegetables over medium heat until hot to the touch. Add salt and pepper to taste and serve.

SAUTÉED CHERRY TOMATOES

 24 cherry tomatoes
  2 tbsp. unsalted butter
     Several sprigs of fresh basil
       (or any other fresh herb
       you may have; dried herbs
       work, too)
     Salt and pepper

Prick each cherry tomato with a pin to prevent the tomato skins from bursting, and remove the green tops. Sauté in the butter till hot and sprinkle with the chopped herb, salt, and pepper. Serve.

CHARCOAL-GRILLED BREAD

  1 loaf of French bread
  1 garlic clove
     About ½ cup good
       green olive oil

Slice the bread into ½-inch pieces and rub each side with the garlic. Grill over a medium-low fire and then pour a little of the olive oil on each piece.

PEAR CAKE (see page 70)

Smoked Goose Salad
Butternut Squash Soup
Sun-Dried-Tomato Bread
Chocolate Cake

Serves four

The next two menus involve using smoked goose. I like to smoke our geese because I never really found a method of roasting that made them taste as romantic as the recipe made them sound. Geese are big, tough birds in general, and even though they are terrific fun to shoot, I'd rather eat a black duck any day. So the smoking helps considerably. There are, of course, several types of smoking methods and many types of smokers. We use a hot smoke technique and a charcoal cooker. The charcoal cookers are a little bit more difficult to control than electric ones but definitely produce the desired results. We suggest following the manufacturer's directions on how to rig the cooker. Use a piece of green, fruit-tree wood on the coals; this will affect the taste. Use beer or wine in the water. It appears to have absolutely no effect on the taste but aesthetically is much more pleasing. Do not smoke the goose for as long as is recommended. We usually do our geese for only an hour even though much more is recommended. The length of time is greatly affected by the outside temperature where the smoker sits. Just remember that it is always possible to cook something more but impossible to uncook an overdone bird.

SMOKED GOOSE SALAD

1 smoked goose
  Rind from 1 orange
4 celery stalks
1 apple
½ cup walnuts, toasted and
    chopped fine
½ cup walnut oil
1 tsp. shallots, chopped fine
1 tbsp. vinegar
1 tsp. prepared mustard
1 tsp. tarragon
  Salt and pepper
  Lettuce leaves (Boston or Bibb
    or any type that would make
    a nice bed of lettuce)

110

Remove the meat from the bones of the goose. The skin of a smoked goose is worth saving as it contains much of the flavor, so leave it on the meat. Cut the meat into bite-size pieces and set aside. Peel the orange, making sure not to get any of the white pith. Blanch and julienne the peel. Set aside. Peel the celery stalks and apple and cut into nice size pieces. Toast the walnuts. Combine the goose, orange rind, apple, celery, and walnuts. Make a vinaigrette in the blender with the walnut oil, shallots, vinegar, mustard, tarragon, salt, and pepper and pour over the goose mixture and toss. Check for seasoning and serve on a bed of lettuce.

BUTTERNUT SQUASH SOUP

 1 butternut squash
 ¾ cup unsalted butter
 1 tbsp. thyme
 1 tsp. ground nutmeg
 2 cups chicken stock
 1 cup heavy cream
 Salt and pepper

Peel the squash so there is no beige, hard skin on it. Remove the seeds and any of the stringy darker insides with a spoon. Cube and sauté the squash in ½ cup of butter over a medium-low heat until the squash is very soft. Purée the squash in a blender or food processor and strain it back into the sauté pan. Add the remaining ¼ cup butter, thyme, nutmeg, and stock and cook gently, stirring with a wire whisk, until all ingredients are well combined and hot. Add the cream and stir for another minute or two. Season to taste with salt and pepper and serve.

SUN-DRIED-TOMATO BREAD (see page 54)

CHOCOLATE CAKE (see page 72)

Smoked Goose in Cold Pasta Salad
Pepperoni Bread
Almond Cake

Serves four

The goose and pasta salad in this menu requires the use of grapes. Grapes, generally speaking, should be peeled if they are to be used in a cold salad. However, you will notice I have not said that here. I envision this menu for a Sunday supper with one's spouse and favorite friends and where a modest amount of effort over the meal is desirable. Peeling grapes for a meal like this seems silly. If, however, the Queen of England is coming for lunch, it is advisable to peel the grapes, as they will blend better in the salad.

SMOKED GOOSE IN COLD PASTA SALAD

1 smoked goose
½ cup hazelnut oil
2 tbsp. red wine
3 tbsp. cream
1 tsp. prepared mustard
Salt and pepper
½ lb. pasta
½ cup green, seedless grapes
½ cup red grapes

Remove the meat from the bones of the goose. The skin of a smoked goose is good and can be left with the meat. Cut the meat into bite-size pieces and set aside. Combine all the remaining ingredients but the pasta and grapes in the blender to make a vinaigrette. Cook the pasta *al dente* and let cool but not become cold. Toss the pasta, goose meat, grapes, and vinaigrette together and check for seasoning.

PEPPERONI BREAD

3 cups all-purpose flour
1 pkg. dry yeast
1 tsp. salt
⅔ cup pepperoni, chopped

In a medium-size bowl, mix 1 cup of the flour with the yeast and add enough warm water (not hot water) to make a moist and cohesive ball. Fill the bowl with warm water so the ball is covered. Let sit 5 to 15 minutes until the ball pops to the surface.

Meanwhile, take the remaining amount of flour (this can be all white flour or a mixture such as ⅔ white and ⅓ whole wheat) and put it on top of the counter. Make a trench in the middle of the pile and add the salt. Add the chopped pepperoni to the flour trench. You will need to add more water, fluffing it into the flour with your fingers. The mixture should be slightly cohesive but not wet, as the yeast/flour ball will be quite wet. When the ball has risen to the surface of the water, scoop it out and set in the middle of your pile of flour. Knead the ball and the flour together and continue to knead for 8 minutes or so.

Put the dough in an oiled or floured bowl with a towel over it and place in a warm spot to rise 2 hours or until doubled in bulk. Punch down and let rise again, or shape then bake in a preheated oven at 425° till done (35 to 40 minutes). Remember that it can rise and be punched down four times; after that the yeast dies. Also, after the first rising it can be punched down and left to rise slowly overnight in the refrigerator.

ALMOND CAKE (see page 42)

Christmas Goose Anytime
Pine Nuts and Raisin Cognac Stuffing
Sautéed Mustard Greens
Cooked Apples
Cornsticks
Good Floating Island

Serves four

Despite the fact my taste buds prefer smoked goose, my mind and heart belong to Dickens. Nothing sounds better than a roast goose. Maybe it's because I expect so much that I've been disappointed, but also because so many recipes for goose have clearly never been designed for a wild goose. Wild geese are fatless and dry out easily when cooked if they are not basted and stuffed with other types of fat. They do not need to be cooked for hours; quite the contrary. Also, the cavity of the bird must be meticulously cleaned if you plan to use a stuffing (which is desirable to aid in keeping the meat moist), as blood will not enhance the taste of any stuffing I know about. (I have suggested making more than enough stuffing in this recipe so some can be cooked outside of the bird, since we cannot always be sure the goose is free of blood.) Also, I'd suggest not shooting at the lead bird in the vee, as he is the toughest and oldest of all the birds and will not taste as good. (As I write this, I smile. I'd like to meet the enthusiastic hunter who can resist and be patient enough to not take aim at the lead goose.) Hope for a shot at a lone goose and then try this very nice recipe.

CHRISTMAS GOOSE ANYTIME

       1   cup onion, chopped fine
       1   small celery stalk, chopped fine
       1   lb. sweet Italian sausage,
               chopped
     1½   tsp. fennel seeds
       ½   cup (1 stick) unsalted butter
       ¼   cup cognac
       ¼   cup golden raisins, soaked in
               hot cognac
       5   tbsp. pine nuts, toasted
     1½   cups raw rice, cooked
       ¼   cup chopped parsley
       ¼   tsp. dried thyme
           Salt and pepper
       1   egg
       1   Canada goose (about 6 or 7 lbs.
               dressed)
       1   additional stick of butter plus
               cheesecloth to cover the bird

To make the stuffing, sauté the onion, celery, sausage, and fennel seeds together in the butter till everything looks a light brown. Add the cognac, raisins, nuts, rice, parsley, and thyme and toss with salt and pepper. Let cool. Beat the egg and mix into the stuffing. Pack half of the stuffing or so into the cavity of the bird and truss it tightly. Melt the remaining stick of butter, soak the cheesecloth first in water (and wring out) and then in butter, and spread over the goose. Roast at 350° for about 1 hour, or 10 minutes per pound, basting frequently.

Place the other half of the stuffing mixture in a baking dish and cook in the same oven with the goose for the last half hour of the bird's roasting.

SAUTÉED MUSTARD GREENS

       1   bunch mustard greens
       2   bacon strips
           Salt and pepper

Remove any of the large stems (larger than a pencil) from the mustard greens and wash the greens. Fry the bacon until almost crisp and remove from the pan. Add the mustard greens to the frying pan with the bacon fat still in it and cook quickly with the lid on for a few minutes till wilted. Chop up the bacon and add it to the greens. Season with salt and pepper.

COOKED APPLES (see page 76)

CORNSTICKS (see page 50)

GOOD FLOATING ISLAND

12　egg yolks
¼　tsp. salt, plus a pinch more
2　plus a scant ¼ cups
　　　granulated sugar
3　cups medium cream
2　tbsp. vanilla or liqueur
　　　(Grand Marnier, Tia Maria,
　　　or rum are good)

(The custard may be made the day before.)

To make the custard, whisk together the egg yolks, ¼ teaspoon salt, and 1 cup of the sugar until they are just combined. Add the cream and mix well, trying not to make any foam. Pour into a heavy-bottomed saucepan and heat over a medium flame. Stir constantly as it will get hot slowly and then thicken quite suddenly. Watch carefully, and as soon as it thickens remove from the heat and pour through a strainer. Whisk till cool. Add the vanilla or liqueur and refrigerate at least 1 hour. To make the islands, beat the egg whites, with the pinch of salt, until soft peaks are formed. Then add ½ cup sugar and beat until the whites are smooth and stiff.

Now caramelize the remaining sugar. Put ⅔ cup sugar and ½ cup water into a frying pan and cook over a high heat until it foams and bubbles and becomes a golden caramel. Remove immediately from the heat and use as it will continue to darken and become stiff. If it becomes too hard, add a little water and warm over a low heat.

Smooth the custard into a low serving dish and spoon the whites on top in blobs to form the islands. Take a fork and dip it into the caramelized sugar. Criss-cross the islands of whites with the caramelized fork, dipping it every time a criss or cross is made.

This dessert can sit finished for about an hour if the egg whites have been beaten enough.

Mixed Bag

Several years ago, Ed and I went smallmouth bass fishing in Maine. I was a novice fisherman and depending on Ed and this trip to change that status. After several easy days of watching an eaglet and his mother, listening to the loons at night, and learning about emersion into wilderness, Ed began the campside sessions on casting. Soon enough we paddled down the lake to test the knowledge. Ed made several casts at his chosen spot, caught a fish, threw him back, and then pointed to the spot and suggested I give it a try. I remember being disappointed by this learning procedure.

Surely determining where the fish are and catching them because you have made that discovery is one of the most enjoyable aspects of fishing. Ed knew that and has since written quite eloquently in *Gray's Sporting Journal* about the episode. And he is the best of teachers. But even so, instruction has an element of straightforward indoctrination whether it is in fishing, hunting—or cooking.

We have tried to be instructional but not definitive in this book, believing in the need for experimentation and discovery. Unfortunately an imperious tone is too often found in cookbooks, either because the printed word makes it all seem absolute or because the author writes it to sound so. There are no absolutes in cooking game; that is why it is hard and fun to do.

There are also too few game cookbooks where the author confesses to being ignorant on a specific topic. At one point during the writing of this book, Cintra turned to me and said, "Well, I'm not the dessert queen, you know." Good as she is, desserts are not her forte. So better to repeat her good recipes than throw in ones we don't know much about (the readers will catch you every time anyway).

I do not know how to cook every type of game. That is why this chapter is thin by comparison to the "Upland Birds," "Water Fowl," and "Venison" chapters. I have tried to write about what I know. And tried to say so when I don't have first-hand knowledge. And tried to leave what I don't know entirely out of the book.

Tempting as it is to try and sound smart about all game cooking, it would be a lie. And I definitely need to reserve my lying for the catching and shooting tales rather than the cooking and eating dissertations.

Roast Leg of Mountain Goat
Blue Cheese Polenta
Mixed Green Salad
Plum Cake

Serves four

ROAST LEG OF MOUNTAIN GOAT

1 leg of goat
2 garlic cloves
2 tbsp. rosemary
¼ cup oil
½ cup (1 stick)
   unsalted butter

Clean off all fat from the leg with a little knife. Peel and sliver one of the cloves of garlic. Cutting slits in the meat, insert, at a slight angle, the slivers of garlic and ¼ teaspoon of the rosemary. Then rub it all with the oil and the rest of the rosemary and let stand in the refrigerator overnight wrapped in foil. Bring to room temperature before roasting. Preheat the oven to 400° and roast for 30 minutes (or about 10 minutes per pound). Then let sit for 15 minutes or so before carving. An hour or even a day before cooking the goat, make a compound butter by whipping together the butter, the last garlic clove chopped fine, and the rosemary, also chopped fine. Salt and pepper to taste. Wrap in plastic wrap and shape into a log, place in the refrigerator. When the leg is ready, sprinkle with salt and pepper and serve with the compound butter.

BLUE CHEESE POLENTA (see page 25)

PLUM CAKE (see page 99)

Braised Bear
Baby Artichokes
Fava Beans, Peas, and Pancetta
Fresh Fruit

Serves four

I have never actually hunted bear although I have cooked it several times and have been in camp with bear hunters (we were fishing). We had a bear carcass near our duck camp in Alaska (the local Indians had taken the edible meat and left the rest). And we once came upon some bear hunters while we were hunting partridge.

The bear hunters were tracking with dogs and had an eerie resemblance to the folks they hired to do the movie *Deliverance*. The dead carcass near our duck camp proved an inconvenience. The two retrievers with us loved to roll in it and then cuddled up at night near us for warmth from the Alaskan fall air. Our bear hunting friends, camping near us while we were land-locked-salmon fishing, caused only the greatest of amusement. They were left early one morning to huddle over bait (garbage) in hopes of attracting a bear while their guide and only means of getting out of the woods went off . . . to get drunk. As darkness fell, the hung-over guide tried desperately to remember where he had parked his "sports." The night passed and so did many hours of aimless four-wheel driving through a lot of the Maine backwoods. The bear hunters were eventually found with black-fly bites as big as base-balls and stories of the thrill of sitting over garbage while the springtime sun heated up—and then went ominously down. A little bleary-eyed but amaz-ingly cheerful. I remember wondering what the appeal was for those bear hunters. Certainly my brief encounters with bear hunting have left me with no great desire to do it.

My bear-*cooking* experiences have, however, been slightly more persua-sive—conjuring great images of the lumbering creatures lurking through the wonderful woods of Maine or Michigan or Alaska. The meat must be cooked long (for fear of any possible trichinosis) and therefore is cooked with many herbs, spices, and, in this case, much garlic. It is very aromatic—wonderful for the pre-meal anticipation.

This menu is designed for spring bear as it is the only time fava beans or the baby artichokes are available. Also, don't let the amount of garlic scare you. After it cooks for so long it takes on a very mild and sweet flavor.

BRAISED BEAR

8	lbs. bear meat, cut into 2-inch cubes
½	cup corn oil
1	onion
3	carrots
1	large stalk of celery
1½	sticks of unsalted butter
1	bottle of good red Rhone wine
2	cups veal or chicken stock
40	garlic cloves, peeled
2	tsp. thyme
1	bay leaf
	Salt and pepper
	A few parsley stems

Brown the meat in the corn oil and set aside. Discard the oil. Chop the onion, carrot and celery and sauté in the same pan as the bear with 2 tablespoons of butter. Add the browned bear meat to the vegetables and pour in the wine and stock. Bring it to a boil and then reduce to a simmer. Add the garlic cloves, thyme, and bay leaf to the meat mixture. Cover the pan with foil, pressing down so there is no space between the liquid and the foil and the foil is tight over the sides of the pan. Now cover with the lid and continue simmering until done, about 2 to 3 hours or when a skewer comes out of a piece of meat easily. Skim off any fat. Remove the meat and discard the bay leaf. Strain the liquid and purée both the liquid and the vegetables in a blender, in batches if necessary. Return the mixture to the stove and reduce over a medium heat by one-third the quantity. Whisk in the butter and check for salt and pepper. Return the meat and parsley to the sauce and reheat for a few minutes. Serve.

BABY ARTICHOKES

8 to 10 baby artichokes (the very small
artichokes that are about 2 inches
long and which will have no choke)
Juice from 1 lemon (3 tbsp.)
2 tbsp. parsley
1 garlic clove
3 tbsp. olive oil
1 bay leaf
½ tsp. thyme
Salt and pepper
3 to 4 cups chicken stock

Remove the outer leaves of the artichoke. Trim the top and bottoms and cut each artichoke lengthwise into slices about ¼ inch thick. Keep them in a lemon and water bath while preparing. Chop the parsley and garlic very fine and sauté in olive oil. Add the artichokes, bay leaf, and thyme. Salt and pepper to taste and toss. Pour in the chicken broth so that the chokes are half covered. Simmer with the lid on for 20 minutes, turning the artichokes every now and then. Remove the lid and turn up the heat. Stir until the liquid has almost evaporated. Test for seasoning. Place the artichokes on a serving platter and dot with butter. Serve.

FAVA BEANS, PEAS, AND PANCETTA

1 lb. fava beans
4 oz. pancetta
1 box frozen peas, defrosted
(Birds Eye Tiny Tender Peas
are better than most fresh
unless from your own garden)
Salt and pepper
Butter to taste

Remove the fava beans from their pods. Peel the outer skin from each bean. This is very tedious and boring but important and worth doing. Steam the beans till barely done, about 5 minutes. Then dip in ice water. Dice the pancetta into ⅛-inch pieces and sauté over a low heat until it is not quite crispy. Remove it from the pan. Rinse the defrosted peas in cool water and drain well. Put the peas and the fava beans into the pan with the pancetta fat and, over a medium flame, heat through. Put into a serving dish, add salt, pepper, pancetta, and a little butter and toss.

Boar Chops with Pernod and Mustard Butter
Gaufrette Potatoes
Fiddleheads
Raspberry Tart

Serves four

This menu suggests gaufrette potatoes, which require the use of a mandolin—another piece of equipment that has an outrageous price tag but is very chic. Since what we are really suggesting for this menu are homemade French fries or "chips," you can save the mandolin for when the Queen comes to lunch.

To make the fries you simply slice the potatoes and deep-fat fry them. I make a couple of suggestions: Leave the skin on for a stronger potato flavor, use fresh peanut oil each time (re-use the oil only in desperation), and keep the done fries in the oven while the remainder cook.

BOAR CHOPS WITH PERNOD AND MUSTARD BUTTER

1½ sticks unsalted butter,
          slightly softened
1 tbsp. good prepared
          mustard
3 tbsp. Pernod
     Salt and pepper
4 boar chops
2 tbsp. oil

Whip the butter until soft, add the mustard, Pernod, salt, and pepper to taste. Put into plastic wrap and mold into the shape of a cylinder. Place in the freezer for one hour or overnight. Cook the chops quickly in the oil and season each side with salt and pepper after they have browned. Slice the Pernod butter and serve several pats on top of each chop.

FIDDLEHEADS

    1 lb. fiddleheads
       Salt and pepper
    3 tbsp. butter

Cut the stems off the fiddleheads leaving ¾ of the stems. In a large soup pot full of cold water soak the fiddleheads for 5 minutes or so. Then, by the handful, rinse the fiddleheads under the faucet. Pour out the potful of water and repeat the process two or three more times or until the brown chaff has been completely removed. It is very important to remove as much of the chaff as possible because it causes the fiddleheads to be bitter. Bring a quart of salted water to boil and drop in a handful of the fiddleheads. Cook 3 to 4 minutes or until they're just tender. Scoop them out and plunge them into ice water to stop the cooking. Drain the fiddleheads in a colander and wrap them in an old towel. Repeat this until you have cooked all the fiddleheads, changing the boiling water with each handful of fiddleheads as more chaff will come off in the boiling water. Finally, sauté the fiddleheads quickly in the unsalted butter and serve seasoned to taste with salt and pepper.

RASPBERRY TART

1 sheet Pepperidge Farm puff pastry or your own	½ tbsp. *framboise*
	3 tbsp. sour cream
1 tbsp. butter	2 pints raspberries
2 tbsp. granulated sugar	2 tbsp. currant jam
½ pint heavy cream	

Preheat the oven at 425° for at least 20 minutes.

Roll out the pastry and fit into a heavily buttered porcelain tart or quiche dish. Roll the rolling pin over the top to cut the extra pastry off the edges. Let rest in the refrigerator for 1 hour. Prick the pastry with a fork and then flatten a piece of foil tightly over it. Put dry beans, peas, or pastry weights on top of the foil. Cook in the lower part of the hot oven for 7 minutes then carefully open the oven and remove the foil and weights. Sprinkle with sugar and continue cooking for at least 5 minutes until the crust is a light brown with a shiny, caramelized surface. Then remove from the oven and let cool 1 minute. Slide the pastry out of the dish onto a cake rack to cool completely. Whip the cream. About halfway through whipping add the *framboise* and the sour cream. Spread over the pastry shell. Arrange the raspberries on top of the cream attractively (peaches, blueberries, or any fruit are good, also). Melt the currant jam over a low flame. Remove and let cool slightly. Add a dash of the liqueur you used in the cream. With a 2-inch pastry brush, paint the raspberries with the jam mixture. Serve immediately as it will become soggy if you try to hold it.

Roast Sheep
Sautéed Watercress
Pasta with Chestnuts and Pine Nuts
Poached Prunes and Apricots with Cognac and Cream

Serves four

This is one of those menus that whenever I read it, I salivate. We had sheep one night on our duck hunting trip in Alaska and the fond memory of it still lingers. Although, in retrospect, I have wondered if this was because we had had Ron Rau's Gizzard Stew and military C rations (coffee, Type II) the previous evening.

It is all relative, nonetheless. The following is a wonderful meal.

ROAST SHEEP

3 to 4 lbs. rolled loin roast
2 tbsp. oil
2 tbsp. cognac
1½ cups veal stock
1 garlic clove, chopped
4 tbsp. unsalted butter
Peel from 1 lime, blanched
  and julienned
Salt and pepper

Clean any fat off the roast and brush the roast with the oil.

Roast the sheep in a hot 450° oven for 1 to 1½ hours according to your taste. Remove the roast from the pan to a warm serving platter. Deglaze the pan with cognac and then add veal stock, chopped garlic and reduce to one-half the amount. Whisk in butter and lime rind. Season with salt and pepper and serve over sliced sheep.

SAUTÉED WATERCRESS

3 bunches watercress
3 to 4 tbsp. unsalted butter
Salt and pepper

Cut each bunch of watercress into 2-inch lengths (the bunches should be cut approximately into thirds). Sauté the watercress in the hot unsalted butter uncovered for a second or two, then cover for 2 minutes. Remove the lid, season with salt, pepper, and a little more butter, and serve.

PASTA WITH CHESTNUTS AND PINE NUTS (see page 59)

POACHED PRUNES AND APRICOTS WITH COGNAC AND CREAM

12 orange rind slivers
12 lemon rind slivers
 1 bottle of good white wine
   Several cloves
½ lb. good quality pitted and
   dried prunes
½ lb. dried apricots
 1 cup cream
⅛ cup cognac or Armagnac

Peel an orange and a lemon with a potato peeler making sure not to get any white pith. Put 12 of the shavings from the orange and 12 from the lemon into a pan with the wine and cloves. Bring the mixture to a boil and let simmer for a few minutes. Add the prunes and apricots, remove from the heat and let sit for 48 hours or more in the refrigerator.

When ready to serve, whip the cream only lightly with the cognac in it and pass with the fruit.

Braised Rabbit
Sautéed Cucumbers
Red Peppers with Basil
Clafoutis

Serves four

Rabbit is shot and eaten more than any other game in this country. I find it quite good but often very bony. The other problem with rabbit is a disease they carry called tularemia or "rabbit fever." This is transmitted to humans who either eat it or handle an infected rabbit. However, our very knowledgeable friend Bob Elman writes in his excellent book, *Hunters Field Guide,* published by Alfred A. Knopf, that the effects of tularemia have been greatly exaggerated. Rarely is the disease fatal (only in about 6 percent of the cases according to my encyclopedia), and it is easily treated with streptomycin. He does suggest wearing rubber gloves when field dressing a rabbit. And it is advisable to cook the rabbit well. This disease is not reserved for wild rabbits—the friendly butcher shop rabbit can also be infected.

BRAISED RABBIT

1	rabbit
4	tbsp. oil
1	carrot, peeled
1	small onion
½	small celery stick
6	parsley stems
½	piece bacon or pancetta
2	tbsp. unsalted butter
1½	cups wine (about)
1½	cups veal or chicken stock (about)
	Pinch of thyme
1	bay leaf
1	pint heavy cream
2	tbsp. dried basil
	Salt and pepper

Cut up the rabbit into pieces and brown quickly in the oil. Remove the oil. Chop the carrot, onion, celery, parsley stems, and bacon and sauté in the butter. Add the rabbit pieces, except for the breast, and pour enough wine and stock in equal parts to cover two-thirds of the rabbit. Bring this to a boil, turn down to a simmer, add the thyme and bay leaf, and cover with aluminum foil, pressing down and fitting it closely to the rabbit and liquid and bringing it over the sides of the pot for a good seal. Continue cooking on simmer until done (about an hour) or when a skewer inserted into the meat comes out clean. The breast meat should be added to the pot about 10 to 15 minutes before all is done. Meanwhile, in another pan, reduce the pint of cream to 1 cup and add the basil. Season the cream mixture with salt and pepper and set aside. Remove the rabbit pieces to a warmed serving platter and discard the bay leaf. Strain the liquid and return it to the pan to reduce to half its quantity. Add the reduced basil-cream mixture and check for seasoning. Season with salt and pepper and pour over the rabbit.

SAUTÉED CUCUMBERS

8 cucumbers
Salt and pepper
2 tbsp. unsalted butter
1 tsp. oil
Sprinkle of dill

Cut and peel the cucumbers in half lengthwise and scoop out the seeds with a teaspoon. Cut into ¼-inch slices and place in a colander. Sprinkle with salt and let drain for 40 minutes. Rinse the cucumber in cold water. Meanwhile melt the butter in a frying pan and add the oil. When it is hot, add the cucumber and sauté till just tender. Season with salt, pepper, and the dill.

RED PEPPER WITH BASIL

2 red peppers, seeded and
    julienned
3 tbsp. unsalted butter
1 tsp. basil
½ tsp. lemon juice
Salt and pepper

Sauté the red pepper in hot butter for just a minute. Add the basil and lemon juice and toss. Season with salt and pepper.

CLAFOUTIS (see page 9)

Rabbit Salad
Black Olive Bread
Baked Apples with Crème Anglaise

Serves four

RABBIT SALAD

1 rabbit
2 tbsp. oil
¼ cup veal or chicken stock
2 tbsp. red wine vinegar
¼ cup walnut oil
1 shallot, chopped fine
 Salt and pepper
2 tbsp. hazelnuts, chopped
 Bittergreen (chicory, escarole,
  radicchio)

Brush the rabbit with oil and cook in a preheated oven at 350° for about an hour. Remove the rabbit and cut all the meat from the bones and then into bite-size pieces. Now, with the stock, deglaze the pan in which the rabbit was cooked. Turn the heat to low. In a blender, whiz together the vinegar, oil, and shallot, taste for salt and pepper, and then add it to the stock in the pan. Toast hazelnuts a few minutes in the oven then wrap in a towel to steam and rub off the skins. Chop coarsely and reserve. Toss the rabbit meat and bittergreens together with the walnut oil and stock mixture. Sprinkle the hazelnuts in and check for salt and pepper. Serve immediately.

BLACK OLIVE BREAD

     3 cups all-purpose flour
     1 pkg. dry yeast
     1 tsp. salt
     ½ cup pitted black olives
     1 tsp. thyme

In a medium-size bowl, mix 1 cup of the flour with the yeast and add enough warm water (not hot water) to make a moist and cohesive ball. Fill the bowl with warm water so the ball is covered. Let sit 5 to 15 minutes until the ball pops to the surface.

Meanwhile take the remaining amount of flour (this can be all white flour or a mixture such as ⅔ white and ⅓ whole wheat) and put it on top of the counter. Make a trench in the middle of the pile and add the salt. Chop the olives coarsely and add to the flour trench. Add the thyme. You will also need to add a couple tablespoons of water, fluffing it into the flour with your fingers. The mixture should be slightly cohesive but not wet as the yeast/flour ball will be quite wet. When the ball has risen to the surface of the water, scoop it out and set in the middle of your pile of flour. Knead the ball and the flour together and continue to knead for 8 minutes or so.

Put the dough in an oiled or floured bowl with a towel over it and place in a warm spot to rise 2 hours or until doubled in bulk. Punch down and let rise again or shape and bake in a preheated oven at 425° till done (about 35 to 40 minutes). Remember, it can rise and be punched down four times, after that the yeast dies. Also, after the first rising it can be punched down and left to rise slowly overnight in the refrigerator.

BAKED APPLES WITH CRÈME ANGLAISE

          4 apples
          3 tbsp. granulated sugar
             Rind from one orange,
                blanched and julienned
         ¼ cup raisins
             Pats of butter

             For the crème anglaise:
          4 yolks
         ⅛ tsp. salt
         ¼ cup granulated sugar
         ½ cup milk
         ½ cup cream
          1 tbsp. liqueur (Grand
                Marnier is good)
             or vanilla

Bake the apples first. Combine the sugar, orange peel, and raisins together. Core the apples and cut the peel from the top and bottom. Fill each apple with the raisin mixture and dot the top with butter pats. Bake in a preheated oven at 375° for 40 minutes. While the apples cook, make the crème anglaise. Whisk together the yolks, salt, and sugar. Combine the milk and cream and whisk that into the yolks. Cook over a medium-high heat, stirring constantly until it thickens quite suddenly. Remove from the heat, strain, and then whisk till cool. Add the liqueur or vanilla and spoon the crème anglaise over the cooked apples. Can be served hot or cold.

**Boar with Ginger and Orange Sauce
Fried Bread
Fried Sage Leaves
Good Floating Island**

Serves four

Fried sage leaves sounds perhaps peculiar, but these are a delightful taste sensation. The quantity suggested here is really only a minimum requirement. If you have additional large leaves, use them.

BOAR WITH GINGER AND ORANGE SAUCE

A large sprig of rosemary
4 to 5 lbs. roast of boar, cleaned of any fat
¼ cup cognac
2 cups stock (preferably veal)
½ cup fresh orange juice
orange rind peeled with a potato peeler (no white pith)
5 tbsp. unsalted butter
2 tsp. fresh ginger, peeled and julienned
Salt and pepper
Sprigs of watercress

Put the sprig of rosemary in the bottom of a medium roasting pan and put the boar on top. Roast the boar for 1½ to 2 hours at 325°. Remove the roast to a warm platter. Remove the rosemary.

Deglaze the pan with cognac, add the veal stock, and ½ cup of orange juice (be sure to save the rind from the orange). Reduce the liquid by half, whisking continuously. Add the butter and continue whisking. Blanch and julienne the orange rind. Add ginger and orange rind to the stock mixture and remove from the heat. Then add any of the juices from the sliced meat and season with salt and pepper. Serve the boar with the sauce and garnish with watercress.

FRIED BREAD

8 1-inch slices of French or
     Italian bread
4 tbsp. unsalted butter
   Salt and pepper
2 tbsp. fontina cheese, grated, or
     any cheese

Dry bread in oven at 300°. Fry in melted butter. Sprinkle with salt, pepper, and cheese. Put back in oven to just melt.

FRIED SAGE LEAVES

½ cup large sage leaves
2 tbsp. unsalted butter

Fry the sage leaves in butter until they are stiff. Remove with wooden tongs and season with salt. Use as a garnish on or around meat or as an hors d'oeuvre.

GOOD FLOATING ISLAND (see page 116)

Salmon

Salmon is a wonderful fish. Whether you fish for Atlantic or Pacific salmon or pull them out of Lake Michigan, their energy and excitement in the water are unmistakable. A beautiful, flavorful fish that lends itself to many varied recipes, he is surely as interesting and fun in the kitchen as in the water. Except when he is to be poached.

On a trip several years ago to Labrador we were lucky enough to bring home twelve beautiful Atlantic salmon. Obviously recipe versatility was called for, poaching being one of the clear and desirable choices. I learned quickly that you should always release the salmon that are over the size of 24 inches if you intend to poach them. In all of North America (and probably Europe, too) there does not exist a poacher large enough for any salmon I've had the pleasure of meeting. I know this for a fact since I called every kitchen store in the world looking for a poacher over the size of 24 inches. Many of the recipes I found in my cookbooks called for poaching large salmon in the dishwasher(?!) This being too bizarre, I spoke with my professional friends. First, I talked with our French-Canadian publisher friend—a great fisherman, and the person who had accompanied us to Labrador. He had gotten his poacher by welding together two stainless sausage containers found in a remote meatpacking house in northern Quebec. This was not too helpful. I then spoke with my cooking friends, who referred me to restaurant supply houses in East Boston but who suggested that I own a restaurant before attempting to purchase anything there as the prices would require that kind of cash flow.

No, I never found a big poacher. I curled him up in my turkey roaster and cooked him just fine, though. But if you, too, have found that poaching a salmon has lost some of its romantic appeal, these menus with salmon should provide plenty of *ooh-la-la* inspiration.

Whole Poached Salmon If You Must
Green Mayonnaise
Salad of Zucchini and Yellow Squash and Tomato
Grand Marnier Rice Pudding

Serves four

Yes, I realize there are definitely times when poaching a salmon is the only conceivable cooking method. The cooked salmon is then good hot or cold, of course, and looks good and makes you look good. If you plan to poach the fish and serve it cold you may want to consider decorating it the way the guys in the tall white hats do. Let the fish cool after poaching it and peel the skin off the body. Gently scrape the thin layer of gray meat off with a knife. Layer halved slices of cucumber in rows over the body so the cucumber resembles large fish scales. Cherry tomatoes are nice for an eye patch, and, of course, good ol' hard-boiled eggs can be used for the bordering. Use your imagination and plan on this taking a while. But, in my opinion, decorating is completely unnecessary if the salmon is going to be served to fishermen; they like the way he looks just fine.

The rice pudding looks most attractive when served in a glass bowl.

WHOLE POACHED SALMON IF YOU MUST

1 whole salmon, gutted and
   scaled
Your liquid should be ⅔ water
   and ⅓ wine. For each bottle
   of wine add:
½ cup vinegar
2 quarts water
2 onions, chopped
1 carrot, chopped
3 shallots, chopped
Salt and pepper
1 bay leaf
1 tsp. thyme
6 parsley stems
3 whole peppercorns

Combine all the ingredients except for the fish. You may use red wine for a nice change. Cook this court bouillon 30 minutes and let cool. Wrap the salmon well in cheesecloth and, if you decide to remove the head, be sure to cover the end with tin foil. Cook the fish on a rack with the court bouillon reaching just to the rack. Simmer in the oven at 200° for 8 minutes per pound.

GREEN MAYONNAISE

¾ tsp. salt
1 tsp. prepared mustard
4 tbsp. vinegar and lemon juice, mixed
4 egg yolks
2½ cups good corn or peanut oil
A few grinds of pepper
A dash of cayenne pepper
A big handful of de-stemmed
    spinach leaves
3 tbsp. shallots, chopped very fine
1 cup watercress leaves
¼ cup parsley leaves
2 tbsp. dried basil, reconstituted with
    a few tablespoons of hot water

Any dry herbs added should first be blanched in a small amount of water for 30 seconds and puréed. Beat salt, mustard, vinegar, and lemon juice together. Add egg yolks. Whisk until foamy. Slowly add oil. Add herbs near end. Finish up and season to taste. If adding salt, dissolve in a little hot water first. It may all be made quickly and easily in a food processor.

SALAD OF ZUCCHINI AND YELLOW SQUASH AND TOMATO

Salt and pepper
2 tbsp. good vinegar
⅓ cup olive oil
1 tsp. good prepared mustard
Fresh basil leaves—the little-leafed kind,
    if possible, called spiley globe
2 tiny zucchini, julienned
3 tiny yellow squash, julienned
Corn oil or cooking oil
1 head Boston lettuce or 2 Bibb, cleaned
1 tomato, skinned, seeded,
    drained, and julienned

First mix salt, pepper, and vinegar and then add the olive oil, mustard, and basil leaves and zip in the blender for a second or two. Sauté zucchini and yellow squash in corn oil until they just begin to cook. Be sure they keep some of their crispness. Let cool. Toss with lettuce, tomatoes, and dressing, or you can keep the squashes separate and lay the alternate colors out in groups on top of the lettuce. Taste for salt and pepper.

GRAND MARNIER RICE PUDDING

½ cup rice, cooked in water
¼ cup, plus 2 tbsp. water
¾ cup, plus 4 tbsp. Grand Marnier
½ to ¾ cup yellow raisins
¾ cup light cream
¾ cup milk
Peel of 1 orange, grated
1 envelope of gelatin
4 egg yolks
A pinch of salt
⅓ cup granulated sugar
1 cup heavy cream

Rinse the cooked rice in a strainer under warm water and put in 250° oven to dry a little. Fluff with a fork a few times. In a small pot with ¼ cup water and ¾ cup Grand Marnier add the raisins and bring to simmer. Cook until raisins are plump and liquid almost evaporated. Combine the light cream and milk in a small pot and add the grated orange. Bring to scald. Remove from heat and let sit for 40 minutes to infuse the flavor. Strain orange rind out.

Melt the gelatin in a custard cup with 2 tablespoons of water. Set in small pan on low heat to melt. Whisk the egg yolks, pinch of salt, and sugar together. Add the milk and cream mixture to it. While whisking, cook on medium-high or high heat. Add dissolved gelatin and stir constantly until thick. It will become thick quite suddenly. Strain immediately onto rice and stir. Add raisins. Stir. Add 3 tablespoons Grand Marnier. Taste and add more if you like. Whip the heavy cream and add to it any raisin juice and 1 tablespoon Grand Marnier. Whip only to be very soft—no peaks. Stir the custard/rice mixture with a large rubber spatula, resting over a bowl of ice and water. Be sure to let the custard bowl touch the ice water. Stir constantly but lightly as the gelatin sets. Stir until a path through the center of the mixture remains bare for a second. Then stir in ¼ of the whipped cream. Mix well, then fold in the rest of the whipped cream. Gently turn into an oiled mold and let sit in the refrigerator until set. You can do this the day before. Unmold just before serving. Serve alone or with sliced berries topped with a little sugar.

Salmon Scallops
Watercress Salad
Potato Gratin
Grand Marnier Soufflé

Serves four

Using very good prepared mustards that are not too hot and that tout
herbs on their labels is critical to making a good salad dressing. Some cities
(Boston and London for certain) have stores where their sole purpose in life
is to sell different mustards. Next time your rich brother-in-law goes to
London, tell him he can make points by bringing you back some fancy
mustard.

SALMON SCALLOPS

2 tbsp. shallots, minced
¼ cup cider vinegar or lemon juice,
   strained
½ cup very dry white wine
   Salt and pepper
8 ¼-inch salmon scallops, cut from
   fillets, about 2 lbs. in all
2 sticks or 8 oz. unsalted butter at
   room temperature

Combine shallots, vinegar, wine, a little salt, and a grind of pepper.
Simmer slowly until reduced by one-third. This you can do ahead. Sauté the
salmon very quickly in a couple of tablespoons or so of butter, to count of 3
or 4 each side. Remove to platter or plates. Spoon fat out of pan. Add the
vinegar mixture to the fish pan. Scrape around for goodies and on very low
heat whisk in the butter slowly to make a foaming sauce. Taste for seasoning.
Add salt and pepper if necessary. Serve over fish.

WATERCRESS SALAD

1 garlic clove, peeled and crushed
2 tbsp. wine vinegar
1 tsp. prepared mustard
1 tsp. soy sauce
  Salt and pepper
⅓ cup good quality olive oil
1 head Boston lettuce or 2 Bibb,
   washed
1 bunch watercress without stems,
   washed
½ head red lettuce, washed

Rub salad bowl with garlic. Combine in the blender the vinegar, mustard, soy sauce, salt, and pepper and zip on high for a second or two. Add olive oil and blend again. Toss with the greens and serve with a crusty bread and butter and a couple of cheeses if you like.

POTATO GRATIN

1 clove garlic
1 tbsp. unsalted butter (soft)
4 to 6 Idaho potatoes
2-plus cups cream
  Salt and pepper
  Nutmeg, whole to grate
¼ cup fontina cheese, grated
   (optional)

Rub a medium-size baking dish with the peeled garlic clove. Let dry. Then grease with the butter. Peel and slice potatoes very thin. Make a layer of potatoes covering the bottom. Cover with cream. Season with salt, pepper, and nutmeg. Add another layer of potatoes, putting in the cheese here if you like, then more cream, salt, pepper, nutmeg, etc. Top with a layer of cream. Bake in a 300° oven for at least an hour or until butter starts to bubble around the edge. Let sit 10 minutes at least before serving.

GRAND MARNIER SOUFFLÉ

5 tbsp. granulated sugar, plus
   some for dusting
3 tbsp. flour
1 cup milk
1 vanilla bean
   Grated rind of one small
   orange (optional)
4 eggs, separated
2 tbsp. soft unsalted butter,
   plus some for buttering
   mold
4 tbsp. Grand Marnier
   Pinch salt
1 extra egg white
   Confectioners' sugar

Butter and sugar a 6-cup soufflé mold. Stir the flour with a tablespoon or so of the cold milk. Bring to a boil the rest of the milk with 4 heaping tablespoons of sugar and the vanilla bean. Remove from heat and let sit for 10 minutes. Stir in flour mixture (and orange rind if used). Stir over medium-high heat until mixture thickens. Stirring continually until it just boils, remove from heat. Continue to stir. Add the egg yolks one by one to sauce. Whisking well after each addition, whisk in the butter and the Grand Marnier. Beat the 5 egg whites and a pinch of salt together until it reaches the soft peak stage. Add 1 tablespoon sugar and beat until stiff and a whole egg in its shell will sit on top of the whites sinking in only ⅓ of the way. Stir ¼ of the whites into the milk, yolk, sugar mixture and then fold in the rest of the whites. Put in mold. It should only be ¾ full. Cook at 375° for about 15 to 20 minutes. Then, during the last 10 minutes of cooking, open the oven door and quickly sprinkle the top with confectioners' sugar. Do this a few times for a glaze. Soufflé will be done in about ½ hour in all. Be sure it is cooked through. Serve immediately, of course.

Salmon Medallions with Black Olive and Basil Butter
Fiddleheads with Fried Bread Crumbs
Julienned Carrots
Poached Pears and Figs
Sugar Cookies

Serves four

In *Gray's Wild Game Cookbook* (page 65 in this combined volume), there is quite a long description of the Chet Reneson method of cleaning fiddleheads. The method involves dressing in full sou'wester outfit and tearing down a long lake in a motorboat, holding up each fiddlehead as you speed along, in hopes of getting the chaff off. This description has produced several letters from readers, either querying what the heck were fiddleheads or suggesting their own rather bizarre and unprintable techniques for removing the chaff from fiddleheads.

Fiddleheads are unfurled baby ferns, very delicious greens. It is possible to get the chaff off by plunging them in boiling water for a few minutes and then draining and rinsing and patting them dry on a towel that you intend to throw away after the fiddleheads are clean. This must be repeated multiple times and is very tedious work. Try to pick the ones that are clean or find them already clean and in cellophane at your grocer.

SALMON MEDALLIONS

4 salmon steaks about ¾ inch
     thick
3 tbsp. unsalted butter
     Salt and pepper

To prepare the salmon medallions, first slice from a whole, cleaned salmon four ¾-inch steaks. This can be done with a still-frozen, but gutted, fish by using a saw. This has the advantage of giving you just what you need at the time and returning the rest of the salmon to the freezer for future use. Or, with a fresh fish, use a sharp knife and a cleaver to get through the backbone. Now with a pair of small pliers remove all needle bones from the four steaks. You can feel these by running your fingers over the flesh. Remember to do both sides. With a very sharp knife remove the skin and the center backbone from each salmon steak; now you will have two pieces from each salmon steak. Lay the pieces down as if they were still attached and then flip one upside down so that the fat parts face each other and the thin parts go off in opposite directions. Now wrap the thin parts around in their natural curve (they will both be going in the same direction) and push in four toothpicks to hold together. You should now have a round, boneless salmon steak called a medallion. You can do all this in the morning, and then put the medallions on a plate covered with some plastic wrap in the refrigerator until dinner. To cook the salmon, melt the butter in a frying pan over medium-high heat. Put the salmon in and cook this first side for 4 to 6 minutes, the second side for just a few minutes (remember fish continues to cook even though it's been removed from the heat, so remove the salmon when the center of each medallion is still a little bit darker pink). Place each medallion on a warm plate and season with salt and pepper. Put the compound butter (see below) immediately on top.

BLACK OLIVE AND BASIL BUTTER

1 stick unsalted butter
2 tbsp. dried basil, reconstituted
    in 2 tbsp. hot water
4 oil-cured black olives, pits
    removed and chopped fine
Salt and pepper
Lemon juice

Let the butter soften and then whip it till fluffy. Squeeze out the water from the reconstituted basil and add basil to the butter. Combine the butter and basil with the chopped olives. Add salt, pepper, and lemon juice to your taste and then whip again. Turn the butter mixture out onto a large piece of plastic wrap and roll it up, shaping it as you roll into a log. Freeze for 24 hours, bringing it out of the refrigerator an hour or so before the salmon is cooked. Slice butter and use a tiny cookie cutter to cut the butter pats for atop the salmon. (The remainder of the butter can be used in soup or as a nice sandwich spread. Keeps 1 month in the freezer.)

FIDDLEHEADS WITH FRIED BREAD CRUMBS

1 cup clarified unsalted butter
¼ tsp. chopped garlic
3 tbsp. hard bread crumbs
    Salt and pepper
1 lb. fiddleheads, cleaned and
    blanched
2 tbsp. unsalted butter

For the bread crumbs, heat the clarified butter and add to it the garlic and bread crumbs. Sauté until the bread crumbs are a nice golden brown and then season with salt and pepper. Now sauté the blanched fiddleheads in 2 tablespoons of butter until they are hot. Toss the bread crumbs and fiddleheads together and check for seasoning. Serve immediately.

JULIENNED CARROTS

8 to 10 nice-size carrots
2 tbsp. unsalted butter
1 tbsp. fresh parsley, chopped fine
    Salt and pepper

Scrape the outside of each carrot with a vegetable peeler and cut into 2-inch lengths. Now julienne into ⅛-inch sticks. Blanch in boiling water for about 5 minutes or until just tender and then drain. Sauté the carrots quickly in butter, adding the parsley, salt, and pepper to your taste.

POACHED PEARS AND FIGS

1 vanilla bean, split
2 cloves
2 cups water
½ cup granulated sugar
¼ lb. dried figs
½ lb. dried pears (Fresh, still-hard
      pears can be used, too. In this
      case, peel and core the pears.)
   Crème fraîche

Bring to a boil the first four ingredients and let simmer 5 to 10 minutes. Add the figs, cover, and cook very gently until they are soft, about 45 minutes. Add the pears and continue to cook for another 15 minutes. Remove the fruit and reduce the syrup over a high heat by one-quarter. Serve with the syrup and crème fraîche.

SUGAR COOKIES

¾ cup unsalted butter, softened
½ cup granulated sugar
¼ tsp. salt
1 egg
1 tsp. grated orange rind
   Dash of vanilla
2 cups cake flour
   Cinnamon-sugar sprinkles

Cream the butter into the sugar and salt. Whip till fluffy. Add 1 egg, orange rind, and vanilla and mix. Blend in the flour. Refrigerate the dough, covered, about an hour until it is firm. Roll out in small batches and cut with a cookie cutter. Sprinkle with cinnamon sugar and bake at 350° till just starting to brown around the edges (about 7 minutes or so).

Fresh Mozzarella Slices
Grilled Whole Salmon
Rice Pilaf
Peas and Artichoke Hearts
Raspberry Tart

Serves four

A good homemade tart pastry is, to my way of thinking, one of the most difficult items to make. Little French girls learn at their mothers' sides and have the advantage of years of practice. Big American girls learn at the side of their cooking instructor and anonymously leave piles of gray dough on the instructor's doorstep in frustration and anger. If you master the technique for good tart pastry you will most certainly be rewarded by the *oohs* and *aahs* of your guests. I do believe that pastry making is something that cannot be described in a cookbook; you must see someone do it. Consequently, if you haven't had the chance to observe an expert at work, use frozen Pepperidge Farm pastry sheets. They are a whole lot better than gray piles of dough.

FRESH MOZZARELLA SLICES

As a first course, thinly slice fresh mozzarella or otalegio cheese. Drizzle good olive oil on it and sprinkle with cracked black pepper. Serve with homemade bread.

GRILLED WHOLE SALMON

Clean the salmon and remove the head. Also scrape the scales off. Wash the cavity well with fresh water and sprinkle the cavity with salt, pepper, and your choice of herbs. Brush the salmon's skin with olive oil or butter. Heat the grill till very hot, a gas grill for 20 minutes. While this is happening, measure the girth of the fish at the thickest point. Calculate the number of inches times ten and that's your approximate total cooking time for both sides of the fish.

RICE PILAF

½ cup unsalted butter
2 cups rice
4 cups hot chicken stock (If using
cubes to make stock, Knorr
is preferable.)

Melt the butter in a large pan with a lid. Sauté the rice in the butter until quite hot and add the stock. Lower the heat to a simmer and put a towel over the pan and then the lid. Cook about 25 minutes depending on the depth of the pan. The rice is done when the grains are plump and separate and all the liquid has been absorbed.

PEAS AND ARTICHOKE HEARTS

2 8-oz. cans of artichoke hearts
in brine
2 lbs. fresh peas
2 oz. pancetta, chopped fine
3 tbsp. unsalted butter
Salt and pepper

Several hours before using, drain the artichoke hearts and rinse in lukewarm water. Let sit in a bowl of cool water, changing the water at least twice to remove any tinny taste. Drain and slice into quarters. While you're waiting for the artichokes to bathe, shell the peas. Blanch in boiling salted water for a minute or two, drain and plunge into ice water. Drain again and set aside. In a large saucepan, combine pancetta and butter and fry on medium heat for a few minutes. Add the artichoke hearts and heat thoroughly. Add the peas and cook till hot. Season with salt and fresh cracked pepper.

RASPBERRY TART (see page 123)

Salmon Hash Patties
Sage Bread
Three Green Salad

Serves four

I do believe that the different species of salmon are different from each other in taste. Certainly the Pacific salmon taste different from the Atlantic and the everywhere salmon, the coho, different from them. The meat of the Atlantic salmon is quite a bit paler than other salmon and seems to have a lighter, more delicate flavor. I prefer the Atlantic salmon. Is that because I live on the Atlantic ocean? But for this recipe the best salmon would be the more hearty-flavored coho; or actually the best salmon for this recipe is the one that has been cooked and in your refrigerator and needs to be used up.

SALMON HASH PATTIES

1 very small onion, chopped fine
1 small celery stick, chopped fine
¼ cup unsalted butter
2 cups leftover cooked salmon, no
   bones or skin, and flaked
2 eggs, beaten lightly
1 large Idaho potato, cooked and
   mashed
   Salt and pepper
   Flour for dredging

Sauté the onion and celery in 2 tablespoons of the butter until they are wilted. Place the salmon in a mixing bowl with the cooked onion and celery plus the eggs and potato. Season with salt, pepper, and a little chopped parsley if you like. Form into patties and dip lightly in flour. Sauté in the remaining butter until golden.

SAGE BREAD

1 package yeast
2⅓ cups all-purpose unbleached
    white flour
⅔ cup whole-wheat flour
1 tsp. salt
1½ tsp. dried sage (not ground)
1 tsp. oil

In a medium-size bowl, mix the yeast with 1 cup of the all-purpose flour and enough warm water to form a cohesive ball of dough, but keep it gooey. Mark an **X** on top and then fill the bowl with warm water. Let sit 5 to 15 minutes and the ball will pop up to the surface. While the sponge rests, mix the remaining flours, salt, and sage together. Add the oil and enough room-temperature water to form another ball, but this one should be very dry. When the sponge pops up, scoop it out of the water and add it to the dry ball. Knead together for 6 to 8 minutes or until the dough is firm and elastic. Let rise in a lightly-oiled bowl covered with a towel for about 2 hours or until doubled in bulk. Punch down and then shape into a loaf by flattening it out and rolling it up tightly. Then again flatten it in the other direction and roll it up, pinching loose ends together. This will allow the bread to keep its shape. Place on floured baking sheet and make slashes with a knife on top of the loaf. Let rise till almost doubled in bulk. It should take less time this rising, approximately an hour or so. Preheat oven to 400° for 30 minutes. If you use baking tiles put them in; if not, put in another baking sheet to preheat also. Just before baking, re-slash the bread and sprinkle baking sheet with cornmeal. Then carefully roll bread off onto hot baking surface. Bake for 35 to 40 minutes. Let cool on a rack.

THREE GREEN SALAD

3 tbsp. wine vinegar
  Salt and pepper
2 tsp. good prepared mustard
¼ tsp. garlic, chopped fine or
  squeezed through a press
  A dash of soy sauce
½ cup olive oil

1 tbsp. mayonnaise
  At least three different
    greens: endive, water-
    cress, Boston lettuce,
    or whatever is available
    to you
6 strips of cooked bacon

Combine the vinegar, salt, pepper, mustard, garlic, and soy sauce. Add the oil and mix well. Now add the mayonnaise and mix well again. Toss dressing with the greens. Crumble the bacon into the salad and toss again.

Leftover Salmon Salad
Tuscan Muffins
Another Grand Marnier Soufflé

Serves four

Why do we have two Grand Marnier soufflé recipes in this book? Recipes have different styles and suit individuals differently. That's why so many cookbooks are sold. The end result for each of these soufflés is the same, a delicious desert, but you may find one recipe is easier and produces tastier results than the other. Try them both and stick with whatever works for you.

LEFTOVER SALMON SALAD

2 cucumbers
2 ripe tomatoes
2 small zucchini
2 tbsp. corn oil
  Cooked salmon, broken into
  chunks
  Homemade mayonnaise
    (see page 282)
1 tsp. grated lemon rind
  Fresh basil, preferably small leaf
  Salt and pepper
  Lettuce

Peel and seed the cucumber. Slice into ⅛-inch pieces; salt and let drain. Peel, seed, drain, and coarsely chop the tomatoes. Cut the zucchini in half the long way and then slice into ⅛-inch pieces. Sauté in a little corn oil.

Combine salmon, mayonnaise, lemon rind, and vegetables. Toss lightly but well and season to taste. At the last minute, add basil and tomatoes. Toss carefully again. Taste for seasoning and serve on lettuce.

TUSCAN MUFFINS

2¾ cups all-purpose flour
1 package dry yeast
¼ cup whole-wheat flour
1 tsp. salt
  Several tbsp. of melted
    pancetta fat or bacon fat

In a medium-size bowl, mix one cup of the all-purpose flour with the yeast and add enough warm water (not hot water) to make a moist and cohesive ball. Fill the bowl with enough warm water so the ball is covered. Let sit 5 to 15 minutes until the ball pops to the surface. Meanwhile take the remaining flours and put on top of the counter. Make a trench in the middle of the pile and add the salt. You will need to add water, a few tablespoons at a time, to the pile, fluffing it into the flour with your fingers. The mixture should be slightly cohesive but not wet, as the yeast/flour ball will be quite wet. When the ball has risen to the surface of the water, scoop it out and gather the two doughs together into one cohesive ball, kneading as little as possible. When they are well blended, roll the ball into a cylinder about 2 inches in diameter. With a sharp knife cut off muffins about ½ to ¾ inch thick. Dust one side with flour and set that end on a baking sheet. Make an indentation on the top of the muffins and dribble a little of the fat in each dent. Allow to rise until doubled in bulk. Bake in a preheated oven of 400° for 35 minutes. Serve while hot.

150

ANOTHER GRAND MARNIER SOUFFLÉ

        4   tbsp. sugar and some for
              dusting
        3   tbsp. flour
        1   tsp. grated orange rind
        8   tbsp. milk
        4   egg yolks
        1   tbsp. vanilla extract
     4½   tbsp. Grand Marnier liqueur
        5   egg whites and a pinch of salt
              Butter to grease the soufflé
              dish

In heavy saucepan mix sugar, flour, orange rind, and milk slowly together. Bring slowly to a boil and stir till mixture thickens. Remove from heat and cool slightly. Then add yolks one by one, beating after each addition. Add vanilla extract and liqueur. In separate large bowl, beat salt and egg whites until they hold a whole uncooked egg, letting the egg sink in only ¼ to ⅓ of the way. Stir ⅓ of the egg white mixture into the base, mixing well. Then fold in the remaining whites. Have ready a buttered and sugared 6-cup soufflé mold. Fill with the soufflé, tap on counter once to release any large air pockets, and cook in a 400° preheated oven for 30 to 35 minutes.

Smoked Salmon Salad
Fried Broccoli
Fresh French Whole-Wheat Bread
Fruit and Cheeses

Serves four

Fresh homemade bread is the best. In France you learn to truly appreciate how fresh bread (that means only a few hours old) enhances the meal. The bakeries there bake bread twice a day and you buy your bread twice a day. I've read that an average French person will eat a pound of bread a day. I find this completely understandable having lived with their bread for a while. Although it is not in our tradition to go out twice a day for bread, it is possible to find very fresh bread at local gourmet shops or bakeries. This is worth the trip for this meal.

SMOKED SALMON SALAD

      1 orange
      1 red onion, peeled and sliced thin
         Olive oil
2 to 3 tbsp. Armagnac
         Salt and fresh ground pepper
      4 portions of smoked salmon
         (about 2 cups)

Cut both ends off the orange. Stand the orange on one of the squared off ends and with a large, very sharp knife, cut away both the peel and the pith (the white part) from the top to bottom. When finished, you will have a completely peeled orange. Now separate and remove the sections (a small knife is best to cut between the sections). Place orange pieces on a plate and set aside.

Place the peeled, sliced onion in a small saucepan with a lid. Add a bit of olive oil. Steam over low heat till partially cooked (to remove the onion taste) but still a wee bit crunchy. Raise the lid and toss in the Armagnac. Replace the lid and remove from the heat to steep for a few minutes. Divide the onion between four plates, using your judgment as to quantity. You may not need it all. Season with salt and pepper. Top with the smoked salmon. Dribble with good green olive oil and place the orange segments around the edges.

FRIED BROCCOLI

      1 head broccoli, separated into
         florets with 1- to 1½-inch
         stems
      ½ cup flour
         Salt and pepper
         Grated lemon rind from
         1 lemon
      1 beaten egg
         Milk to moisten to the right
         texture
         Olive oil for frying

Blanch the broccoli in boiling water until it is almost tender, but not quite. Refresh the broccoli in ice water, drain and let dry. Now combine the flour, salt, pepper, lemon rind, egg, and enough milk so the mixture is a good-consistency batter. Dip the broccoli in the batter. Fry in hot olive oil. Drain on paper towels and serve at once with a lemon wedge if desired.

Salmon Calzone
Green Salad
The Best Brownies

Serves four

    Cintra has the nice tradition of giving brownies as a birthday present. This is a particularly nice gift when your birthday is in the summer and the children are away at camp. It also is a particularly nice gift because they are particularly nice brownies.

    Calzone is a loaf of bread with stuff in the middle (usually meat or fish). It is very good for Sunday suppers, mother-in-law lunches, or cold in a picnic driving to your favorite grouse covert.

SALMON CALZONE

2⅔ cups all-purpose flour
 1 pkg. dry yeast
⅓ cup whole-wheat flour
 1 tsp. salt
 3 tbsp. dried tarragon, revived
      with a few tablespoons of
      hot water
 1 small onion, chopped fine and
      sautéed in 2 tbsp. unsalted
      butter
1½ cups cooked salmon, broken
      into pieces
⅔ cup cooked rice
⅓ cup white wine, seasoned with
      salt and pepper
 1 tbsp. chopped parsley
   Salt and pepper

In a medium-size mixing bowl, mix 1 cup of the all-purpose flour with the yeast and add enough warm water (not hot water) to make a moist and cohesive ball. Fill the bowl with warm water so the ball is covered. Let sit 5 to 15 minutes until the ball pops to the surface. Meanwhile take the remaining flours, and put them on top of the counter. Make a trench in the middle and add salt. Reconstitute the tarragon by mixing it with a little hot water. Put 2 tablespoons of the revived tarragon in the trench (save the third tablespoon for later). You will need to add more water, fluffing it into the flour with your fingers. The mixture should be slightly cohesive but not wet, as the yeast/flour ball will be quite wet. When the ball has risen to the surface of the water, scoop it out and set it in the middle of your flour pile. Knead the flour and the ball together and continue to knead for 5 to 8 minutes or so. Put the dough in an oiled or floured bowl with a towel over it and place in a warm spot to let rise two hours or until doubled in bulk. Punch down and roll out into a 3-inch-by-12-inch rectangle. Sauté the chopped onion and mix all together with the salmon, cooked rice, wine, parsley, and the remaining revived tarragon, and taste for seasoning. Lay on bread and close bread up, tightly pinching seam. Flip so seam is on the bottom. Let rise about 1 hour and bake in a 425° preheated oven (on tiles if you have them, on the bottom oven shelf) for about 35 to 40 minutes. Let cool to room temperature before serving.

THE BEST BROWNIES

    2 squares unsweetened chocolate
    1 stick unsalted butter
    1 cup granulated sugar
    2 eggs
    1 tsp. vanilla
    ¼ cup flour
    ¼ tsp. salt
    1 cup chopped walnuts

Preheat oven to 325°. Melt together the chocolate and butter and then stir in the sugar. Beat together the eggs and vanilla and add them to the chocolate mixture. Now quickly stir in the flour, salt, and chopped nuts. Spread in greased 8-inch-by-8-inch pan and bake 40 to 45 minutes at 325°. Do not over-cook or they will be dry. Cake tester should just come out clean. Let cool in pan. Then cut in squares and remove. The first brownie will be hard to get out and may stick and crumble. Do not be deterred. These are the best brownies.

Saltwater Fish

One of the great advantages of being a fisherman is that you can only come home with the local, and consequently freshest, fish (as opposed to being enticed into trying fresh mako shark when you are at a fish store in Chicago). No matter how adamant the Dallas waiter is that his ten-pound lobster flown in from Nova Scotia is the best in the world, I know that the one-pound lobster I get from my friend who scuba dives for them off a Massachusetts beach is the best. It's not just because it's the freshest, but because now, as a twenty-year resident of New England, I have learned that the biggest lobsters are not necessarily the tastiest, just as I know that the snapper blues (bluefish in the 1- to 2-pound range) are great grilled whole and the regular blues should be steaked.

There is no better guide to the cook than local lore. Ed and I were fortunate to be able to travel to France with our children for a two-week stay with some friends in a chateau. The meals were cooked by madame (the caretaker's wife) but we did the obtaining of the food. We purchased from the local market the only fish large enough to feed us all, a *merlu*. It was a rather ugly looking bottom-feeding type of fish, which turned out to be similar to our hake. Certainly a respectable fish, but not one I would have spent much time on. Madame made a lovely court bouillon and then a simple *beurre-blanc* to go over it, a recipe I would have reserved for salmon. It was wonderful; she knew how to cook her own local fish.

I will not profess to know more than you do about a fish that surrounds you. You will note that I have not included in this book every type of sport-fish that you can eat. I do not know that much and will not include a fish I know absolutely nothing about just for the sake of inclusion. With a fish that is not one of my most familiar fish I have tried at least to use some imagination with it—after all, redfish doesn't always have to be blackened.

157

There is one word of caution that must be thrown into this local lore concept. I spent nearly six months working at a hospital in northern Newfoundland. We lived in the orphanage, which was next door to the hospital and down the street from the fish docks and local fish cannery. We ate cod three meals a day for six months. It was very fresh and it was certainly being cooked by the locals and it was really terrible. I have come to believe that the cod was bad partially because we ate it so much and partially because the cook had no concept of when the fish had finished cooking. Her adage seemed to be, when in doubt cook for five hours, and she was always in doubt. Certainly "doneness" in fish cannot be reduced to precise minutes of time, as with a cake. There are too many variables to each fish for that. His size, the thickness of the fillet or steak, the amount of water left in the fish, and how cold it is all change cooking time. It is definitely better to learn to rely on seeing, tasting, smelling, and touching a fish for doneness. Always, always, a fish should be cut into and tasted before serving. The first bluefish I ever had was served by a hostess whose gas stove had run out of propane but she'd decided to serve it anyway. I nearly never ate bluefish again. Undone fish is really revolting, but taste the fish before you think it's done. It can always be cooked more, but over-cooking is impossible to undo. The cooking times in this book are always to be regarded as approximates, and you will notice that in some cases I have not written a time. This is because your seeing and smelling and tasting the fish are better guides to its doneness than something cast into the words of a book. Don't trust books on this stuff; trust yourself.

Inshore Saltwater Fish

One time I went fishing with David on his 25-foot cabin cruiser. It had been one of those last-minute, it's-such-a-beautiful-day, let's-go-fishing, trips. Ed was working too hard and couldn't go, but I had only to drag along one baby—and find the right fishing equipment in the garage. I was pretty used to saltwater fishing but rarely (if ever) went fishing without Ed. And Ed was king of equipment in our household. He wasn't what you would call manic about the care of the hunting and fishing equipment. In fact he was what you really would call casual. Rust and saltwater corrosion were on intimate terms with all our equipment. But he did have the distinct advantage of knowing where in that great expansive morass of stuff even the tiniest fly would be hiding. I did not have this advantage—if the stuff in front of me looked like it could catch a fish, grab it. What did it matter if we were going mackerel fishing and I had grabbed a surf-casting rod or if the lighter weight rod had white stuff all over the ferrules—they were both fishing rods, weren't they?

The little rod had been real hard to put together, but I'd fixed it up with a jigging rig, David had purchased some Cokes and bait all at the same stop, and the baby was cooing in his little seat on the deck of the boat. We were ready to go. We steamed out of Gloucester Harbor. We spent an hour or two bobbing along, dipping the rods rhythmically, playing with the baby, watching him be lulled to sleep by the rocking of the boat. We talked, and ate, and drank beer, and let the sun beat on us. We would anchor and fish, then move and troll. David got a bluefish right off, then we waited a long time. Then, *wham*, David's jigging rig tugged and wiggled and bent and looked 25 pounds heavier; then *wham*, mine did too! Scrambling for the rods before they'd flip out of the holders, we began to crank and pull, and crank and pull. As the lines shortened we both realized we each had four fish on at once. We were both yelling gleefully back and forth about our prosperity, trying to drive the boat, and get the fish all inside the boat. The baby had tipped over strapped in his chair and lay crying on his stomach with arms and legs flailing, the chair on his back turtle-style. This was worse than a Chinese fire drill! Holding the rod in my right hand, I tried to right the baby's seat with my left. David's fish flopped about on the deck. Suddenly the end of my rod fell off and was shooting down the monofilament. I quickly decided to drop the baby and go for the rod tip. As I was leaning over the side of the boat to grab the other end of the rod, the boat lurched, and there was a moment when I thought I would be joining the fish in the water—instead the butt-end of the rod did. Now I was laughing so hard that I was totally useless in trying to retrieve the rod or land the fish. David came to the rescue, boat-hooked the rod, jammed it back together, and brought the mackerel into the boat. I comforted the baby.

Well-maintained equipment is essential both in fishing and in cooking. A rod that falls apart when it's catching a fish and a knife that is too dull to fillet a fish provide the same sad results: nothing to eat. Both cooking and fishing have a tendency to produce equipment maniacs; this is to be avoided. There is as little reason to fill your kitchen with the superfluous pastry crimpers as there is to fill your tackle box with scent for plastic worms. Just give me my well-oiled green Penn reel and a barbecue grill and we'll call it dinner.

Grilled Bluefish
Grilled Polenta
Chicory and Escarole Salad
Melon Ice

Serves four

Polenta is a wonderful item for getting starch into a menu and diet. A form of polenta, not using the cornmeal but a different grain, was carried by the Roman soldiers when they went to fight against Hannibal. A recipe that has stood the test of that kind of time has got to have merit.

GRILLED BLUEFISH

1½ sticks unsalted butter
    Salt and pepper
3 medium cloves garlic, chopped
    fine
2 tsp. finely chopped fresh sage
1½ to 2 lbs. bluefish fillets, skin on and
    slashed

Make the compound butter in advance. Whip the butter until light and fluffy. Add salt, pepper, garlic, and sage. Mix well and mound onto plastic wrap. Form into a cylinder and freeze for 24 hours. Bring to room temperature before using. Grill fish, flesh side first, 8 minutes per side. When done spread the butter over each fillet and serve.

GRILLED POLENTA

A few slices of pancetta,
     diced
1 onion
½ cup unsalted butter
3 cups milk
1 cup water
1 cup cornmeal
½ tsp. fresh grated nutmeg
    Salt and pepper

Sauté pancetta until just crispy. Save the fat. Chop onion very fine and sauté in the butter until translucent. Add the milk. Bring it to a boil. Combine water and cornmeal. Stir with a fork, then add to the boiling milk. Lower heat to medium and stir continuously until the mixture is so thick that the wooden spoon stands up in it. Remove from the heat and add the pancetta, nutmeg, salt, and pepper to taste. Lightly grease a cookie sheet and spread the polenta into a ½-inch-thick rectangle. Let stand until cool and hardened, several hours. Cut into squares and paint with melted butter and grill until hot and semi-toasted.

CHICORY AND ESCAROLE SALAD

1 tbsp. vinegar
    Salt and pepper
1 small shallot and 1 very small
     garlic clove, chopped extra
     fine
⅓ cup light olive oil
1 tbsp. heavy cream
    Grated rind of 1 orange
1 small head escarole, washed
     and dried
1 small head chicory, washed
     and dried
1 head Boston lettuce, washed
     and dried
1 orange in sections and cleaned
     of membranes

Combine vinegar, salt, pepper, shallot, and garlic. Let stand a bit to dissolve salt, then add oil, cream, and orange rind. Mix well. Toss with lettuces and orange segments.

MELON ICE

3 small ripe cantaloupes (you want
about 3 to 4 lbs. flesh)
3 tbsp. (approximately) Midori
liqueur or melon flavored
liqueur
6 to 8 tbsp. confectioners' sugar
Juice from 2 lemons
A pinch of salt
Enough salt and ice for the ice
cream machine

Discard the melon seeds, remove the flesh and purée in a food processor. Then add the remaining ingredients to the purée tasting it as you go for proper flavor. Stir well, chill, taste again for flavor and balance. Make according to your ice cream machine's directions. If the cantaloupe shells are the right size, chill them and use as individual serving containers. Pack the melon sorbet in 4 of the shells and chill thoroughly. Garnish with mint sprigs or cut a strawberry and fan it out.

Bluefish Broiled with Thyme and Noisette Butter
Asparagus
Perfect Tomatoes with Cognac Dressing
Raspberry Ice and Sugar Cookies

Serves four

Cooking bluefish fast and hot, as grilling or broiling does, is preferable, I believe, over baking or poaching or any other method because bluefish is quite an oily fish and needs the high heat to draw out the oil. For the same reason, bluefish is one of those fish that should never be frozen if it can be avoided.

BLUEFISH BROILED WITH THYME AND NOISETTE BUTTER

1 stick unsalted butter
2 small bluefish fillets
1 tbsp. thyme (preferably fresh)
   Salt and pepper

Heat one stick of butter till foaming and then stir gently with your small whisk over a high heat until the butter begins to turn a light brown. Remove it from the heat and continue whisking. If it begins to turn a darker brown, turn into a cool pot and whisk. If it gets black, throw it out and start again. Paint the bluefish fillets with the butter and sprinkle with thyme. Broil the fish until done and then season with salt and pepper. Pour any remaining butter over the fish and serve with lemon wedges.

ASPARAGUS

3 lbs. asparagus (or 6 to 10 spears
      per person, depending on the
      fatness of the spears)
   Melted butter
   Salt and pepper

Cut or break off the bottom end of each asparagus stalk and peel with a vegetable peeler. Peeling asparagus makes them taste better, look less nasty, and will impress your mother, so it's worth it.

Steam over boiling water until just tender when pierced with a fork. The asparagus should resist the fork just a little. Serve immediately with melted butter and salt and pepper.

164

PERFECT TOMATOES WITH COGNAC DRESSING

1 tbsp. red wine vinegar
1 tbsp. cognac
1 tsp. mustard
Salt and pepper
½ cup light olive oil
¼ cup heavy cream
6 or 8 tomatoes

Mix the vinegar, cognac, mustard, and dashes of salt and pepper. Whisk the cognac mixture together with the olive oil and the cream. Let sit for at least one hour. Immerse each tomato in boiling water for 10 seconds and put immediately into a cold water bath. Peel and slice the tomatoes and arrange attractively on a platter. Lightly sprinkle with salt and pepper and then dribble the dressing over the tomatoes.

RASPBERRY ICE WITH SUGAR COOKIES

8 cups raspberries
1 cup granulated sugar
½ cup water
Pinch of salt
1 tbsp. *framboise* (raspberry liqueur)
Enough salt and ice for the ice cream machine

Clean berries and purée in the blender. You should have one quart of purée. Boil the sugar in ½ cup water for five minutes, then let cool. Add the sugar syrup a little at a time to the purée, stirring all the time and occasionally checking the taste for sweetness. You may not need all of the sugar syrup; sweeten it to your taste. Add the salt and *framboise* and chill. Freeze according to your ice cream machine's directions.

For a good sugar cookie recipe, see page 144.

Broiled Striped Bass with Wild Mushrooms and Tomato
Peas and Artichoke Hearts
Chocolate Roll

Serves four

It sure is a good thing that grocery stores and gourmet shops are carrying a wider selection of mushrooms, both fresh and dried, because I was coming dangerously close to trying to learn to pick my own wild mushrooms. I probably would have ended up dead. Wild mushrooms are a very tricky business, and the best way to learn how to gather the safe ones is to go out in the woods with someone who has identified, picked, and eaten wild mushrooms and is still around to be your guide. Stick to one or two species, like puffballs or morels, which are easy to identify, and don't bother with trying to learn a whole broad range of wild mushrooms. And don't rely solely on books to teach you what each mushroom is. Wild mushrooms are spectacularly good, but good from a store, too.

BROILED STRIPED BASS WITH WILD MUSHROOMS AND TOMATO

1 lb. wild mushrooms—
    chanterelles, morels, etc.
4 tbsp. unsalted butter
    Salt and pepper
1 tsp. fresh thyme leaves
1 tsp. chopped parsley
4 striped bass steaks, about
    ½ pound each
    Olive oil basting oil
    (see page 176)
4 large tomato slices, seeded
    and drained

Clean (don't wash if possible) and chop mushrooms. Sauté in hot butter until just coated. Lower heat. Season with salt and pepper and add thyme. Cover pan and cook for 5 to 8 minutes until juices start to exude. Remove cover and raise heat and sauté, stirring until golden brown. Season to taste and sprinkle with parsley and set aside. Baste steaks lavishly with the olive oil basting oil and broil 6 to 8 minutes each side. Place a tomato slice on top of each steak and brush with olive oil basting oil and broil again until the tomatoes begin to brown, 2 or 3 minutes more. Season with salt and pepper. Top with wild mushrooms and serve at once.

PEAS AND ARTICHOKE HEARTS

2 8-oz. cans of artichoke hearts
    in brine
2 lbs. fresh peas
2 oz. pancetta, chopped fine
3 tbsp. unsalted butter
    Salt and pepper

Several hours before using, drain the artichoke hearts and rinse in luke-warm water. Let sit in a bowl of cool water, changing the water at least twice to remove any tinny taste. Drain and slice into quarters. While you're waiting for the artichokes to bathe, shell the peas. Blanch in boiling salted water for a minute or two, drain and plunge into ice water. Drain again and set aside. In a large saucepan, combine pancetta and butter and fry on medium heat for a few minutes. Add the artichoke hearts and heat thoroughly. Add the peas and cook till hot. Season with salt and fresh cracked pepper.

CHOCOLATE ROLL

6 oz. semi-sweet chocolate
3 tbsp. strong espresso
6 large eggs, separated
¾ cup granulated sugar
Pinch of salt
Dusting of dry cocoa
1½ cups heavy cream
1 tbsp. confectioners' sugar
2 tbsp. liqueur of your choice

Melt chocolate with coffee in double boiler and cool slightly. Beat yolks together and add sugar and continue beating until thick and light. Add chocolate to egg yolk, sugar mixture. Beat whites with a pinch of salt until stiff but not dry. Stir ⅓ of the whites into the yolk, chocolate mixture.

Gently fold the remaining whites into the chocolate mixture with a large spatula. Carefully spread mixture into a 10-inch-by-15-inch jellyroll pan, greased, lined with wax paper, and greased again. Bake 15 minutes in a preheated 350° oven. When done, set pan on rack and cover with a damp kitchen towel. Allow to cool 1 hour and spray with mister one or two times if necessary to keep the cake moist. Sift some cocoa onto a piece of wax paper just a little larger than the jellyroll pan. Turn pan upside down onto cocoa-covered paper and carefully remove cooking wax paper. Beat heavy cream with confectioners' sugar and liqueur until thick. Spread over cake and roll cake up like a jellyroll, leaving seam-side down on serving platter. Chill several hours.

NOTE: *Framboise* would be a nice liqueur to use if you could add a few handfuls of raspberries to the whipped cream before spreading. Grand Marnier, amaretto, etc., even rum is nice.

Striped Bass with Lime Mayonnaise
Snow Peas with Peas
Boiled New Potatoes

Serves four

STRIPED BASS WITH LIME MAYONNAISE

1   very small striped bass (about
    5 lbs.) cleaned, gills removed,
    and head left on or removed
  Thyme sprigs
  Salt and pepper
2   large onions, minced
6   cloves garlic, minced
3   tbsp. unsalted butter

Preheat the oven to 375°. Stuff the cavity of the fish with a few thyme sprigs, season with salt and pepper, and place in a large baking dish. Sauté onions and garlic in butter until onions are translucent but not brown. Pour over fish and bake 50 minutes. Flesh will flake when done. Drain off juices and save. If more than 2 tablespoons, cook these juices until reduced to 2 tablespoons and then strain and reserve for lime mayonnaise.

LIME MAYONNAISE

  3 tbsp. water
  1 tbsp. lime juice
  ½ tsp. salt
  3 grinds pepper from a mill
  3 egg yolks
  ½ lb. unsalted butter, melted
     Grated rind of 3 limes

Combine water, lime juice, salt, and pepper. Cook over medium heat until reduced to about 1½ tablespoons. Reduce heat to low. Add yolks and whisk until mixture is thick and white. Take off the heat and add the warm butter bit by bit. From time to time dribble in the juices from the cooked fish (see above) to prevent the sauce from becoming too thick. Just before serving, add the grated lime rind.

SNOW PEAS WITH PEAS

 1½ tbsp. unsalted butter
  2 lbs. fresh unshelled peas
      (blanched, refreshed in ice
      water, and drained) or 1 box
      frozen peas
  1 lb. snow peas, stems and strings
      from each edge removed, cut
      in half at an angle, then blanched,
      refreshed in ice water, and drained
    Salt and pepper

Heat butter to sizzling and add peas and snow peas. Cook just to heat. Season with salt and pepper.

BOILED NEW POTATOES

Allow 3 small potatoes per person. Sprinkle with chopped parsley and season with salt and pepper.

Broiled Weakfish with Mint and Garlic
Couscous with Wild Mushrooms and Chives
Your Nice Green Salad
Orange Jelly

Serves four

It was not until I was a grown-up that I discovered that in Australia (and probably in several other English-speaking countries) they call Jell-O, "jelly." I can't quite recall what they call our jelly, perhaps just jam. Anyway, it makes it handy that we can use proper English terms for this dessert, because who would want to say they were serving Jell-O for dessert?

BROILED WEAKFISH WITH MINT AND GARLIC

1 tbsp., plus 1 tsp. dried mint
1½ sticks unsalted butter at room
       temperature
Salt and pepper
1 tsp. finely chopped garlic
2 lbs. weakfish fillets
Lemon slices
Mint sprigs for garnish

Revive the mint in warm water. Whip the butter until light and fluffy. Add salt and pepper, garlic, and mint. Mix well and mound onto plastic wrap. Form into a cylinder and freeze for 24 hours. Bring to room temperature before using.

Broil the fish about 5 to 8 minutes. Just before done put several pats of the butter on the fish. Return to broiler to finish. Serve with round slices of lemon, the centers removed and filled with mint sprigs.

COUSCOUS WITH WILD MUSHROOMS AND CHIVES

    8 oz. fresh wild mushrooms, depending
          on what your store carries. Morels,
          chanterelles, porcini, all are fine.
   10 tbsp. unsalted butter
       Salt and pepper
    1 cup chicken broth—Knorr cubes
          are fine
    1 cup couscous
    2 tsp. fresh chives, snipped

Try not to wash the mushrooms too much unless absolutely necessary.
Wipe dry and cut into bite-size pieces. If mushrooms are tiny, leave whole.
Sauté the mushrooms in 4 tablespoons butter until hot and well coated.
Season with salt and pepper, cover pan, and lower heat. Cook in this manner
for 5 to 6 minutes, then remove cover, raise heat, and evaporate liquid. Stir
occasionally until mushrooms become golden brown. Remove from heat and
let stand. In saucepan, bring chicken stock to a boil with 4 tablespoons
butter, salt, and pepper. Stir in couscous, cover pan, and remove from heat.
Let stand about 7 minutes. Mix in mushrooms, 2 to 3 tablespoons butter,
and fluff and mix couscous and mushrooms. Add chives. Season to taste and
serve.

Serve with a gentle green salad. No harsh greens, no garlic, no onions.

ORANGE JELLY

   1½ packages Knox gelatin
    ½ cup cold water
   3½ cups boiling water
    ¾ cup granulated sugar
    1 small can frozen orange juice
    3 tbsp. fresh lemon juice
    1 cup heavy cream
    1 tbsp. confectioners' sugar
    2 tsp. vanilla

Dissolve gelatin in cold water. Add boiling water. Stir thoroughly until
gelatin dissolves. Add sugar. Stir again. Add orange juice and lemon juice.
Mix well and pour into glass container and chill well. This dessert is somewhat soft compared to "Jell-O." Whip the heavy cream with the confectioners' sugar and vanilla. Whip so that it is loose and could still be poured.
Serve with the "jelly."

Redfish
Potato Flan
Salad of Bibb Lettuce and Bittergreens
Chocolate Cake

Serves four

This redfish is another version of that popular Louisiana recipe. It can be made in a skillet but because of the high heat necessary and the quantities of butter, you will probably have half the country's fire departments in your kitchen before you finish. So do it on a gas grill; charcoal is not hot enough. Preheat gas grill hot, hot, hot. For the salad, simply wash and spin dry the two lettuces and use the basic vinaigrette listed in the "Cooking Fish" chapter on page 287. This is no ordinary chocolate cake, so chocoholics take note.

REDFISH

4 redfish fillets, ½ inch thick,
      sliced in half horizontally
      if they are too thick
2 sticks melted unsalted butter
1 tbsp. paprika
¼ tsp. each thyme and oregano
½ tsp. cayenne pepper
½ tsp. each white and black
      pepper, fresh ground
1 tsp. garlic powder
2 tsp. salt

Just before grilling, drown the fillets in the melted butter. Cover the fillets with the last six ingredients and cook 2 minutes each side. When you turn the fish, cover the cooked side with more butter and even more when it is done. This ought to make everyone sit up straight.

POTATO FLAN

1 crushed garlic clove
6 tbsp. unsalted butter (soft)
2 lbs. potatoes, peeled and cut
    very thin (use Idaho potatoes)
    Salt and pepper, fresh ground,
    of course
3 tbsp. chopped parsley (Italian
    parsley if possible)
    Grated rind of 1 lemon
1½ cups onion, sliced thin and
    sautéed in olive oil until
    just golden
¼ cup chicken broth
½ cup heavy cream
    Juice of 1 lemon

Preheat oven to 375°. Rub a medium-size flan, an earthenware baking dish, with the garlic clove. Let the flan dry and cover the bottom and sides with the butter. Make an even layer of potato slices on the bottom. Season with salt and pepper. Now add a parsley, lemon rind, and onion layer, evenly distribute and season with salt and pepper. Keep going and end with potatoes. Mix broth, cream, and lemon juice. Season with salt and pepper and pour over. Bake at 375° for 1¾ hours. Serve hot or lukewarm.

CHOCOLATE CAKE (see page 72)

**Grilled Lemon-Thyme Mackerel
Tomato and Eggplant Tart
Green Salad**

Serves four

Your green salad or ours; see the index for ours.

GRILLED LEMON-THYME MACKEREL

1 stick softened, unsalted
    butter
  Salt and pepper
  Grated rind of 1 lemon
2 tsp. fresh thyme
  Dash of Tabasco
4 little mackerel

Make the lemon-thyme butter ahead. Whip the butter until fluffy and then add the salt, pepper, lemon rind, thyme, and dash of Tabasco. Place in plastic wrap and mold into a log shape. Freeze until an hour before it's to be used, then remove to the refrigerator.

Butterfly fresh mackerel and remove head and tail. Do not baste, but put some sprigs of herbs such as thyme on the coals just before cooking.

Cook flesh-side first and serve with several pats of lemon-thyme butter on each fish.

TOMATO AND EGGPLANT TART

Olive Oil Basting Oil:

 1 cup good olive oil
 8 peeled garlic cloves
1½ tsp. thyme
 1 bay leaf

Tart:

 2 tbsp. fresh basil, cut in slices, or 1½ tsp. dried and revived
1½ tbsp. fresh oregano or ½ tsp. dried and revived
 1 recipe pastry (semi-puff)
 3 cups (approximately) baby eggplant, cut into ⅛-inch slices
   Salt and pepper
 ¾ cup ricotta cheese
 2 tbsp. finely chopped scallions—a little green included
1½ lbs. (about 10) plum tomatoes, cut into ⅛-inch slices—
    let drain while preparing the tart
 ¼ cup olive oil basting oil (see above)

Combine basting oil ingredients and heat on low for 20 to 30 minutes. Remove garlic and keep for whatever.

To revive herbs, place in a small quantity of hot water. Stir and let sit for a few minutes and then use.

This tart may be done in individual tart dishes or one large round one or just laid out on a cookie sheet, which can look very impressive indeed. Butter tart dish(es) or cookie sheet. Roll out pastry. If using cookie sheet, turn edges over to form a little rim. Let rest in refrigerator covered for 1 hour.

Slice eggplant and toss with several teaspoons salt and let sit in a colander for 1 hour to drain. Rinse in cold water and dry.

Mix ricotta with scallions and salt and pepper to taste.

Remove pastry from refrigerator and prick with fork all over except edges. Spread with cheese mixture and lay out tomato and eggplant in overlapping slices. Make circles if in a dish or rows on a cookie sheet. Brush with garlic oil and sprinkle with herbs, salt, and pepper.

Bake in a preheated 425° oven for 15 minutes on the bottom rack. Lower heat to 375°. Move tart to top rack and cook 10 more minutes or until top is browned. As soon as possible, but with all dexterity, remove tart from cooking container to cooling rack.

Serve hot, warm, or at room temperature.

Pasta with Spinach and Artichoke Hearts
Grilled Mackerel
Tuscan Muffins
Raspberries with Crème Anglaise

Serves four

Crème anglaise can be refrigerated after you've made it and saved for instant great desserts as a hard sauce over any fruit.

PASTA WITH SPINACH AND ARTICHOKE HEARTS

1   can artichoke hearts in brine
½   lb. fresh spinach
1   cup cream
    Salt and pepper
6   oz. imported pasta in shapes
     such as bows
    Unsalted butter

Drain canned artichoke hearts and soak in lukewarm water for 20 minutes. Drain. Rinse and soak again. Drain and cut into quarters. Wash the spinach, remove the larger stems, and steam until just wilted. Drain well, press water out with a slotted spoon. Chop spinach medium-fine and set aside. Reduce cream over medium-high heat to ½ cup. Season with salt and pepper. Add spinach and stir well. Add artichokes, stir, and taste seasoning. Cook pasta *al dente*. Season with a few pats unsalted butter, salt, and pepper. Add sauce. Stir well. Serve with grated Parmesan cheese on the side if you wish it to be more than just a vegetable course.

GRILLED MACKEREL

½ stick unsalted butter at room
    temperature
6 anchovy fillets, chopped coarsely
Pepper
A squeeze of lemon juice
2 tbsp. finely chopped parsley
4 pounds mackerel, split and
    boned
Olive oil basting oil (see page 176)

Whip the butter until light and fluffy. Add anchovies, pepper, lemon juice, and parsley. Mix well and mound onto plastic wrap. Form into a cylinder and freeze for 24 hours. Bring to room temperature before using.

Brush the mackerel with olive oil basting oil and grill, flesh-side first. Just before removing from the grill, put several pats of anchovy butter on each fish.

TUSCAN MUFFINS (see page 150)

FRESH RASPBERRIES WITH CRÈME ANGLAISE

4 egg yolks
⅛ tsp. salt
¼ cup granulated sugar
½ cup milk
½ cup cream
1 tbsp. *framboise*
2 pts. raspberries

Whisk together the yolks, salt, and sugar. Combine the milk and cream and whisk that into the yolks. Cook over a medium-high heat stirring constantly until it thickens quite suddenly. Remove from the heat, strain, and then whisk until cool. Add the liqueur and spoon the crème anglaise over the raspberries. Can be served hot or cold.

Offshore Saltwater Fish

We fished in a tournament once and really thought it was terrific fun. It was a bluefish tournament for Grady White boats. We fished over an August weekend off the coast of Lynn, Massachusetts, and were trying to catch the biggest bluefish or the smallest bluefish or the best combined weight over the two days. We caught a shark. Not a mako shark, just a little dogfish shark. This was quite exciting to our hosts who explained that in England (where they were born) "fish and chips" were made out of this type of fish. It was boneless and absolutely delicious.

We did actually catch some bluefish, too. Not enough to win the tournament, but enough to learn a few things. In the last hour of the tournament I was beginning to see a great correlation between the number of fish caught and when the gin and tonics started to be served; also between the size of the fish caught and the number of gin and tonics drunk. At the time, that correlation was very clear, but I can't remember it now. The correlation I do remember concerned the care of the fish once caught. Because we were trying to keep the weight of the fish up, we avoided letting the fish bleed (no bonks on the head), and he was immediately iced. Even at this, the weight dropped dramatically (about 25 percent) from the time he was caught and weighed to the time he had traveled five hours to the dock and been weighed. In photographing fish, you find his colors the best and brightest before he dies. Certainly the taste must change as each hour passes, too.

179

Of course, the quality of flavor as it relates to the freshness of fish is not a particularly novel concept, just one that is uniquely within the fisherman's control and consequently should be managed properly. There is one interesting observation I can make about these big fish. With almost all meat and many freshwater fish, size and age of the animal has as much or more to do with the good flavor as does freshness. It seems that a large, old buck whitetail is not nearly as tasty as the small, tender antelope, or mutton versus spring lamb. This is not dramatically true with these large saltwater fish. A smaller tuna does taste somewhat better but not perceptibly better than one that weighs 75 pounds more. There may be a difference in bonito or tuna, but can it be said that one is better than the other? The consistency in the flavor of the big fish is one reason they are such a pleasure to cook. Barring six martinis before dinner and a burnt swordfish steak, there is virtually nothing that will change the great flavor that is already in the swordfish. It will not be tough or gamey or full of sinew, it is simply marvelous just the way it is.

Japanese Leftover Tuna
Sautéed Watercress
Melon and Fortune Cookies

Serves four

Fortune cookies, of course, cannot be made by us.

JAPANESE LEFTOVER TUNA

Leftover cooked tuna—as much as you
    have. If little, add more of the rest of
    the ingredients; if a lot, decrease
    ingredients
Pepper, fresh ground
Soy sauce
3 cans water chestnuts, drained and sliced
    Sesame oil
1 bag imported Japanese pasta (called soba).
    Available in gourmet and health food
    stores (a buckwheat pasta).
Ponzu sauce or similar sauce

There are many sauces (*tsuyu, kake, jiru,* etc.), hot and not so hot, and if
what you want is unavailable, ask your grocer to order it.

Break up the tuna into small pieces. Season with pepper and soy. Sauté
the water chestnuts in sesame oil and set aside. Cook pasta in water according to directions and then season with sesame oil, soy, and other seasoning.
Toss with fish.

SAUTÉED WATERCRESS (see page 18)

**Fresh Tuna Steaks
Pizza
Green Salad
Blueberries with Crème Anglaise**

Serves four

Fresh tuna is one of the great fish; go out of your way to obtain some. This goes for fresh mozzarella as well. It is really a different cheese from the mozzarella you get in the plastic bags in the supermarket (this is true also of Parmesan cheese), and fresh mozzarella will make your pizza exceptional.

FRESH TUNA STEAKS

2 lbs. fresh tuna steaks
   Any of the compound butters
      you still have in the
      refrigerator, especially roasted
      red pepper butter (page 186) or
      lemon butter (page 185).

Grill the steaks about 6 minutes on the first side, 5 on the second. Just before the steaks are done, put some of the butter on each steak and then again when you are just about to serve it.

PIZZA

1⅓ cups lukewarm water
   1 package dry yeast
   3 cups all-purpose flour
   1 tsp. dried thyme
   1 tsp. salt
      Oil and cornmeal
⅔ to ¾ cup mozzarella, grated—fresh if
      possible. If fresh, thin slices
      are fine.
   2 tbsp. basil, roughly chopped
4 to 6 tomatoes, peeled, seeded, and sliced
      Salt and pepper—fresh ground or
      red flakes
3 to 4 tbsp. good Italian olive oil

182

In a small bowl add the warm water to the yeast. Stir and let stand for 10 minutes. In a large bowl combine flour, thyme, and salt. Make a well in the center and add the yeast and water. Stir well to mix and form the dough. Turn out onto a lightly floured board and knead well for about 5 minutes. The dough will have become smooth and elastic. Place the dough in a large bowl coated with oil. Cover tightly with plastic wrap and let rise for about 1½ hours or until doubled in bulk. Divide the dough into 4 pieces. Roll out into thin circles and set on cookie sheets sprinkled liberally with flour. Put your toppings on. If you use fresh mozzarella, put the cheese on first, then the basil, then the tomatoes, then the pepper and olive oil. Bake in a pre-heated 450° oven. If possible, have tiles on the bottom shelf of the oven preheated for 30 minutes. Sprinkle with cornmeal just before cooking and slide the pizzas onto the tiles. Bake 15 minutes and sprinkle with salt and serve.

BLUEBERRIES WITH CRÈME ANGLAISE

⅛ tsp. salt
4 yolks
¼ cup granulated sugar
½ cup milk
½ cup heavy cream
1 tbsp. liqueur (Grand Marnier
      is good) or vanilla
4 cups blueberries, washed and
      picked over

Whisk together the salt, yolks, and sugar. Combine the milk and cream and whisk that into the yolks. Cook over a medium-high heat stirring constantly until it thickens quite suddenly. Remove from the heat, strain, and then whisk until cool. Add the liqueur or vanilla and spoon the crème anglaise over the blueberries and serve.

Fried Pasta with Water Chestnuts
Grilled Tuna with Lemon Butter
Salad of Melon, Pears, and Cucumbers

Serves four

I discovered to my horror that good oils can go rancid. This seems to be particularly true of the more delicate oils such as hazelnut or walnut oil. Keeping them in the refrigerator is one solution, or splitting the oil and the cost with a friend so there isn't as much to use up is another solution.

FRIED PASTA WITH WATER CHESTNUTS

½ lb. pasta, bows or farfalle are
    nice
¼ cup toasted sesame oil, splash
    of vegetable oil
2 garlic cloves, finely chopped
2 to 3 tbsp. ginger, peeled and
    julienned into matchsticks
¼ cup soy sauce
¼ cup rice wine vinegar
    Salt and pepper
2 cans water chestnuts, drained
    and sliced
4 scallions, julienned and blanched
    for 30 seconds in boiling
    water, then plunged into ice
    water and drained

Cook the pasta until just *al dente*. Drain well. Toss with a little of the sesame oil so the bows won't stick together and set aside. Heat in a frying pan ¼ cup of sesame oil with a splash of vegetable oil till hot. Add the garlic and ginger and stir for a few minutes. Add the pasta and fry it till the edges start to crisp. Now add the soy sauce and the rice vinegar a little at a time over the fried pasta, tasting the pasta as you add. One day you may want more soy, the next more vinegar. You may also want to add more sesame oil. Add salt and pepper as well to taste. Toss in the water chestnuts and fry a little more. Now add the scallions, toss and serve.

GRILLED TUNA WITH LEMON BUTTER

    1 stick of unsalted butter, softened
    2 tsp. lemon juice
    1 tsp. lemon rind, grated
    ½ tsp. dry mustard
       Salt and pepper
    4 tuna steaks at least 1 inch thick,
          about 4 to 6 oz. each
       Oil to paint the fish
       Several sprigs of rosemary

Whip the butter till fluffy. Add juice, rind, mustard, salt, and pepper. Whip till mixed well, then mound onto plastic wrap and roll into a cylinder. Freeze a night ahead then bring into the refrigerator a few hours before serving.

Brush the steaks with oil and lay the sprigs of rosemary on the coals as you put the steaks on. Grill until done, about 7 minutes on the first side and 4 on the second. Remove to a platter and sprinkle with salt and pepper. Top with pats of the lemon butter.

SALAD OF MELON, PEARS, AND CUCUMBERS

    2 tbsp. red wine vinegar
    1 tsp. mustard
    ½ cup hazelnut or walnut oil
       Salt and pepper
    ½ cup hazelnuts, toasted and
          coarsely chopped
    4 pears
       Lemon juice
    1 small melon
    2 medium-size cucumbers

Combine the vinegar, mustard, oil, salt, and pepper in the blender. Turn on high for a couple of seconds and then set aside. Toast the hazelnuts in the oven set at 300°. Remove and cover with a towel for 5 or 10 minutes, then rub off the skins and chop coarsely. Peel, core, and slice the pears and toss with a little lemon juice. Add slices of melon, about an equal amount to the pears. Peel, seed, and slice the cucumbers. Toss the cucumbers, pears, and melon together with the vinaigrette and let sit an hour or so. Just before serving toss in the toasted hazelnuts.

Grilled Swordfish with Roasted Red Pepper Butter
Green and Purple Cole Slaw
Grilled Idahos
Summer Trifle

Serves four

Yes, this chapter suggests only one way to cook swordfish. Grilling is the best way, and suggesting any other technique would be implying that other techniques might be good. There is only one way to cook swordfish and that is to grill it. It is too expensive and too difficult to catch to fool with other techniques. Go with the best.

GRILLED SWORDFISH WITH ROASTED RED PEPPER BUTTER

2 small red peppers
Salt and pepper
1½ sticks or 6 oz. of unsalted, room
    temperature butter
Small spot of Worcestershire
    sauce
2 lbs. swordfish
Good olive oil for basting

Prepare the butter in advance. On a hot grill, roast whole red peppers until blackened on all sides. Remove to a plate and when cool enough to handle, peel off all the skin. Slice open and clean out all membrane and seeds. Chop roughly and purée in food processor. Scason with salt and pepper. With electric mixer, whip butter until light and fluffy. Add pepper purée in small batches to see how much the butter can hold. You want to add as much as you can, but it will depend on how big the peppers are. When you feel it is right, taste, season with salt, pepper, and just a little dash of Worcestershire. Mix well. Mound onto plastic wrap and mold into a cylinder. Freeze for 24 hours and then bring to refrigerator several hours before using.

Baste the swordfish with olive oil and grill on a preheated grill.

Slice the compound butter in ¼-inch slices and give several per portion. I say just slather it on!

186

GREEN AND PURPLE COLE SLAW

- 3 cups finely shredded green savoy cabbage
- 3 cups finely shredded purple cabbage
- 1 large carrot, grated
- ½ tsp. salt
- 2 tsp. prepared mustard
- ¼ tsp. ground pepper
- 1 dash cayenne
- 3 egg yolks
- 2 cups corn oil or good olive oil
- 1 tbsp. hot water
- ¼ cup vinegar
- 2 tsp. granulated sugar
- ¼ cup sour cream
- 2 tsp. lemon juice
- 2 tsp. caraway seeds
- 1 tbsp. dry mustard
- 1 tsp. salt

Keep the cabbages separate. Divide the carrot between them.

Now make a mayonnaise by combining in a bowl: ½ teaspoon salt, the prepared mustard, pepper, and cayenne. Let the salt melt and add the egg yolks. Whisk until frothy and well combined. Add the oil slowly in a dribble until the mayonnaise begins to take and thicken. Then you may add the oil faster. When finished, taste for seasoning and adjust. Add a tablespoon of hot water to finish it off. This also can be made in a food processor. Now add the remaining ingredients to the mayonnaise and divide between the two cabbages. Be sure to dissolve the salt in vinegar first as it will not dissolve well in the mayonnaise. Mix well and taste for seasoning. You will want a nice sweet sour taste. Grate a little black pepper over each and chill for several hours. Mix again before serving.

GRILLED IDAHOS

  1 cup good olive oil
  8 peeled garlic cloves
1½ tsp. thyme
  1 bay leaf
  3 Idaho potatoes, sliced
      lengthwise
     Salt and pepper

Heat on low heat all the ingredients (but the potatoes) for 20 to 30 minutes. Remove garlic. (The softened garlic can now be used for whatever your taste buds tell you; i.e., smearing on the potatoes or on the swordfish before you add the red pepper butter or for the cook to eat atop a piece of French bread.) Baste the potato slices with this olive oil basting oil and grill also. Season with salt and pepper just before serving.

SUMMER TRIFLE

  2 cups light cream
  5 egg yolks
 ½ cup granulated sugar
     Pinch of salt
     Framboise or rum
  1 sponge cake (store-bought is
      okay)
     Raspberry jam (optional)
     Raspberries
     Grated orange rind (optional)

Make a custard by mixing cream, yolks, sugar, and salt together in heavy saucepan. Over a medium-high heat, stir the mixture constantly until it thickens (which it will do quite suddenly, just as a cloud of steam rises from the surface). Remove from heat and pour through fine strainer into bowl and whisk to stop cooking. Cool, stirring occasionally, and add *framboise* to taste.

In your best glass bowl put a layer of sponge cake with jam on it if you like. Spoon in cool custard just to cover. Spread profusely with raspberries (grate on a little orange rind if you like). Add more cake, then more custard, and finish with raspberries. Be sure the berries of each layer show off in an orderly manner through the glass. Chill overnight.

Corn Chowder
Grilled Swordfish Steaks
Grilled Artichokes
Apricot Ice

Serves four

If you have access to the little tiny artichokes (we find them in Boston's Italian North End in the spring, and they are available in parts of California, too), they would be good to use in this recipe.

CORN CHOWDER

1	large onion, chopped fine
1	small rib celery, chopped fine
2 or 3	potatoes, peeled and diced
1	large green pepper, diced
1	tbsp. bacon fat
6	tbsp. unsalted butter
2	qts. light cream
½	bay leaf
	Salt and pepper
	Pinch basil
2½	cups cooked corn
4	tbsp. cornstarch (optional)

Garnish:
¼ lb. cooked ham
Pimento
Parsley

Sauté the onion and celery until translucent. Add potatoes and green pepper. Toss in fat and butter and add light cream. Add bay leaf, some salt and pepper, and a pinch of basil. Let simmer until potatoes are done, approximately 30 minutes. Add 2½ cups corn and taste for seasoning.

If you should wish to have a thicker soup, just before serving: Mix 4 tablespoons cornstarch with ⅔ cup soup. Stir and add mixture back into the hot soup. Stir gently. Bring to a boil and serve.

Garnish each soup plate first with: ¼ lb. cooked ham, diced and sautéed and divided among the plates, and some finely chopped pimento. Sprinkle the top of the soup with chopped parsley.

189

GRILLED SWORDFISH STEAKS

4 good-sized swordfish steaks

Baste with olive oil or butter and a few grinds pepper. Grill on a pre-heated grill. Serve with lemon wedges and melted butter; reserve some for the artichokes as well.

GRILLED ARTICHOKES

4 large artichokes
Olive oil

Trim stems of artichokes to ½ inch. Slice off the tops with a knife and then with a scissors cut off each sharp thorn, about ⅛ to ¼ of the leaf. Steam for 30 to 45 minutes. They are done when a leaf pulls off easily—and you want them to be done! When cool enough to handle, cut into quarters and remove the choke. Paint with olive oil and grill to desired brownness.

APRICOT ICE

4 17-oz. cans of apricot halves
   in heavy syrup. Drain well
   and reserve the syrup.
   Pinch of salt
2 medium-size lemons for the
   juice
   Splash of white rum (1 tbsp.)
   Salt and ice for your ice cream
   machine

Purée the apricots in a food processor. Add a pinch of salt, ¾ of all the lemon juice, the rum, and about ⅔ cup of the apricot syrup. Taste for balance. You may want more sweetness (syrup) or tartness (lemon juice) or rum. Prepare as your ice cream machine says for ice. Remember you use less salt than for ice cream. Decorate with fresh mint if you like or a pint of fresh raspberries.

Kingfish with Lime Butter
Banana Chips
Tomatoes, Red, Green, and Yellow Peppers
Potato Cake
Real Tuttifrutti

Serves four

KINGFISH WITH LIME BUTTER

1½ sticks of unsalted butter
2 shallots, chopped very fine
Grated rind of 2 limes
1 clove garlic, chopped very fine
Salt and pepper
1½ lbs. kingfish

The lime butter should be in readiness in your freezer for the happy moment when the fisherman comes home. So at least 24 hours before you expect the fish to arrive, whip the butter until fluffy and white. Add the shallots, lime rind, garlic, salt, and pepper and mix well. Check the taste and add more salt and pepper if necessary. Turn out onto a piece of plastic wrap, wrap it up and shape into a log. Freeze it, making sure it goes into the refrigerator one hour before serving.

Fillet the kingfish, leaving the skin on one side. Each fillet should be no more than 1 inch thick. Grill over charcoal a few minutes on each side. Remove from the grill and put pats of the lime butter on top.

BANANA CHIPS

3 or 4 medium-green bananas (about 1 lb.)
2½ inches of corn oil or peanut oil

Slice the bananas either lengthwise or across, whatever is your fancy, so the chips are ⅛ inch thick. Heat the oil till it is 375° and fry a few pieces of banana at a time for about four minutes. Make sure you turn them once during the cooking. They should be a nice golden brown when done. Remove to drain on paper towels. Serve with your favorite tropical drink.

TOMATOES, RED, GREEN, AND YELLOW PEPPERS

                    Olive oil
            2   red peppers, seeded and
                    julienned
            2   green peppers, seeded and
                    julienned
            2   yellow peppers, seeded and
                    julienned
            2   tomatoes, very ripe, seeded
                    and julienned
                Fresh coriander or chopped
                    parsley
                Salt and pepper

Splash a bit of the olive oil in two frying pans and sauté the red peppers in one pan and the green and yellow peppers in the other. Sauté until they are just done and still a little crunchy. Add some of the tomatoes to each pan along with the coriander and heat through. Season with salt and pepper. You can stir them all together now or arrange in an attractive pattern on a serving platter.

POTATO CAKE

            2   lbs. all-purpose potatoes
       2 to 5   tbsp. corn oil
            1   freshly grated nutmeg
                Salt and pepper
            2   tbsp. unsalted butter

Peel and slice the potatoes very thin, about 1/16 inch thick. You can use a food processor for this if you like. Keep the slices in ice water until you're ready to use them, then rinse under cold water and dry on a kitchen towel. Heat half of the oil in a 10- to 12-inch skillet. Add the potatoes and sauté until lightly brown all over, about 10 minutes. Season with the grated nutmeg, salt, and pepper. Stir again. Press the potatoes with a spatula or spoon into a flat layer in the pan and cook 5 more minutes, shaking the pan every now and then. Then invert the potato cake onto a lightly oiled plate and add the other half of the oil to the pan. Return the potato cake to the pan with the unbrowned side down. Finish cooking, about 5 to 10 minutes more, or until potatoes are completely brown but tender. Slide cake onto a platter and spread soft butter on top.

REAL TUTTIFRUTTI

2 grapefruit
2 oranges
½ pineapple
1 papaya
1 banana
8 tbsp. orange liqueur
Mint for garnish

Cut the ends off the grapefruit and oranges and stand on end. Then with a sharp knife cut off the remaining peel. Separate into sections, making sure the connecting tissue is left behind. Core and pare the pineapple half and cut into small pieces. Core, pare, and seed the papaya and cut into small pieces. Slice the banana. In a bowl combine all of the fruit and sprinkle the orange liqueur over it. Let it marinate in the refrigerator several hours. Serve garnished with mint.

Rice and Parsley Soup
Mako Shark Steaks with Lemon Dill Butter
Green Beans with Sesame Seeds
Sauternes

Serves four

RICE AND PARSLEY SOUP

6 tbsp. unsalted butter
1 small onion, chopped
4 Idaho potatoes (baking),
    parboiled for 15 minutes,
    then grated (skins and all)
    through the round holes
    of a grater
2 quarts water
1 tsp. salt
¼ tsp. fresh ground pepper
    Fresh nutmeg
4 vegetable or chicken bouillon
    cubes
5 tbsp. chopped parsley
¾ cup uncooked rice—Italian is
    best, but regular okay
1½ cups Parmesan cheese

Melt 3 tablespoons of the butter. Cook the onion until translucent over medium heat and continue cooking until just starting to turn golden. Then add potatoes, water, salt, pepper, a few grates of nutmeg, bouillon cubes, and half of the parsley. Bring slowly to a boil and add rice. Cover and lower heat until rice is just cooked *al dente*—about 20 minutes. Give one or two quick grinds in food processor if you like. Correct seasoning. Add butter, cheese, and remaining parsley.

MAKO SHARK STEAKS WITH LEMON DILL BUTTER

1½ sticks of unsalted butter at room
     temperature
2 tsp. dried dill, revived in a little
     hot water
1 tsp. lemon juice
1 tsp. grated lemon rind
   Pinch of cayenne pepper
   Salt and pepper
4 good-size shark steaks, 1 inch
     thick
   Flour for dusting

In advance, whip 1 stick of butter until fluffy. Add the dill, lemon juice, lemon rind, cayenne, salt, and pepper. Whip until well mixed and then turn out onto plastic wrap and roll up like a small log. Freeze for 24 hours. Bring to refrigerator a few hours before using.

Dry steaks with paper towels. Season lightly with salt and pepper, and dust lightly with flour, shaking off excess. Heat 4 tablespoons sweet butter over medium-high heat until sizzling. Add steaks and cook 8 minutes first side and 6 to 8 minutes the second side. They should be nice and golden brown. Place on warm plates or platter and top with ½-inch slices of the compound butter. Let sit a few seconds so the butter starts to melt before serving or run under the broiler.

GREEN BEANS WITH SESAME SEEDS

1½ lbs. green beans, ends removed
     (If beans are quite long, cut
     in half on the diagonal.)
1½ tbsp. sesame seeds
3 to 4 tbsp. unsalted butter
   Salt and pepper

Blanch the beans until *al dente* in a large quantity of boiling salted water. Refresh in ice water and drain. This may be done several hours before serving time and then wrap the beans in a dish towel and refrigerate. Toast sesame seeds on medium heat in a heavy skillet. Just as they start to turn a golden color, remove from the heat and transfer to a plate or bowl. Just before serving time, melt the sweet butter until hot. Sauté the beans, stirring until heated through. Add sesame seeds, season with salt and pepper. Toss and serve.

Capered Dolphin
Red, Green, and Yellow Pepper Salad
Sweet Pastry with Jam

Serves four

CAPERED DOLPHIN

1½ sticks unsalted butter
    Salt and pepper
 1 large clove garlic, chopped
 1 tsp. grated lemon rind
1½ tbsp. chopped capers (the big
        ones are best), well rinsed first
        if salted
 1 tsp. finely chopped parsley
1½ to 2 lbs. dolphin fillets

In advance make the compound butter. Whip the butter until light and fluffy. Add salt, pepper, garlic, lemon rind, capers, and parsley. Mix well and mound onto plastic wrap. Form into a cylinder and freeze for 24 hours. Bring to room temperature before using.

Broil the dolphin for about 10 minutes (depending on thickness of steaks) and put a little of the caper butter on top two-thirds of the way through.

RED, GREEN, AND YELLOW PEPPER SALAD

 3 large peppers of each color, cored, seeded,
        julienned, and the red peppers kept
        separate from the yellow and green
 3 tbsp. corn oil or olive
    Salt and pepper
⅓ cup red wine vinegar or balsamic vinegar
 1 tsp. prepared mustard
 2 shallots, chopped very fine
 1 tbsp. dried tarragon, revived in a little
        hot water
⅔ cup good olive oil, added last

Sauté peppers, yellow and green together, red separately, in olive or corn oil until just *al dente*. Season with salt and pepper and toss with a dressing made from the remaining ingredients. Blend dressing well. Toss peppers all together and serve at room temperature.

SWEET PASTRY WITH JAM

½ cup unsalted butter
⅓ cup granulated sugar
   Pinch of salt
1 tsp. grated lemon rind
2 or 3 eggs
1 cup all-purpose flour
½ cup corn flour
1 tsp. baking powder
1 jar of jam

Cream butter and add sugar, salt, lemon rind, and 1 egg. Mix well. Mix flour, corn flour, and baking powder together and add to the butter mixture by flattening it against the side of the bowl with a large spatula, sort of squeezing it into the butter and sugar, and then flatten and shape into a cake shape. Wrap dough in plastic wrap and chill for several hours. Roll out to ¼- to ⅜-inch thickness on a floured surface. If it is too difficult, roll between wax paper. Chill and then remove the wax paper for the cutting. Cut 3- to 4-inch ovals, squares, etc. Gather scraps and reroll to get as many cookies as possible. Paint the surface of each piece with thin layer of beaten egg (you may need 2 whole eggs to do all). Spoon a tablespoon or so of jam (apricot or raspberry jam are good classics, but try fig, marmalade, etc.) in the center of the dough. Fold it over and seal by pushing down with the tines of a fork around the edges, excluding the folded edge. Now paint the tops with beaten egg. Place cookies on buttered baking sheets. Bake in preheated 350° oven until golden, about 20 minutes. Cool on racks. You will be surprised how many of these little delectables people can eat.

Pina Coladas
Banana Chips
Wahoo Steaks Shish Kebab
White Rice
Grilled Pineapple with Orange Ice

Serves four

See page 191 for Banana Chips recipe. You know how to make white rice.

WAHOO STEAKS SHISH KEBAB

1½ tbsp. dried oregano, reconstituted
½ to ⅔ cup olive oil
Juice of 1 lemon
A pinch each of salt and pepper
¼ tsp. chopped garlic
4 good-size wahoo steaks, 1½ inches
thick, cut into squares
1 green pepper, in pieces
2 sweet red peppers, cut in large pieces
1 large sweet onion, cubed
8 to 12 firm cherry tomatoes

Combine oregano, oil, lemon juice, salt, pepper, and garlic and marinate fish cubes for several hours. Assemble shish kebabs, putting cherry tomatoes on last. Grill, turning once. Paint with marinade; serve with white rice. Also, these steaks may be served with any of the compound butter sauces listed with other firm-fleshed fish steaks.

GRILLED PINEAPPLE WITH ORANGE ICE

1 fresh pineapple skinned, cored,
and cut into 1-inch slices
Sprinkles of Grand Marnier
1 pint orange ice

Sprinkle the pineapple slices with Grand Marnier and grill quickly until hot and slightly browned. Lay on a plate and top each slice with a scoop of orange ice.

Fish From the Tropics

I have fished now quite a few times in tropical places. And I've caught very few fish. I've not been sorry for that.

There was the time in Jamaica with Ed and Patrick and Marcie when we went up the Black River looking for tarpon and saw a large swirl created by a very large tail but nothing more. There was the time in Tortola when a friend of mine threw his fishing gear, tackle bag and all, into a wave on an outgoing tide. Frustration, I guess, at the wiliness of the fish. There was the time when I was twelve out in front of my grandparents' house on the Gulf of Mexico with my brother and sister and grandfather when even shrimp wouldn't catch fish. And then, most recently, on Green Turtle Cay, when it was too windy for me to even attempt a bit of fly casting.

But I've never really been sorry for the absence of fish in those places. Maybe I hark back to my first time saltwater fishing. About eight years old, I remember standing on some coral rocks casting out to sea at dusk and cranking back, endlessly casting and cranking, casting and cranking with the odd tug here or nibble there. What was that! I would follow that line down to where it disappeared into the water and think about the bait (or plug or fly) dancing along flashing in front of fish, lots of fish, and fantasize about what would finally grab the hook. The fantasy played along so extravagantly and with such great mystery that I think I forgot that I wasn't catching fish—and I'm sure I was happier for it. Many times since, my mind has made that trip to the Bahamas, sometimes while fishing and sometimes while not. And although I can think of no better fish to eat than pompano or snapper, I think I prefer the slow, sweet, magical tropics with no fish to eat—just fantasies.

But in case you must come back to reality, these menus will help.

Grilled Pompano with Mint and Orange Rind
Brown Rice with Pine Nuts and Green Beans
Green Salad
Sauternes and Sugar Cookies

Serves four

Pignoli nuts, or pine nuts as they are called in English, are a perfectly wonderful nut to add to boring vegetables and should probably be kept on hand at all times. Madame Cintra demands that all nuts be cooked (roasted or sautéed) if they are used in a recipe. This is a common demand of real cooks. A word of caution: pine nuts burn quite easily if you try to roast them. Sauté them, as they are expensive, and avoid the risk of burning them.

Serve a mild green salad with no bitter greens and sauternes and sugar cookies for dessert. (See page 144 for cookie recipe.)

GRILLED POMPANO WITH MINT AND ORANGE RIND

2 tbsp. dried mint, revived
1½ sticks unsalted butter
Salt and fresh ground pepper
 to taste
Grated rind of 1 orange
Dash of Tabasco sauce
1 lb. pompano fillets, skin
 removed

Reconstitute the mint in warm water. Whip the butter until light and fluffy. Add salt, pepper, grated orange rind, Tabasco, and mint. Mix well and mound onto plastic wrap. Form into a cylinder and freeze for 24 hours. Bring to room temperature before using. Grill the pompano a few minutes on each side.

Just before done, put a few pats of the butter on the fish and add some more after.

BROWN RICE WITH PINE NUTS AND GREEN BEANS

2¼ cups water
1 tbsp. salt
1 cup brown rice
¼ cup pine nuts
1 tbsp. unsalted butter
½ lb. green beans
 Salt and pepper
2 to 3 tbsp. noisette butter
 (see index)

Bring 2¼ cups water to a boil and add the salt and rice. Cover and reduce heat and cook until tender, about 30 to 45 minutes. Sauté the pine nuts in 1 tablespoon unsalted butter until golden brown. Mix together the rice and nuts and add the green beans, which you've cut on the diagonal into ½-inch pieces and blanched for 1 minute. Add salt and pepper and a little noisette butter, about 2 to 3 tablespoons.

Grilled Red Snapper with Lime Butter Sauce and Grilled Pineapple
Bibb Salad
Cornbread
Coconut Ice Cream

Serves four

Ice cream is very satisfying to make at home even when you live, as we used to, in the state that has more ice cream parlors than any other. In Massachusetts it is very easy to get fresh, homemade ice cream. I do not think it is worthwhile to either crank by hand or spend a lot of money on a fancy ice cream maker. The extremes are unnecessary. Just buy a $30 electric machine; that will do the job nicely.

GRILLED RED SNAPPER WITH LIME BUTTER SAUCE AND GRILLED PINEAPPLE

2   tbsp. vinegar
¼   cup white wine
    Salt and pepper
2   shallots, chopped fine and
        sautéed in butter
8   oz. unsalted butter, plus 1 tbsp.
        (for sautéing the shallots)
4   fillets of red snapper
8   very thin slices of pineapple,
        peeled and cored
    Rind of one lime (Peel with
        potato peeler, being sure
        to remove only the green
        rind and none of the white
        pith. Cut into pieces the size
        of matchsticks and blanch in
        boiling water for 2 minutes.)

Combine the 2 tablespoons vinegar, wine, salt, and pepper with the cooked shallots and reduce by one-half to two-thirds. Now with the vinegar-wine reduction at a hot but not boiling temperature, add the butter in small bits, whisking constantly. The sauce will become foamy and white. Paint the fish and the pineapple lightly with the butter sauce. Put the pineapple on the grill a little before the fish. You will want it chewy and lightly caramelized. Grill fish until done. Put the remaining butter sauce under the fish on the plate with the pineapple around. Sprinkle a little of the lime rind on top.

BIBB SALAD

2   tbsp. red wine vinegar
½   cup good olive oil
1   tsp. prepared mustard
    Salt and pepper
4   heads Bibb lettuce, cleaned
    A few snips of chive

Combine vinegar, oil, mustard, salt, and pepper in a blender and zip on high for a second or two. Toss with the lettuce and chives.

CORNBREAD

1½ cups cornmeal
2 tsp. baking powder
1 tsp. salt
2 tbsp. granulated sugar
¼ cup flour
1 tbsp. finely diced sweet red
    pepper
3 tbsp. bacon drippings
2 eggs
1 cup buttermilk

Sift together the cornmeal, baking powder, salt, sugar, and flour. Sauté the red pepper in the bacon fat. Beat the eggs, add the buttermilk and red pepper along with the bacon drippings. Now combine this with the dry ingredients. Bake in a 425° oven for 15 to 25 minutes (depending on whether you cook the cornbread in buttered corn stick molds or muffin tins).

COCONUT ICE CREAM

2 cups whole milk
1 cup granulated sugar
1 cup grated coconut
6 egg yolks
1 cup heavy cream, chilled
1 tbsp. coconut liqueur (a
    coconut flavored rum or
    white rum)
Enough ice and salt for the
    ice cream machine

Bring the milk, ½ cup of the sugar, and the coconut to a boil. Just as it boils, remove from the heat. Cover pot and let rest until cool.

Combine the egg yolks and the other ½ cup sugar and mix with whisk or electric beater until thick and creamy. Add the cooled coconut milk mixture to the egg yolk mixture. Mix well. Return to heat in heavy-bottomed saucepan, and over medium heat stirring constantly, cook until it thickens, which it will do quite suddenly (between 5 to 10 minutes). Pour into a large bowl and stir for a few minutes to stop cooking. Add the heavy cream, the liqueur, and stir well to mix. Chill mixture well, stirring from time to time. Make according to your ice cream machine's directions. Serve with chocolate cookies.

Saltwater
Bottom Fish

One of the greatest aspects of saltwater fishing is that in the ocean, more than any other place, a fisherman can be surprised by what he catches. How many times have we all gone out for bluefish and returned home with flounder? Sometimes this is a result of needing to be versatile with fishing methods; sometimes the surprise happens as we're reeling in. It sure does seem sometimes that flounder will just jump onto your hook saying, "Take me, eat me, I'm yours."

Too many times we as fishermen are disappointed with catching something different from what we set out to catch. In Alaska the exclamation, "A grayling! Oh no, where's the rainbow!" has been heard more than once. And certainly in Gloucester Harbor there have been times when it seemed like my fellow fisherman was almost literally shaking his rod trying to get that flounder off the hook. Better to look at that fish as something to eat and cook than as an unexpected intruder onto your hook.

The three fish in this chapter are often considered such intruders. Perhaps because they are so plentiful and relatively easy to catch, they are also sometimes a bit disappointing to catch. But since all three are delightfully flavored fish and are best tasting when absolutely fresh, as fresh as only a fisherman can make them, then you must approach them from a cook's vantage. Their frequency and occasionally unexpected appearance make them ideal for testing new recipes. And although the menus listed here for cod, flounder, and sea bass are well suited to them, any, yes any, of the other fish recipes will work. Rarely is there a recipe in the book that will not work well on some species of fish other than the one it calls for. To determine applicability of one fish recipe to another kind of fish, consider the type of fish it is listed for. A recipe for a nice delicate brook trout will work well also on small-mouth bass. Went out for striper and came home with weakfish? Use the same recipe you were planning for striper on the weakfish. We have tried to group the fish by chapters according to likeness—not only likeness of habitat and species characteristics but also according to what recipes will work equally as well on all species within that chapter. In mixing species and menus, be concerned mostly with matching the proper cooking technique with the size or proper cut. Grilled fillet of black-fin flounder will end up dripping onto the coals. This thoughtful improvisation in the kitchen is very similar to matching the hatch on the river and will breed the same success and feeling of satisfaction. It's worth catching a mess of flounder for that. Just find someone else to clean them!

Chinese Grilled Flounder with Noodles
Sautéed Watercress
Pear Sorbet with Fortune Cookies

Serves four

Sautéing greens was a revelation to me. It can be done not only with watercress, but with spinach and parsley. It's very tasty and easy and solves that age-old problem of what to do with the remaining bunch after you've used the three sprigs for garnish.

CHINESE GRILLED FLOUNDER

  1 tbsp. lemon juice
  2 tbsp. soy sauce
  1 tbsp. rice wine vinegar
  1 large garlic clove, chopped fine
  1 piece ginger, peeled, chopped fine
  1 shake red pepper flakes
  ¼ cup corox oil (may substitute with
     more expensive sesame oil)
  1½ lbs. flounder, skinned, trimmed
     and in 1-inch pieces and put
     on grilling skewers
  1 lb. oriental pasta
  1 lb. mushrooms
  1 tbsp. sesame oil
3 to 6 scallions, green part only, cut into
     1-inch pieces
  ¼ cup peanuts or cashews, toasted in
     corn oil and coarsely chopped
  Salt and pepper

Blend the lemon juice, soy sauce, vinegar, garlic, ginger, and red pepper flakes in food processor, adding the corox oil last. Pour over fish, let rest several hours. Wrap the fish with the juices in foil and grill on a preheated grill, 2 to 3 minutes per side. Cook and drain the pasta and place the fish on top of it. Sauté the mushrooms quickly in the sesame oil. Remove from the heat and add the scallions and nuts. Season with salt and pepper. Top the fish with the nut and mushroom mixture and any leftover marinade. Serve with noodles.

SAUTÉED WATERCRESS

3 bunches watercress
3 to 4 tbsp. unsalted butter
Salt and pepper

Cut each bunch of watercress into 2-inch lengths (the bunches should be cut approximately into thirds). Sauté the watercress in the hot unsalted butter uncovered for a second or two, then cover for 2 minutes. Remove the lid, season with salt, pepper, and a little more butter, and serve.

PEAR SORBET

1 cup water
1 cup granulated sugar
1 qt. ripe pears peeled, cored,
    and puréed
2 tbsp. lemon juice
    A pinch of salt
1 tbsp. pear liqueur
    Salt and ice for the machine

Boil the water and sugar together 5 minutes. To puréed pears, add sugar syrup to taste, lemon juice to taste, a pinch of salt, and pear liqueur. Chill mixture, then freeze according to your ice cream machine's directions, but use less salt than recommended so ice crystals won't form. Serve with fortune cookies.

Gray Flounder
Sautéed Spinach
Fried Bread

Serves four

GRAY FLOUNDER

2 large carrots or 8 tiny ones,
   julienned
3 sticks celery, julienned
1   potato, julienned
1 tbsp. orange rind, julienned
   and blanched for 30 seconds
1 tsp. garlic, finely minced
2 tbsp. unsalted butter
4 flounder fillets
1½ cups heavy cream
1 tbsp. clam juice
   Salt and pepper

Sauté the vegetables, orange rind, and garlic in the butter until just barely tender. Set aside. In a stove-to-table container, set some vegetables on the bottom of the dish. Arrange fish on top. Reduce the cream by boiling it in a frying pan until it is halved, then add the clam juice to the cream and whisk. Pour over the fish. Add the remaining vegetables on top of the fish—criss-cross or put in little bunches if you wish. Cook at a simmer uncovered for about 5 minutes. Season fish with salt and pepper and serve on heated plates.

SAUTÉED SPINACH

1 lb. spinach
2 tbsp. unsalted butter
   Salt and pepper
   Fresh grated nutmeg

Rinse and dry spinach. Remove stems and sauté in butter until just wilted. Season with salt and pepper and a few grates of fresh nutmeg.

FRIED BREAD (see page 132)

Fish Chowder
Common Crackers
Green Salad
Gingerbread

Serves four

Cod is a wonderful fish if it is eaten very fresh; some people prefer it to haddock. It certainly is plentiful and caught easily by saltwater fishermen. Most of the recipes in this book would be appropriate to try on cod, but if you do not have a fresh cod or you have caught so much and had to freeze the fish, this recipe is perfect to use.

FISH CHOWDER

½ as many potatoes as fish,
      peeled
½ lb. unsalted butter
1 8-lb. cod (approximately),
      cleaned and cut up
   Salt and pepper
   Pinch thyme
1 can evaporated milk
½ pint all-purpose cream
1 qt. milk

Slice potatoes and put in kettle with some butter and a little water to cover. Bring to a boil and simmer about 10 minutes. Add cut up fish and salt and pepper to taste. Add more water to cover and a pinch of thyme and cook 30 minutes or until fish is tender. Stir in more butter, 1 can evaporated milk, and cream. Add regular milk to obtain the fluid level you want. Taste for seasoning. Set aside and do not let boil again. Serve with fried salted pork and common crackers.

GINGERBREAD

½ cup unsalted butter
⅔ cup light brown sugar
1 egg
1½ cups all-purpose flour
1¼ tsp. ground ginger
1 tsp. ground cinnamon
¾ tsp. ground cloves
1 tsp. baking soda
½ cup unsulphured molasses
½ cup boiling water
Confectioners' sugar
1 cup heavy cream
Dash of rum

Preheat the oven to 350°. Butter a 13-inch-by-9-inch-by-2-inch baking pan. Put a piece of wax paper on the buttered bottom and butter that and dust with flour.

Whip butter until fluffy. Add sugar and mix well. Add egg and blend well. Sift flour with spices and baking soda and set aside. Combine molasses with boiling water. Alternately add flour mixture and water and molasses mixture to the butter, sugar, egg mixture. Pour batter into prepared baking pan and cook about 25 to 30 minutes or until cake tester comes out clean. Cool in pan on wire rack. Then remove from cake pan. This can be made ahead and stored for several days if tightly wrapped and kept at room temperature. Just before serving, dust with confectioners' sugar. Serve with lightly whipped cream and add a dash of rum to the cream.

Grilled Sea Bass with Sun-Dried Tomatoes, Pepper, and Garlic
Straw Potato-Corn Cake
Green Salad
Honey Ice Cream

Serves four

Sun-dried tomatoes have become a little bit more common an ingredient in recent years but still may have to be purchased from a gourmet shop. My own taste dictates the purchase of the more expensive sun-dried tomatoes, the ones packed in olive oil, not the ones simply dried and salted. The salt is too over-bearing, and I like to use the oil in which the tomatoes have been packed in salad dressings and other recipes within the menu to "tie" the tastes together. When you make the vinaigrette for your salad in this menu (see the index in this book if you can't think of a good salad on your own) use some of the oil from the sun-dried tomatoes.

GRILLED SEA BASS WITH SUN-DRIED TOMATOES, PEPPER, AND GARLIC

1   3-pound sea bass, butterflied
      (that is, skin left on, head
      and tail removed), boned,
      and split (remove scales)
    Salt and pepper
1   sprig fresh basil or 1 tsp. dried
1   sprig fresh thyme or 1 tsp. dried
1   small onion, sliced fine
½   cup olive oil
2   cloves garlic, minced
1   large green pepper, cored and
      chopped into ½-inch pieces
½   cup sun-dried tomatoes in oil,
      roughly chopped (If they are
      not in oil: in a small pot add
      the tomatoes, 1 cup olive oil,
      1 small clove garlic, and a pinch
      thyme. Heat until hot and keep
      warm for 20 minutes or until
      tomatoes have plumped. Drain
      off oil and reserve for another use.
      It's great in salads.)
    Handful chopped parsley

Dry fish and season with salt and pepper. Stuff with basil and thyme. Wrap tightly in foil and refrigerate for 2 to 4 hours. Make the sauce ahead of time: Sauté onion in olive oil over medium-low heat until translucent. Add garlic, peppers, and tomatoes. Cook until peppers are done to taste. Season with salt and pepper and a handful of chopped parsley. Let sit 20 minutes at least to meld flavors. Preheat grill. Do not remove foil from fish and cook 15 minutes one side and 12 minutes on the other. Test for doneness. Remove the herbs from the fish and spoon the sauce over it. Serve with a green salad.

STRAW POTATO–CORN CAKE

1½ lbs. baking potatoes
4 tbsp. unsalted butter
2 tbsp. oil
6 tbsp. creamed corn
Salt and pepper

Peel potatoes, cut into ⅛-inch slices and then into ⅛-inch matchstick strips, or easier still, cut into matchstick juliennes in your food processor. In a 10-inch nonstick pan, heat half the butter and all the oil until hot, add half the potatoes, and spread around the center on top of the potatoes about 6 tablespoons cold creamed corn. Season with salt and pepper. Then add the rest of the potatoes. Season with salt and pepper and press down with spatula. Cook until the bottom is browned, by which time the whole cake will move as one. (Be sure you squish those potatoes down occasionally.) When the bottom is golden brown, lower the heat and cover and cook 7 minutes to cook the center of the cake. Remove cover and raise the heat. Flip the potato cake over and add a little more butter and brown the other side.

HONEY ICE CREAM

2 cups milk
⅓ cup very aromatic and high
   quality honey
6 egg yolks
⅔ cup granulated sugar
1 cup heavy cream, chilled
   Enough ice and salt for the ice
      cream machine
   Crystallized lavender flowers for
      decoration (These can be
      purchased at a gourmet shop.)

Bring milk and honey slowly to the scalding point while stirring. Remove from heat and cool, stirring occasionally. Mix egg yolks and sugar together and beat until a light ribbon is formed. The mixture will be thick and creamy. Combine egg-sugar together with the milk-honey, whisking just to mix. Using a heavy-bottomed saucepan, return to medium-high heat and stir constantly until the mixture thickens. Remove immediately from the heat and pour through a fine strainer into a large bowl and cool, stirring occasionally. Add heavy cream and mix well. Chill mixture thoroughly. Make ice cream according to your ice cream machine's instructions. Serve garnished with crystallized violets.

Stir-Fried Snow Peas with Broccoli
Black Sea Bass Chinese Style
White Rice
Fortune Cookies

Serves four

I thought you would know how to cook white rice so I did not include a recipe for it. Also, I have found that rice lovers all have their own very definite ideas as to what brand, converted or not, or how sticky or dry the rice should be. Fortune cookies need to be bought.

STIR-FRIED SNOW PEAS WITH BROCCOLI

> 1 head of broccoli
> 2 tbsp. sesame oil
> 2 tbsp. unsalted butter
> 1 lb. snow peas, ends and
>   strings removed
> Salt and pepper

Remove bite-size flowerettes from the broccoli and blanch. Heat the oil and butter together and add the snow peas and flowerettes. Stir constantly till hot and season with salt and pepper.

BLACK SEA BASS CHINESE STYLE

    3 lbs. of black sea bass; the
          average size is 1 to 3 lbs.,
          so 2 smaller or 1 bigger
    2 tbsp. dry sherry
    ¼ cup plus 2 tsp. soy sauce
       Salt and pepper
    3 tbsp. corn oil
    2 tbsp. sesame oil
    4 tbsp. peeled and julienned
          ginger
    5 scallions, white and green parts,
          cleaned, in 1-inch pieces
    1 clove garlic, chopped fine
    3 tsp. cornstarch, mixed in ¼ cup
          cold water
    1 tsp. granulated sugar

Bone, clean, wash, and dry the fish and leave head and tail on. Score the fish on both sides and lay it on a large piece of foil. Combine the sherry and 2 teaspoons of soy sauce to make a basting liquid. Sprinkle the fish with the liquid and a grind of pepper and fold up carefully to encase all liquid. Steam over boiling water in steamer for 15 minutes. Meanwhile, in heavy saucepan, heat the two oils until hot. Lower heat and add ginger. Cook 1 to 2 minutes. Add scallions and garlic and cook 20 seconds. Add soy sauce, the ¼ cup water plus cornstarch, and sugar. Stir well and set aside. Remove fish from foil as soon as cooked, saving the juices. If there is a lot, reduce the liquid to 5 to 6 tablespoons. Add to the ginger, garlic soy sauce. Season with salt and pepper. Pour over fish. Serve on a decorative platter.

Freshwater Fish

I had a rather eclectic relationship with fish as a child. I have very far away memories of the commercial fishing boats on Lake Michigan, walking the beaches looking for the metal floats washed up from their nets, and my parents eating delicious "whitefish" for breakfast. But by the time I'd become old enough to catch the fish, the Great Lakes had become barren of edible fish and my greatest source and opportunity for catching and eating fish was gone. My parents resorted to eating fish that had been "brought in." The fish stores liked to claim that the fish had been flown in, but we could tell from the aroma and taste of the fish that it had actually traveled by wagon train and come down the Erie Canal. Fresh they were not. There were many years which passed where I stood firm on the belief that fish was not very tasty. In bits and pieces I began to learn something about fishing on my annual trips to Florida, but fishing and eating fish remained separate concepts for me for a long time.

The idea that the best fish to eat is the fish you've caught, and vice versa, came to me in two quick, hard lessons. As a teenager cruising on a sailboat in the North Channel, I discovered something I'd never done before: fishing in Lake Superior. The lake was still rather barren of fish and I completely unknowledgeable about freshwater fishing. I was reduced to catching the little rock bass that lay along the pier where we were moored. The minnows netted proved excellent bait and I caught literally 50 or 60 little rock bass. Catch-and-release was not a known concept to me, especially for rock bass, and the little fish lay scattered on the dock. A passing gentleman, seeing the litter of dead fish, exclaimed, "I hope you intend to eat every one of those." It was as if an enormous tidal wave of realization came over me: *Most people eat what they catch!* And as I looked at all those dead fish I understood what a dreadful thing I had done. Only the excuse of providing sustenance could have absolved me.

217

Clearly there was no brain in this pathetic fisherman but I was at least now armed with a new conscience (and primed for the concept of catch-and-release). I did have the good sense to travel East and marry a fisherman. Although at this point I realized that morally it was tasteless to not eat what you caught and kept, I still was a little slow to understand the selfish benefits to it all. Ed and I were invited up to Maine to a friend's lovely old log cabin for fishing. We had the place to ourselves. The seven-hour car ride had been long, especially the last hour on dirt roads. We felt particularly welcomed as we drove up to the house and saw the caretaker waiting for us with a little stringer of native brook trout. He had just finished building a fire and was breaking off sticks to skewer the fish as we were unloading the car. We sat by the water eating the roasted brook trout. I had had brook trout in restaurants in the Midwest before; were these fish related? Impossible. As that wave of conscience had washed over me, so now did a new wave of eating delight. A freshly caught, wild fish, simply cooked; this surely was the ultimate taste treat. From there to catching the fish myself and eating it fresh, the lesson was forever locked in my mind, heart, and taste buds.

I have never tasted a fresh fish that I didn't like. Much of this cookbook is concerned with cooking and eating very fresh fish and is written on the premise that a good, fresh fish need not have much done to it. The fresher the fish, the simpler the recipe for its preparation. Do not let yourself get enticed for the sake of culinary art into cooking sauces and court bouillons and complicated programs for a fresh fish. There's no need to over-cook. Save all that for the rest of the menu or an old fish. Relax, and think of fresh fish as your chance to cook the simplest but most delicious food there is.

I have in many of the menus here tried very hard to keep the fish recipes simple because that is what makes the fish taste best. Sometimes I have made the rest of the menu more complicated to keep up your interest in cooking, but on other occasions I've complemented the simplicity of the fish recipe with a simple menu: Pumpkinseed-Fish-On-A-Stick with Homemade Chocolate Chip Cookies. If only that had been my first meal of a fish I'd caught, it never would have taken me twenty-five years to love to fish and eat the fish I catch.

The Stream Fish

I think God really wanted us to eat the fish we catch, but He realized there were a bunch of pigs in the crowd and so He invented the sport fisherman: A creature who would find it appealing just to catch the fish and would figure out a whole lot of excuses why we all should put the fish back and not eat it. The fishermen have used both guilt, as in the case of the striped bass (our chemical effluents have been killing the fry in the Chesapeake), and reason very effectively to make us put it all back.

When we go fishing in Alaska for rainbow trout, the guides are very proud of the fact that they may have had to kill only one trout, or maybe none at all, that summer. They are very protective of those trout and tell the fisherman that they aren't worth catching to eat anyway because they don't taste very good. A trout that doesn't taste good; is this possible? Oh, yes, it's because the rainbows feed on carcasses of the dead salmon. They must taste terrible feeding on that stuff. If this logic followed we would want to reduce our fish intake considerably. Note the lovely aroma and appeal of your chum bucket some time; and doesn't that sea worm look scrumptious? Unlike the duck that feeds on wild rice or the antelope that grazes on sage-scented grasses, fish are not known for their gourmet diets. It probably is a little difficult to honestly say that carcass-eating rainbows taste any worse than the ones that eat lemmings or salmon eggs or insects.

There is perhaps more correlation between where the fish lives and his flavor than to how his diet affects his taste. It does seem that the little brookies, the Dolly Varden, grayling, or rainbow trout that swim in the beautiful wild waters of Alaska or British Columbia, or Montana or Maine are better eating than hatchery trout.

Or is it simply that we like to catch the fish in those places? God did intend for us to eat the fish we catch.

**Breakfast Trout
Cornbread**

Serves four

BREAKFAST TROUT

4 ⅛-inch slices of pancetta
    (Italian cured bacon)
4 12-oz. trout, cleaned, whole
    Salt and fresh ground pepper
1 cup flour
½ cup clarified butter
1 tbsp. plus 2 tsp. pancetta fat
20 cherry tomatoes
    Lemon wedges

Slice the pancetta into ½-inch strips and sauté on low heat until almost crisp. Set on towels to drain. Rinse trout, drain; sprinkle with salt and pepper. Dredge in flour; shake off excess. Fry in hot butter and 1 tablespoon pancetta fat 3 to 4 minutes per side. Set on warm plates when done and sauté cherry tomatoes in same pan, adding 2 teaspoons pancetta fat to the pan. Reheat the pancetta strips with the tomatoes. Divide among the plates and garnish with lemon wedges.

CORNBREAD (see page 204)

Trout Fried
Stuffed Risotto Tomatoes
Zucchini
Strawberry Sponge

Serves four

TROUT FRIED

4 slices of French bread or a
    generous ½ cup of bread
    crumbs
2 tbsp. flour
2 trout, boned and filleted
1 egg
1 tsp. oil
1 tsp. water
¼ tsp. thyme
4 tbsp. unsalted butter
    Salt and pepper
    Lemon wedges

Process four slices of dry French bread in your food processor and sift through a wire mesh strainer. Put the flour on a plate and dust both sides of the fish. Combine the egg, oil, water, and thyme and using a pastry brush, paint the fillets with this mixture. Now dip the trout into bread crumbs and rest on a cake rack to dry. This can be done ½ hour before cooking. (If you leave the skin on, put flour only on the skin side. Use the egg mixture and crumbs for the flesh side only.) Heat the butter in a large skillet until very hot. Put in fish and cook only a few minutes on each side. It will be very crispy on the outside and moist on the inside. The fish may be kept warm for a few minutes. Season with salt and pepper and serve with lemon wedges.

STUFFED RISOTTO TOMATOES

4 medium-size tomatoes, ripe
  but firm
  Salt and pepper
  Dribble of oil
  Risotto (see page 289)
2 tbsp. tomato purée
2 tbsp. Parmesan cheese
  Sprinkle of bread crumbs
  Dots of butter

Remove tomato tops and carefully scoop out seeds. Sprinkle with salt and pepper. Dot with oil and bake at 425° for 5 to 6 minutes. Remove from oven, drain juices and save. Make risotto according to the directions on page 289. Stir in the purée, Parmesan cheese, and the juices you reserved from the tomatoes. This can be done several hours ahead. Stuff tomatoes and sprinkle with fresh bread crumbs. Dot with butter and bake at 425° for 10 to 15 minutes.

ZUCCHINI

8 5- to 6-inch firm zucchini
2 to 3 tbsp. unsalted butter
1 small clove garlic, chopped fine
  (optional)
  Salt and pepper

Cut both ends off the zucchinis. Cut in half lengthwise and then in half again so that each zucchini is in 4 long pieces. Cut each piece into ⅛-inch-thick strips and then cut the strips in half. You now have zucchini that looks like pasta. Melt butter. When very hot, add zucchini and garlic. Cook over medium-high heat until soft. Season with salt and pepper and serve.

STRAWBERRY SPONGE

  1 supermarket sponge cake
  3 tbsp. *framboise,* Grand Marnier,
       or rum
  4 egg yolks
  ⅓ cup granulated sugar
  ¼ tsp. salt
  1 cup heavy cream
  1 tsp. vanilla extract
     A sprinkle of fresh strawberries
     Several tbsp. melted currant
       jelly

Paint the sponge cake with a tablespoon or so of the *framboise* if you have it or Grand Marnier or even rum will do. Mix the egg yolks and sugar in a bowl with a whisk. Add salt and cream. Mix well but do not whisk to a foam. Transfer to a heavy-bottomed saucepan. Put over high or medium-high heat and stir constantly with a wooden spoon (that means touching the bottom of the pan as you stir) until the custard begins to thicken and the surface of the custard becomes very smooth. Pour immediately through a strainer into another bowl and whisk to cool to stop the cooking. Then add two tablespoons of the liqueur and the vanilla and chill for several hours, stirring occasionally. Spread the custard on the cake base and top with strawberries and glaze with the melted currant jelly. If not served at once, it may be chilled for a bit. Just bring it out of the refrigerator 15 minutes or so before eating.

Serves four

Fava beans are hard to find, especially anywhere outside of California, but worth a hard search. Skip the canned version.

POACHED STEELHEAD TROUT WITH LEMON BUTTER SAUCE

½ cup plus 2 tbsp. vinegar
1½ quarts water
1 tbsp. salt
2 peppercorns, crushed
Pinch thyme
½ bay leaf
1 onion, thinly sliced
1 carrot, sliced
¼ cup white wine
Salt and pepper
2 shallots, chopped fine and
sautéed in butter
4 steelhead trout steaks, ¾ to
1 inch thick. One steak per
person should do, depending
on the size of the fish.
8 oz. unsalted butter, plus
1 tbsp.

Make a court bouillon by combining ½ cup vinegar, water, 1 tablespoon salt, peppercorns, thyme, bay leaf, onion, and carrot and bringing to a boil. Cook 45 minutes. Strain and let cool.

Now combine together the 2 tablespoons of vinegar, wine, salt, pepper, and cooked shallots and reduce by one-half to two-thirds. Set aside.

Return the court bouillon to the stove and bring to a boil. Plunge the fish steaks in. Bring back to boil. Cover and remove from the heat. The steaks should take 7 to 8 minutes. Drain the fish and place on warm plates.

Return the vinegar-wine reduction to heat and at a hot but not boiling temperature, add the butter in small bits, whisking constantly. The sauce will become foamy and white. Serve immediately on the fish.

FAVA BEANS WITH ASPARAGUS

3 to 4 lbs. fava beans
1 lb. asparagus
2 tbsp. unsalted butter
Salt and pepper

Fava beans are a wonderful spring vegetable. Big supermarkets will probably carry them as well as Italian markets. A lot of tedious work is involved in preparing them, so you may only eat them once a year, but it's worth it for the taste and the fact that they mean spring is here. Remove fava beans from their pods. Peel the outer skin from each bean (it is worth it, I promise). Steam until just done—about 5 minutes. Refresh with ice water and drain. Remove the tips from the asparagus and use the stalks for soup. Blanch or steam the tips until just done. Refresh in ice water and drain. This can all be done in the morning. Cook the butter until sizzling (you could use one-half bacon fat if you wish). Add beans and asparagus. Cook until vegetables are heated through. Season with salt and pepper. Serve.

STRAWBERRIES WITH CRÈME ANGLAISE

4 egg yolks
⅛ tsp. salt
¼ cup granulated sugar
½ cup milk
½ cup heavy cream
1 tbsp. liqueur (Grand Marnier is good) or vanilla
1 pt. fresh strawberries, cleaned and hulled

Whisk together the yolks, salt, and sugar. Combine the milk and cream and whisk that together with the yolk combination. Cook over a medium-high heat, stirring constantly until it thickens quite suddenly. Remove from the heat, strain and whisk cool. Add the liqueur or vanilla and spoon over the strawberries.

Trout with Noisette Butter
Sautéed Cucumbers
Dilled New Potatoes

Serves four

TROUT WITH NOISETTE BUTTER

4 trout
1 tbsp. corn oil
   Salt and pepper
   Flour for dredging
8 tbsp. unsalted butter
   Lemon juice

Clean the fish, removing intestines and gills. Wash and dry the fish, rub with oil, and sprinkle with salt and pepper. Dredge in flour and shake off excess. Cook 4 tablespoons butter over medium heat until it is a very pale brown. Remove from heat and it will continue to cook a little more. If it appears to be turning color too fast, pour it into a cool pan to stop the cooking. Set this browned, or noisette, butter aside for the sauce. Heat remaining 4 tablespoons of butter and all of the oil together on medium-high until just about to sizzle. Add the trout and sauté until one side is golden and then turn and finish the other side. Remember, the second side will take a little less time. Serve the fish immediately, sprinkled first with lemon juice, and then pour on the hot noisette butter.

SAUTÉED CUCUMBERS

4 cucumbers, peeled, halved,
    seeded, and cut into
    ¼-inch-thick slices
2 tbsp. unsalted butter
    Salt and pepper

Sauté cucumbers in the hot butter until just tender. Season with salt and pepper.

DILLED NEW POTATOES

3 potatoes per person
    Salt and pepper
1 tbsp. chopped dill

Boil or steam the new potatoes and then sprinkle with the salt, pepper, and dill.

Streamside Trout with Potatoes
The Best Brownies

Serves four

For the best brownie recipe, see page 156.

STREAMSIDE TROUT WITH POTATOES

4 ⅛-inch-thick slices of pancetta
(Pancetta is a cured Italian
Bacon. It is round in shape,
carried by most delicatessens
and may be eaten cooked or
uncooked. If you can't or
don't wish to bring it on your
fishing trip, then cook it at
home and bring the rendered
grease.)
4 stalks celery, cleaned and
chopped
4 medium potatoes, cleaned
and chopped with skin on,
cut into bite-size pieces
Salt and pepper
4 trout, cleaned and scaled

Slice the pancetta into ½-inch strips and sauté till almost crisp. Spoon out a little of the fat into a cup (reserved to cook the fish in), add the celery and potatoes to the rest. Cover and cook till nicely browned, turning once or twice. Season with salt and pepper. Push aside and add the extra fat and the fish. Cook the fish until the tails are just crispy and season with salt and pepper.

Grilled Char with Tarragon and Shallot Butter
Pasta with Fresh Corn and Basil
Sautéed Cherry Tomatoes
The Best Brownies

Serves four

GRILLED CHAR WITH TARRAGON AND SHALLOT BUTTER

1½ sticks unsalted butter
Salt and pepper
1 dash Worcestershire sauce
1 tbsp. dried tarragon
3 or 4 shallots, finely chopped
4 char steaks
Oil for basting

Make the compound butter in advance. Whip the butter until light and fluffy. Add salt, pepper, Worcestershire, tarragon, and shallots. Mix well and mound onto plastic wrap. Form into a cylinder and freeze for 24 hours. Bring to room temperature before using. Brush the char with oil and cook 6 to 8 minutes per side. Place pats of the compound butter on each steak and serve.

PASTA WITH FRESH CORN AND BASIL

1 lb. pasta
1 cup heavy cream, reduced by
half
1 tsp. dried basil, cooked with
the cream
1½ cups cooked fresh corn
Salt and pepper
Pinch cayenne pepper
Fresh basil for garnish

While the pasta is cooking, reduce the cream with the dried basil. Add cooked corn. Season with salt, pepper, and cayenne and combine with the cooked pasta. Check for seasoning again and serve garnished with lots of fresh basil.

SAUTÉED CHERRY TOMATOES

24 cherry tomatoes
2 tbsp. unsalted butter
   Several sprigs of fresh basil
      (or any other fresh herb
      you may have; dried herbs
      work, too)
   Salt and pepper

Prick each cherry tomato with a pin to prevent the tomato skins from bursting, and remove the green tops. Sauté in the butter till hot and sprinkle with the chopped herb, salt, and pepper. Serve.

THE BEST BROWNIES

2 squares unsweetened chocolate
1 stick unsalted butter
1 cup granulated sugar
2 eggs
1 tsp. vanilla
¼ cup flour
¼ tsp. salt
1 cup chopped walnuts

Preheat oven to 325°. Melt together the chocolate and butter and then stir in the sugar. Beat together the eggs and vanilla and add them to the chocolate mixture. Now quickly stir in the flour, salt, and chopped nuts. Spread in greased 8-inch-by-8-inch pan and bake 40 to 45 minutes at 325°. Do not over-cook or they will be dry. Cake tester should just come out clean. Let cool in pan. Then cut in squares and remove. The first brownie will be hard to get out and may stick and crumble. Do not be deterred. These are the best brownies.

Pan Poached Grayling
Sautéed Potatoes with Chanterelles and Thyme
Green Salad
Fresh Fruit with Lightly Whipped Cream
Almond Cookies

Serves four

    When I think of eating grayling, I always think of a streamside meal. This would be a good menu streamside, especially if you did the chopping of herbs and whatnot before leaving home and had them ready to go sealed in a plastic bag. Then lay the grayling fillets in foil, pour the wine over them and dump the prechopped herbs, parsley, celery, and shallots from their plastic bag over the fish and seal the foil. Wrap again and cook in the coals of a wood fire. The potatoes and chanterelles can be done in a frying pan over the coals, too. The fruit and cookies should be prepared ahead and ready to go. Just whip a little cream and you have a most elegant streamside dinner.

PAN POACHED GRAYLING

         2 tsp. finely chopped shallots
         1 small rib celery, peeled and diced
         1 tsp. chopped parsley stems
    3 to 4 tbsp. unsalted butter
       ⅔ cup white wine
         4 grayling fillets
            Salt and pepper
            Optional—any chopped fresh herbs,
               such as tarragon, parsley, chives

Sauté the shallots and celery with parsley stems in 1 tablespoon butter. Add the wine and simmer for a few minutes. Add the fish. Cover and reduce heat and cook until just tender. Remove the fish and reduce the liquid by half over high heat. Lower the heat and whisk in 2 to 3 tbsp. sweet butter. Season with salt and pepper. Stir in the herbs if you've chosen to use any. It is fine without. Pour over fish and serve.

SAUTÉED POTATOES WITH CHANTERELLES AND THYME

         2 cups chanterelle mushrooms,
               coarsely chopped
         1 tbsp. bacon fat
         5 tbsp. unsalted butter
         4 medium potatoes, peeled,
               washed, dried, and cut
               into medium chunks
            Salt and pepper
       ½ tsp. thyme

If you are using dried mushrooms, rinse them quickly in cold water and revive them in a small amount of hot water or hot chicken stock. (You may save the liquid for another dish as it will become permeated with the flavor of the mushrooms.) In a large heavy-bottomed saucepan melt bacon fat and 3 tablespoons of the butter until hot and sizzling. Add potatoes and sprinkle with salt and pepper. Cover and cook slowly. Let them brown slowly as they cook, stirring from time to time. At the same time, sauté the mushrooms in 2 tablespoons unsalted butter for 1 minute over medium-high heat. Lower the heat and sprinkle with salt and pepper and cover. Cook until juices exude, then remove cover, raise heat and evaporate juices, stirring all the while. Add the mushrooms to the cooked potatoes and sprinkle with thyme. Taste for seasoning and serve.

GREEN SALAD

      1 tbsp. vinegar
      1 tsp. prepared mustard
      ½ cup oil
      1 tsp. basil
         Salt and pepper
      1 head Boston, red, oakleaf , or
            Bibb lettuce (no strong tastes)

Blend all but the lettuce in the blender on high-speed. Toss with the lettuce.

FRESH FRUIT WITH LIGHTLY WHIPPED CREAM

For the fresh fruit, whip 1 cup cream lightly with a little liqueur or rum and 1 teaspoon confectioners' sugar.

ALMOND COOKIES

      ¾ cup unsalted butter, softened
      ½ cup granulated sugar
      ¼ tsp. salt
      1 egg
      ½ tbsp. orange rind
         Dash of almond extract
      2 cups cake flour
         Cinnamon-sugar sprinkles

Cream the butter into the sugar and salt. Whip till fluffy. Add 1 egg, orange rind, and almond extract and mix. Blend in the flour. Cover the dough and refrigerate until it is firm. Roll out in small batches and cut with a cookie cutter. If you have it, use a fish cookie cutter to flatter the fishermen. Sprinkle with cinnamon sugar and bake at 350° till just starting to brown around the edges (about 7 minutes or so).

233

Leftover Char Risotto
Green Salad
Tuscan Muffins
Apricot Crème Brûlée

Serves four

Cintra and I have had our disagreements with this dessert about how long to cook the custard in the oven. I think we have disagreed partially because our ovens cook differently (hers is much hotter than mine) and partially because she is of the belief that custard should be quite soft. I like it any which way. Actually, I have determined after some experimentation that how long it cooks in the oven is somewhat dependent on how long you cook it on top of the stove. The 25 minutes specified here requires a short (3 to 5 minutes) amount of cooking on top of the stove. If you are willing to be quite diligent and stir the cream and egg mixture constantly until it is very hot, the cooking time in the oven should be reduced to 20 minutes or less, depending on how you like your custard.

LEFTOVER CHAR RISOTTO

         1 green pepper
         2 red peppers
         4 oz. unsalted butter or a mixture
               of butter and olive oil
         2 onions, chopped very fine
      1½ cups Italian arborio rice
   4 to 5 cups hot fluid, either stock (veal
               or chicken), water, or a
               combination of both
         2 tbsp. chopped Italian parsley or
               thyme
      1½ cups any leftover char, broken into
               pieces, fat and bones removed

First, halve the peppers and take out the seeds (or use whole). Place them cut-side down on a piece of foil in the broiler and broil them 2 to 3 minutes until the skins are black. Remove and let cool. Peel the black skin off, remove the seeds, and slice the peppers into pieces keeping colors separate.

Then in a heavy-bottomed, wide saucepan, heat butter. Sauté onions until translucent. Add rice. Cook, stirring until it becomes very white, shiny, and very hot to touch. Then, over medium-high heat, add only enough stock so that the rice is just covered. Holding the handle of the saucepan, firmly swish the rice around and around. Do this every 2 to 3 minutes, keeping a low simmer going in the pot in between. This is so the rice won't stick. (If you weaken and stir the rice, then you must continue to stir until done.) As soon as you can distinguish the grains of rice again, then add another ½ cup of fluid. Keep swirling the pot and adding more fluid as it becomes absorbed. Taste when you feel it is nearly finished. It should be firm to the bite and of a tender, creamy texture—not too dry and not too runny. In the meantime, sauté the peppers separately (red from green) in a little butter and sprinkle thyme or parsley over them. Combine the risotto, peppers, and char and check for seasoning.

TUSCAN MUFFINS (see page 150)

APRICOT CRÈME BRÛLÉE

8 to 10 dried apricots
1 cup apple juice
6 eggs
5 tbsp. granulated sugar
3 cups heavy cream
1 tbsp. vanilla extract
½ cup light brown sugar

In a small heavy-bottomed saucepan, cover apricots with just enough apple juice to cover the tops; use good apple juice. Bring to a low simmer and cook with a lid until the apricots become very soft and mushy. Let cool and purée in a food processor. Separate the eggs and combine the yolks well with the white sugar and cream. Heat the mixture until very warm over a medium heat, stirring constantly. Remove from the flame and add the vanilla. Spread apricot purée on bottom of baking dish. Then pour cream mixture through a strainer over the apricots. Put the dish into a roasting pan and surround it with an inch or so of boiling water. Bake it in a preheated oven at 300° for 25 minutes or until the custard is just setting around the edges but is still soft around the middle. Remove from the oven and let sit in the water bath until cool. Then refrigerate the custard for at least two hours or overnight. Just before serving sprinkle the custard with the brown sugar and put under a very hot broiler for a few seconds. If you cannot get your broiler hot enough, put the dish in cracked ice so the custard won't overcook while the brown sugar forms a nice hard crust.

Walleye and Pike

I t has been said that necessity is the mother of invention. It is also the mother of some terrific meals.

We were visiting our friends Dave and Kim, who run a fish camp in the Bristol Bay region of Alaska. Dave and Ed were flying the last two guests into Dillingham and were to pick up supplies for the next couple of days. Kim and I had the luxury of lolling about camp for the few hours they were to be gone. We talked a lot about cooking: what it was like to cook every day for a camp full of fishermen, what problems were unique to cooking in the bush, what were some of her fish recipes. The talk was fun, but the two hours the men were supposed to be gone were stretching into three. Kim had wanted to get dinner cooking but needed the supplies to do so. The in-the-bush game of trying to hear the airplane's motor first was beginning to grow old with mirages of noises building, then destroying, expectations. At long last the engine of Dave's Beaver could truly be heard. It was quite late but the daylight hours were still long in Alaska. The tardiness excuses were made, and we waited for the supplies to be brought in. What, no groceries? There was then a very quiet "discussion" between Dave and Kim. "I gave you a grocery list!" "No you did not!" It didn't really matter, of course, who was supposed to give what to whom or who had lost what, the deed was done. (I am happy to report to all the ladies in the audience that the next day when I was fishing with Dave, he was searching in his pockets for a twist-on and found the slip of paper he had so heartily denied having had the night before.) We were now faced with nothing to eat for dinner and the nearest restaurant or grocery store many hundreds of miles away. Ah, but we had a river full of fish lying before us.

237

We were obliged with a wonderful pike. Kim make Pike Puffs, her own great tempura-like concoction that quickly became nearly my favorite fish recipe that she does. Dinner was spectacular.

Rarely am I truly hundreds of miles away from the nearest grocery store. But there are times with the New England weather or my own fatigue that the grocery store might as well be a hundred miles away. I get the greatest pleasure out of figuring out what I can make from what's left in the pantry. It's a game of letting the imagination run wild, with certain restraints. It also is a game that has forced the creation of many a great recipe and is terrific mental and culinary exercise for when the fisherman returns home not with the anticipated salmon, but with pike. Don't run for this cookbook, improvise!

Cool Vegetables with Herb Mayonnaise
Pike Couscous
Grilled Pineapple

Serves four

Some people don't know about couscous. It is a grain, similar to grits or rice, which comes from North Africa. It is a nice alternative and is delicious.

COOL VEGETABLES WITH HERB MAYONNAISE

As a first course, blanch a large variety of vegetables (broccoli, green beans, squash, carrots, and cauliflower) and serve with a spiced or herb mayonnaise (see index for mayonnaise). This can be arranged on individual plates or presented as a centerpiece to be eaten with each person having his or her own bowl of mayonnaise.

PIKE COUSCOUS

       2 cups chicken broth
      10 tbsp. unsalted butter
      ¼ tsp. cumin
      ¼ tsp. coriander, ground
         Salt and pepper
       2 cups couscous
       2 pounds pike fillets, skinned
           and cut into 2-inch pieces
       2 scallions, green part only,
           chopped
         Parsley, chopped fine
       1 tsp. lemon rind, grated

In a saucepan, bring the chicken broth to a boil adding 6 tablespoons
butter, the ground cumin, and coriander; add salt and pepper. Stir in the
couscous, cover pan, remove from the heat, and let stand for 5 minutes. In a
frying pan, sauté the fish and scallions in 3 to 4 tablespoons butter over
medium-high heat for 4 minutes. Season with salt and pepper. Add the hot
fish and scallions, parsley, and lemon rind to the couscous. Toss well with a
fork, fluffing up the couscous at the same time to break up any lumps. Taste
for seasoning, adding more salt and pepper if necessary and serve in large
soup plates.

GRILLED PINEAPPLE

       1 medium-size ripe pineapple
       1 tbsp. brown sugar
       2 tbsp. Grand Marnier or
           Cointreau

Cut off the top, bottom, and the sides of the pineapple with a large sharp
knife. Remove the core and slice in thin slices, ¼ inch thick or less. Grill
until they start to brown. Sprinkle with the brown sugar and liqueur at the
last minute and serve.

Sautéed Walleye with Noisette Butter and Shallots
Couscous
Broiled Tomatoes
Blancmange

Serves four

Broiled tomatoes are just that; slice them and run them under the broiler for a few minutes and season.

SAUTÉED WALLEYE WITH NOISETTE BUTTER AND SHALLOTS

        8 shallots, peeled and sliced thin
2 to 3 tbsp. unsalted butter
        2 lbs. walleye fillets, dusted with flour
        1 stick unsalted butter, cooked until
              noisette—see page 254
           Salt and pepper

Cook the shallots in 1 tablespoon unsalted butter until they just start to turn a golden color and set aside. Sauté the fish in the butter and top with shallots and the noisette butter. Season with salt and pepper.

COUSCOUS

        1 cup chicken stock
6 to 8 tbsp. unsalted butter
           Salt and pepper and a pinch
              cayenne
        1 cup couscous
           Chopped parsley

In saucepan bring stock to a boil and add 4 tablespoons butter, salt, pepper, and cayenne. When melted, stir in couscous, cover pan, and let stand 5 minutes. Add 2 to 3 more tablespoons soft butter and let stand another minute covered. Then fluff the couscous with a fork and season well with salt, pepper, and chopped parsley.

241

BLANCMANGE

1 envelope gelatin
1 tbsp. water
1 cup whole milk
3 cups heavy cream
⅔ cup granulated sugar
¼ tsp. salt
3 tbsp. Green Chartreuse
   liqueur

Combine the gelatin and the water in a small custard cup. Set in a small frying pan filled with hot water on low heat. This way the gelatin will melt without lumps. Combine milk and cream in a heavy-bottomed saucepan and scald. Remove from the heat, add the sugar and salt, and stir to dissolve. Add the dissolved gelatin, scraping the little custard cup well. Mix thoroughly by stirring and add 3 tablespoons Green Chartreuse. Pour blancmange into individual serving dishes and chill overnight.

Walleye *en Papillote*
Pasta with Parmesan and Romano Cheeses
Green Salad with Oil and Vinegar
Honeydew Ice

Serves four

To use fresh grated cheeses in the pasta recipe is quite essential. Try not to cheat by using pre-grated, dried-up old stuff. Fresh pasta is also a nice touch, but I believe we are all getting quite tired of making it ourselves, especially since it is possible to buy fresh pasta in the grocery store now. So unless the queen is coming to dinner, or you've got a small child crazy to crank the pasta machine, buy this ready-made.

WALLEYE *EN PAPILLOTE*

1	onion, very thinly sliced
3	shallots chopped fine
4	tbsp. unsalted butter, plus extra for buttering paper hearts
	Salt and pepper
⅔	cup white wine
	Rind of ½ an orange, with as little of the pith as possible, julienned and blanched
	Parchment paper
1½ to 2 lbs.	walleye fillets
4	sprigs tarragon

Sauté the onions and shallots in the butter until translucent and starting to brown. Season with salt and pepper and add wine. Reduce the mixture until it becomes syrupy. Add orange rind (12 pieces) and remove from heat. Cut 4 pieces of parchment paper into hearts, 12 inches long and 10 inches wide at the top (the widest part) and lightly butter. Divide fish onto the 4 pieces of parchment, setting the fish onto the right side of the heart. Divide up the onion, shallots, orange rind on top, and top this with a nice size sprig of tarragon. Fold up heart. Bring the left side over to the right side and seal the edges with many little narrow folds to keep the heart closed. When you get to the tip, twist it tight and tuck it in. Bake on a baking sheet in a pre-heated 400° oven for 10 to 15 minutes. Put directly on plates and open each heart at the table. The aroma with the tarragon and orange rind will be delicious.

PASTA WITH PARMESAN AND ROMANO CHEESES

1 lb. fresh fettucini pasta
  Salt and large cracked black
    pepper
6 tbsp. unsalted butter at room
    temperature
½ cup fresh grated Parmesan
    cheese
½ cup fresh grated Romano cheese

Cook pasta according to directions and drain. Toss with salt, pepper, and butter, then cheeses. Serve at once.

Have a green salad of Boston and Bibb lettuces with just oil, balsamic vinegar, salt, and pepper.

HONEYDEW ICE

1 or 2 honeydew melons (you want
    about 3 to 4 lbs. of flesh)
3 tbsp. Midori liqueur or melon
    flavored liqueur
6 to 8 tbsp. confectioners' sugar
    Juice from 2 lemons
    A pinch of salt
    Enough ice and salt for the
      ice cream machine

Open the melon, discard the seeds, and purée the flesh in a food processor or blender. Add to the purée the remaining ingredients, tasting as you go to make sure the flavor is to your liking. Stir well, chill, taste again for flavor and balance. Make according to your ice cream machine's directions.

Pack the melon sorbet into parfait glasses and chill thoroughly. Garnish with mint sprigs or a strawberry cut and fanned out.

244

Crimped Walleye Steaks with Béarnaise Sauce
Cabbage Patch Pasta Salad
Apple Tart

Serves four

CRIMPED WALLEYE STEAKS WITH BÉARNAISE SAUCE

          2 onions, chopped fine
          1 carrot, chopped fine
          3 shallots, chopped fine
          3 tbsp. unsalted butter
        ½ cup vinegar
          1 bottle dry red wine
      1½ qts. water
          1 tbsp. salt
        10 white peppercorns
          1 bay leaf
          1 tsp. dried thyme
  12 to 16 parsley stems
          4 walleye steaks, 1⅓ inch thick
             Salt and pepper

Sauté the onions, carrot, and shallots in butter. Combine with the vinegar, wine, water, salt, peppercorns, bay leaf, thyme, and parsley stems and cook at a simmer for 30 minutes. Let cool. Now to cook the fish, bring the court bouillon to a violent boil. Arrange the fish steaks on a rack placed into the court bouillon and bring back to a boil; cover and remove pan from heat. Let sit 8 to 10 minutes. Drain, season with salt and pepper and serve with sauce.

BÉARNAISE SAUCE

¼ cup good wine vinegar
½ cup white wine
1 tbsp. dried tarragon, revived in
    a little hot water
3 medium shallots, chopped fine
1 tbsp. chopped parsley
    Salt and fresh cracked or ground
      pepper
3 egg yolks
½ lb. unsalted butter, melted
1 tsp. fresh tarragon, chopped
1 tsp. fresh parsley, chopped

Bring the vinegar, wine, revived dried tarragon, parsley, salt and pepper to a boil. Reduce heat and on a low simmer, cook until reduced by two-thirds (this may be done ahead and refrigerated). Lower heat to the lowest and add yolks, one by one, whisking very fast. Remove from heat, add warm, melted butter very slowly and continue to whisk. Strain through coarse strainer into bowl and add fresh chopped tarragon and parsley. Taste for seasoning; if you need to add more salt, mix it first with boiling water to dissolve before adding.

CABBAGE PATCH PASTA SALAD

½ lb. cooked pasta
2 tbsp. toasted sesame oil
1 cup julienned savoy cabbage
    Corn oil for sautéing
2 red peppers, julienned
2 yellow peppers, julienned
2 cups snow peas, destrung and
    cut in half on the diagonal
2 tbsp. vinegar
1 tsp. prepared mustard
    Salt and pepper
1 tsp. soy sauce
1 tbsp. fresh coriander, chopped
½ cup olive or corn oil

After you've cooked the pasta, toss it with the sesame oil. Sauté the cabbage very briefly in a little corn oil. Sauté red and yellow peppers separately in corn oil until cooked but still retaining some crunch. Blanch, drain, and dry the snow peas. Now make a dressing by zipping in the blender for a few seconds the vinegar, mustard, salt, pepper, soy sauce, chopped fresh coriander (if you can get it), and olive or corn oil. Toss all ingredients together with the dressing and taste for seasoning.

APPLE TART

1	recipe for short pastry, or frozen pastry
5	McIntosh apples
	Cinnamon and sugar
2 to 3	tbsp. unsalted butter
1	cup heavy cream
1	tbsp. confectioners' sugar
1	tbsp. Calvados

Preheat oven to 425°. Roll pastry thin and rectangular in shape. Place on buttered aluminum cookie sheet. Let rest 1 hour in the refrigerator. Peel, core, and slice apples thin. Arrange overlapping in any design on pastry. Sprinkle liberally with cinnamon and sugar and dot with butter. Bake till edges of pastry are nicely light brown. Slide onto cooling rack. Check bottom of pastry to see if it's sufficiently browned. Serve hot or cold, with whipped cream with a little confectioners' sugar and some Calvados in it.

Laura's Wild Mushroom and Potato Flan
Lemon-Lime Walleye
Green Salad
Drunk Melons

Serves four

The recipe for the green salad can be found in your head or by perusing the index in this book for a good vinaigrette that will go over fresh lettuce.

LAURA'S WILD MUSHROOM AND POTATO FLAN

8 oz. wild mushrooms, cleaned
and coarsely chopped (oyster
mushrooms are good for this
and readily available at many
grocery stores)

2 tbsp. butter, plus some for
buttering the pan

⅔ cup cooked potatoes, coarsely
chopped

Salt and pepper

Pinch of thyme for the potatoes

1½ cups milk

½ cup cream

3 whole eggs

2 egg yolks

Preheat the oven to 325°. Sauté the mushrooms in 2 tablespoons of butter. Season the cooked potatoes with salt, pepper, and a pinch of thyme. Have a kettle of boiling water ready. This recipe may be made in a 4-cup ring mold or in individual ½-cup capacity custard cups (use 8). Whichever is used, butter heavily with unsalted butter and set into a cake or roasting pan. Scald milk and cream. Cool a bit and slowly add to the beaten whole eggs and yolks, stirring constantly. Season well with salt and pepper and strain into a pitcher. Pour a bit into each mold. Divide the mushrooms and potatoes into each mold and add the rest of the custard. Pour the boiling water into the roasting pan around the edges so the mold(s) will have water coming two-thirds up the sides. Cover the large pan lightly with tinfoil and cook 15 to 20 minutes. A custard is a custard. Do not overcook. It will continue cooking after being removed from the heat. A knife inserted halfway down should just barely be clean. Let sit 5 minutes in the mold(s) and unmold by running a knife around the edge. Garnish around the edge with sautéed watercress.

LEMON-LIME WALLEYE

1½ sticks unsalted butter
    Grated rind of 2 limes, green
      part only
    Grated rind of 1 large lemon,
      yellow part only
1 garlic clove, very finely chopped
2 tsp. finely chopped parsley
    Salt and pepper
2 lbs. walleye fillets

Whip butter till soft and fluffy. Add the rest of the ingredients, except the fillets. Season to taste. Mix well. Mound onto plastic wrap. Form into a cylinder. Freeze 24 hours and bring to room temperature before serving. Grill or broil the walleye, adding some of the compound butter just before finished cooking and then slather with more after cooking. Serve at once.

DRUNK MELONS

2 very ripe melons (They may be
    two different varieties.)
    Sprinkle of confectioners' sugar
½ cup champagne brandy
½ cup Curaçao
    Mint leaves

Remove a lid off the most attractive of the melons. Take out all seeds and scoop out the melon in small pieces. Cut the second melon in half and dice in large pieces or scoop. Put all melon pieces in a bowl. Sprinkle with the confectioners' sugar, champagne brandy, and Curaçao. Stir and let sit for about an hour. To serve, put back in the melon shell, top with mint, and cover with lid.

Shad, Catfish, and Smelt

Shad and smelt are quite pretty little fish and when the run is on, fishing for them is truly an event. Clear, but long-ago, memories of fishermen at night ringing the shores of Lake Michigan with their torches and constant activity testify to the spectacle aspects of smelt fishing. Catfish are certainly as tasty as shad or smelt but certainly are not as pretty. Catfish are quite ugly, and the saying that the bravest man in history is the first man to have eaten a lobster probably holds true for the first man to have eaten catfish too.

This is a problem, eating something that is ugly, particularly when you are involved in catching it and preparing it. Once, when we had just started teaching our very small children how to fish, we made the mistake of catching a very ugly fish. We'd walked to the tidal brook near our house and fished off the bridge with closed-face reels and bait. It was very exciting when the line got heavier and we began to reel the fish in, only to see this prehistoric thing which actually croaked at us on the end of the line; it is a wonder that our children ever wished to fish again. We did have the opportunity to teach them immediately about catch-and-release.

As the catfish will testify, the outside appearance has nothing to do with the inside flavor. Really only in the case of an unknown species (as with the fish on the bridge) or with an obviously sick fish should ugliness be a deterrent to eating. This business of picking the parasites off the fish in order to get to the meat, although a closet practice, is something that is definitely disgusting and a waste of time. Yes, we know that the cooking will probably kill anything harmful, that restaurants are known to remove the parasites from the fish and serve it to the customer who is none the wiser, and that the parasites will not harm the meat once removed. But why do this? It's revolting and takes away the appetite. Even if we get someone else to remove the little bugger while we retire from the kitchen, we still know it was there, don't we? There are more fish in the sea; feel no guilt at tossing it out. We all take enough risk as it is eating commercially prepared foods. Why risk the good name of freshly caught, personally cared for, and healthy fish for the sake of one not-too-healthy fish? It surely is better to save a strong stomach for skinning a catfish than de-bugging a salmon.

Fried Smelts with Noisette Butter
Fried Parsley
Grilled Pineapple with Strawberries

Serves four

FRIED SMELTS

3	eggs
2	tsp. corn oil, plus enough for deep-fat frying the fish
2	tsp. water
	Salt and pepper
2½	cups bread crumbs
2	tsp. thyme
16 to 20	smelts (depending on size and appetite), cleaned with the heads off. There is no need to bone them as the bones are easily removed at the table.
1	cup flour

In Imperial Rome these fish were cooked in a custard. We believe they are better fried. Combine the eggs, 2 teaspoons of corn oil, water, salt, and pepper and set aside. Now make the bread crumbs by taking French or Italian bread cut into slices and drying them in the oven at 300°. Then reduce to crumbs in a food processor. Strain for uniformity of size and mix with the thyme. Rinse and dry smelts. Dredge in flour and shake off excess. Paint with egg mixture and roll in bread crumbs. Let rest on a cake cooling rack while the rest of the meal is prepared. They may be deep-fried for about 1 minute (until golden) with the oil at 375° or you may fry them in an electric frying pan at 400°. In either case, after cooking drain on paper towels. They may be kept warm in the oven on racks.

NOISETTE BUTTER

2 sticks unsalted butter
1 tbsp. lemon juice

Cook the unsalted butter in a heavy-bottomed saucepan constantly stirring until light brown. Remove from heat and let it continue to brown a bit more. (If it is browning too fast, pour the butter into another pan.) Stir in the lemon juice.

FRIED PARSLEY

1 large bunch parsley, washed
    and dried very well
Corn oil or clarified unsalted
    butter
Salt

Deep fry the parsley in some corn oil in a heavy saucepan or sauté in some clarified butter until just crisp. Drain well on paper towels and sprinkle with salt just as you serve it.

GRILLED PINEAPPLE WITH STRAWBERRIES

1 pint strawberries
1 tbsp. confectioners' sugar
2 tbsp. Grand Marnier or
    Cointreau
1 medium-size ripe pineapple
Mint leaves

Hull the strawberries and slice in half if large. Sprinkle with confectioners' sugar and Grand Marnier or Cointreau, toss and let sit several hours. Cut off the top, bottom, and the sides of the pineapple with a large sharp knife. Remove the core and slice in thin slices about ¼ inch thick or less. Grill until they start to brown and caramelize. To serve, place 4 slices of pineapple slightly overlapping on a plate and fill the center holes with the strawberries. Garnish with fresh mint if you can and be sure to provide fruit knives as well as forks, for the pineapple will be somewhat chewy.

254

The Best Catfish
Green Salad
French Bread

Serves four

For a salad, you can invent one yourself, or refer to the index in this book for an interesting vinaigrette. Use it on the most healthy looking greens you can find in the grocery store. French bread, of course, can be purchased successfully everywhere. But as anyone who has spent a little time in France knows, the fresher the better. It is easy to make yourself. Just use a white bread recipe and a French bread pan. Be sure to brush the crust several times in the cooking with cold water so a hard crust will form.

THE BEST CATFISH

⅔ cup all-purpose flour
½ tsp. dried thyme
¼ tsp. salt
   A pinch of dried sage, plus 1 tsp.
⅛ tsp. cayenne pepper
4 grinds fresh black pepper
1½ to 2 lbs. catfish fillets, cut into strips
   1½ inches long and ½ inch
   to ¾ inch wide
1 medium size eggplant, peeled and
   cut into 1½-inch-by-½-inch pieces,
   salted, and left to drain in a
   colander 10 minutes
5 tbsp. unsalted butter
5 tbsp. corn oil
2 boiling potatoes, peeled and cut into
   1½-inch-by-½-inch pieces (keep
   in cold water)
2 garlic cloves, chopped fine
1 tsp. grated lemon rind

Combine the flour with the thyme, salt, a pinch of sage, and both peppers. Dredge fish well in seasoned flour and shake off all excess. Let rest on cake cooling racks until ready to cook. The eggplant should now be rinsed, drained, dried, and tossed in flour. In a heavy-bottomed skillet (2 pans at once is easiest), start with 1 tablespoon butter and 1 tablespoon of oil. Heat until sizzling and add catfish (not to be crowded) and sauté until browned. Set aside on warmed platter. Sauté eggplant and potatoes in separate pans until golden. Add together. Melt any remaining butter (or use more) in empty pan and add the garlic. Sauté for 1 minute, then add 1 teaspoon dried sage, the catfish, eggplant, and potatoes. Grate lemon peel over it all. Toss well and season to taste with salt and pepper.

Fried Catfish
Cole Slaw
Baked Grits
Broiled Persimmons

Serves four

There is nothing as basic as catfish, or grits, or cole slaw. They are as basic as a hamburg and just as easy to wreck. Care and attention should be paid to these recipes for the best results. All are delicious but dependent on being properly prepared.

FRIED CATFISH

    2 eggs
    2 tsp. milk
    2 tsp. oil
    2 tsp. salt
    ½ tsp. fresh ground pepper
    2 lbs. catfish fillets, pat dry
       Flour for dusting
    2 cups cornmeal, yellow or white
       Bacon fat
       Corn oil

Mix eggs, milk, oil, salt, and pepper. Season fish very lightly with salt and pepper. Dust fish with flour. Paint with egg mixture and roll in cornmeal. Let rest on cake cooling racks until ready to cook. In heavy skillet, melt a combination of bacon fat and corn oil to ⅛ inch deep. When the oil is hot, fry fish until brown on one side and repeat for other side, but not quite as long.

COLE SLAW

Deli-bought, your mom's recipe, or see page 187.

BAKED GRITS

1½ tsp. salt
¾ cup grits
3 cups boiling water
2 eggs
⅛ tsp. cayenne
½ lb. grated sharp cheddar cheese
4 tbsp. unsalted butter, sliced
    into thin pats

Add the salt and grits to the boiling water and cook until done or the consistency of bubbling oatmeal. Remove from the heat and let cool slightly then add the eggs, cayenne, butter and cheese. Check the seasoning and then place in a buttered baking dish and cook in a preheated oven at 350° for 1 hour.

BROILED PERSIMMONS

4 persimmons—not too ripe
4 tbsp. unsalted butter
2 tsp. granulated sugar
   Sherry

Cut persimmons in half. Broil till warm. Remove seeds and top each half with butter and sugar. Return to broiler and cook till butter is melted. Sprinkle with sherry and serve.

Sorrel Soup
Shad Roe
Pink New Boiled Potatoes
Rhubarb Fool

Serves four

SORREL SOUP

6 shallots, finely chopped
6 tbsp. unsalted butter
4 cups sorrel, clean and coarsely
   chopped
1 quart hot chicken stock
½ tsp. salt
   Fresh ground pepper
4 tbsp. flour
2 cups heavy cream
   A squeeze of lemon juice

Sorrel is one of the first things up in the garden. Sauté shallots in 2 tablespoons of the butter until soft and transparent. Add sorrel. Stir once or twice. Lower heat and cover and cook until the sorrel has completely wilted. Add chicken stock, salt, and pepper. Simmer gently about 15 minutes. Blend in processor. Melt the 4 tablespoons of butter. When sizzling, add the flour. Cook on medium heat for 4 minutes, stirring constantly. Take off the heat and add the hot stock mixture. Pour in about a cup, whisk to mix, then add the rest, stirring. Bring back to a simmer. Remove from heat, add heavy cream, and chill. Before serving, adjust to taste with salt, pepper, and lemon juice.

SHAD ROE

4 sets of shad roe
   Flour for dredging
   Salt and pepper
4 tbsp. unsalted butter

Wash 4 sets of roe. Do not separate the sets unless they are already separated, and if the roe are large you will need less. Remove clots, etc. Gently parboil if you like for about 4 minutes to toughen the outer membrane a little so it is less apt to burst. Let cool and then roll in flour seasoned with salt and pepper. Sauté 4 to 5 minutes per side in the butter. Serve with lemon wedges.

259

SHAD

If you are going to eat the shad, serve it with a white butter sauce. Try to get someone else to bone it, as it is very difficult. Salt and pepper each side of the fish. Spread with soft butter and squeeze the fish back together and broil it 6 minutes per side.

PINK NEW BOILED POTATOES

      1 stick unsalted, softened butter
         Salt and pepper
      1 tsp. chopped chives
      3 new potatoes per person

Combine the softened butter with the salt, pepper, and chives. Boil the new potatoes for about 20 minutes. Drain and crack open. Spread with the butter mixture.

RHUBARB FOOL

      3 lbs. young rhubarb
      1 cup granulated sugar
         Zest of 1 lemon, grated
   1½ tsp. vanilla extract
      2 cups heavy cream
      2 tsp. confectioners' sugar
     ¼ tsp. ground cloves

Peel the rhubarb using a sharp knife. There is an almost transparent outside skin which comes off very easily. Then slice stalks into very thin slices. This is most easily done when the rhubarb is held bunched together. In a heavy saucepan with a lid, place the rhubarb and the sugar and cover tightly and cook over low heat for 10 to 15 minutes. Remove the lid and raise heat and cook until excess liquid has evaporated, stirring constantly. It will become thick like applesauce. Be sure to stir it or the rhubarb will scorch. When ready, remove from the heat and add lemon zest and vanilla and set aside to cool. Whip until stiff the cream with the confectioners' sugar and the ground cloves. Fold the rhubarb in gently and chill.

Bass and Panfish

We sure have tried a lot of methods for preserving fish. We've tried freezing the fish whole, we've tried freezing the fish just cleaned, we've tried freezing the fish fillets or steaks. We've tried smoked fish and we've tried dried and salted fish, we've tried canned fish. Ted was kind enough to make a presentation one time of some beautiful yellow perch that he had handily frozen whole in a wax milk carton filled with water. The perch were delicious, but I fear his preservation technique may be dying out with the innovation of plastic milk cartons.

One time when we were fishing for Atlantic salmon we caught more than anticipated and had to commandeer styrofoam fishing boxes from an abandoned fishing camp and pack them with Arctic snow. The merits of this procedure were in question until we put it inadvertently to the test. The bush pilot forgot to show up for a day or two, and we missed the weekly train. There was quite a bit of Arctic slush oozing out of the boxes onto the carousel of Air Canada when we arrived in Boston, and the condition of the fish was dubious. But miraculously, the fish, which were then refrozen, were wonderful.

The relative merits of all these preservation techniques are difficult to assess. The reality is that they all impose on the fish certain taste elements that alter the fresh flavor of the fish. Smoked fish does not taste like fresh fish, nor does frozen fish. This is not to say that frozen fish is bad; it is simply different. And those differences vary in value; to some people frozen fish is worthwhile and to others not so, depending on taste, of course.

Some fish, I do believe, stand up better to freezing or smoking or salting or canning than do others. Certainly the salmon are the most resilient of all fish to any preservation method you can think of, as is evidenced by the Air Canada salmon. If you've never tasted a fish fresh before, what have you to compare it to when you eat it smoked or salted for the first time? This was true of the yellow perch Ted gave us. Indeed they were good, but I didn't know till some time later how good they could really be.

One thing is for certain: the species of fish in this chapter are my five top candidates for which avoidance of freezing, smoking, salting, or canning remains sound advice. These fish are plentiful, relatively easy to catch, are well distributed geographically, and are the very best when eaten fresh.

Chicken Consommé
Almond Butter Smallmouth Bass
Sautéed Tomatoes
Fried Bread
The Pretty Easy Dessert

Serves four

CHICKEN CONSOMMÉ

1 small onion, thinly sliced
3 carrots, peeled and chopped small
1 stick celery, chopped small
1 tbsp. unsalted butter
8 cups clear chicken broth (If you do not
     have homemade, use the least-salty
     canned you can find.)
1 bunch watercress, just the leaves

Sauté the onion, carrots, and celery in the unsalted butter over medium-low heat until the onion is translucent. Then add the hot broth, bring to a boil and simmer for 30 to 40 minutes. Strain carefully. Keep hot. When ready to serve, divide the watercress leaves into each soup plate and add the hot broth.

ALMOND BUTTER SMALLMOUTH BASS

¼ cup (approximately 2 oz.) whole almonds
1½ sticks butter unsalted and room temperature,
     plus 2 to 3 tbsp.for frying the fish
2 tsp. finely chopped parsley
½ tsp. grated orange rind
    Salt and pepper
2 lbs. skinned bass fillets, broiled

Make the compound butter 24 hours ahead by placing on a cookie sheet and toasting the almonds in a 300° oven until they turn a light beige. Remove from oven and cool. When completely cool, put in blender or food processor and blend until they become powder. Whip the butter until soft and fluffy. Add the powdered almonds, parsley, orange rind, salt, and pepper and mix well. Taste for seasoning. Then mound onto plastic wrap. Roll into a cylinder and pop into the freezer. Bring to refrigerator or to room temperature a few hours before serving time. Place pats of butter on broiled bass and serve.

SAUTÉED TOMATOES

4 large tomatoes—ripe and tasty
2 to 3 tbsp. good olive oil
Salt and freshly cracked pepper
Chopped parsley or thyme

Dip the tomatoes one by one in boiling water. Count to 10 and then dip in ice water. Peel, cut in half, scoop out seeds, remove core, and let drain for 10 minutes. Heat olive oil until water drops sizzle. Add tomatoes cut-side down and cook until juices start evaporating and the bottom browns. Turn and finish. Serve cut-side up, sprinkled with salt, pepper, and the parsley and/or thyme.

NOTE: If the tomatoes are too huge, which homegrown ones can be indeed, then cut them in thick slices.

FRIED BREAD

8 1-inch slices of French or
    Italian bread
4 tbsp. unsalted butter
    Salt and pepper
2 tbsp. fontina cheese, grated, or
    any cheese

Dry bread in oven at 300°. Fry in melted butter. Sprinkle with salt, pepper, and cheese. Put back in oven to just melt.

THE PRETTY EASY DESSERT

There are several commercial water ices that are quite nice. Take 1 or 2 flavors and pack them into a mold, one inside the other, and serve with berries or fruit sprinkled with liqueur. For example: raspberries with *framboise* or peaches with Grand Marnier. Place on the platter around the edge. To unmold ice, cover mold for a few seconds with a hot, wet towel. The ice should just slip out. Place in the middle of the fruit.

Little Fried Perch
Cucumber and Tomato Slices with Basil Vinaigrette
Rosemary's New Potatoes

Serves four

There is a difference in potatoes. In general, the smaller, thinner-skinned potatoes are sweeter and need less cooking. The bigger and thick skinned potatoes are good for baking. Potatoes should be purchased according to how you plan to cook them, not according to whether you caught the fish in Idaho or Maine.

LITTLE FRIED PERCH

2 or 3	perch per person
2 to 3	cups milk
	Flour for dredging
4	tbsp. oil
	Parsley bunches
	Salt and pepper
	Lemon wedges

Gut the small fish with a sharp knife using the point. Wash them. Dry them and soak in a little milk for 10 minutes. Drain. Roll in flour and fry in very hot oil for 4 minutes. Set on paper towels to drain. Fry some bunches of parsley. Drain. Sprinkle fish with salt and pepper. Serve immediately with lemon wedges.

CUCUMBER AND TOMATO SLICES WITH BASIL VINAIGRETTE

2 cucumbers, washed and sliced
2 tomatoes, washed, peeled, and
   sliced
½ cup oil
½ tsp. prepared mustard
2 tbsp. vinegar
1 tsp. basil, fresh or revived in a
   little hot water
Salt and pepper

After slicing the cukes and tomatoes, arrange attractively on a platter. Now zip the remaining ingredients in the blender. Check the vinaigrette and adjust to suit your taste. Dribble over the tomatoes and cucumbers.

ROSEMARY'S NEW POTATOES

3 new potatoes per person
1 tbsp. fresh rosemary
2 tbsp. melted butter
Salt and pepper

Steam or boil the new potatoes. Sprinkle with rosemary, melted butter, salt, and pepper.

Perch Fillets
Bay Potatoes
Sliced Tomatoes
Fruit

Serves four

PERCH FILLETS

1½   sticks, plus 4 tbsp. unsalted butter
4   shallots, finely chopped and sautéed
     till translucent
2   tbsp. tarragon, finely chopped
1   tsp. Worcestershire sauce
     Salt and pepper
8 to 12   perch fillets
     Flour for dusting

Whip 1½ sticks of butter till soft and fluffy. Sauté the shallots till translucent. Combine the shallots, whipped butter, tarragon, Worcestershire, salt,
and pepper and mix well and season to taste. Mound onto plastic wrap.
Shape into a cylinder and freeze 24 hours. Bring to room temperature before
using. Dust the perch with flour and sauté in hot, sweet butter. Serve with
pats of compound butter on top.

BAY POTATOES

½ cup red wine vinegar
    Salt and pepper
1½ lbs. white boiling potatoes, peeled
    and whole
¾ cup olive oil (good quality)
3 garlic cloves, medium-size and
    coarsely chopped
4 to 5 dried bay leaves, coarsely chopped
    Balsamic vinegar
1½ tbsp. chopped parsley

Bring a large saucepan of water to a boil, add the vinegar and some salt. Drop in the potatoes, reduce heat to a simmer, and cook till potatoes are done but firm. Drain and when cool enough to handle, cut into 1-inch pieces; heat the olive oil, add the garlic and the bay leaves; bring to a simmer, lower the heat to the lowest, and cook for 15 to 20 minutes. Remove the bay leaves and discard. Mash the garlic and return it to the warm oil. Pour over the potatoes. Toss, add a little balsamic vinegar, salt, pepper, and chopped parsley and toss again.

Red, White, and Green Largemouth Bass
Fried Tomato Slices
Fried Bread
Poached Peaches with Raspberries

Serves four

RED, WHITE, AND GREEN LARGEMOUTH BASS

1 small white onion, roughly
   chopped
1 small red onion, roughly
   chopped
1 tbsp. unsalted butter
1 fresh green scallion, chopped
   into ½-inch pieces
1 tbsp. parsley, chopped fine
2 lbs. largemouth bass fillets
   Olive oil
   Salt and pepper

Sauté the white and red onions in butter until the white is translucent. Add scallion and cook for a few minutes more. Add parsley, stir, and set aside. Baste fish with oil and sprinkle with salt and pepper. Broil until golden. Heat onions and season with salt and pepper and serve on top of the fish. Pour any juices from the pan over the fish.

FRIED TOMATO SLICES

4 to 6 ripe but firm tomatoes
1 egg, lightly beaten
Salt and pepper
Pinch of thyme
1 cup fine bread crumbs
Unsalted butter

Slice the tomatoes ¼ inch thick. Sprinkle the beaten egg with salt, pepper, and a pinch of thyme. Dip each tomato slice first into the egg mixture and then into the bread crumbs. In a heavy skillet melt the butter until sizzling and then add the tomatoes and brown on both sides. Serve at once.

FRIED BREAD

8 1-inch slices of French or
Italian bread
4 tbsp. unsalted butter
Salt and pepper
2 tbsp. fontina cheese, grated, or
any cheese

Dry bread in oven at 300°. Fry in melted butter. Sprinkle with salt, pepper, and cheese. Put back in oven to just melt.

POACHED PEACHES WITH RASPBERRIES

4 cups water
2 cups granulated sugar, plus 2 tbsp.
for sprinkling
1 tsp. lemon juice
1 vanilla bean, split down the middle
4 perfect peaches, big ones
1 qt. fresh raspberries
Framboise

Slowly bring the water, sugar, lemon juice, and vanilla bean to a boil. Simmer 5 to 10 minutes. Add the peaches unpeeled. Return the syrup to a simmer and let cook about 5 to 8 minutes. Remove peaches to a rack and let cool. Peel when still slightly warm and then chill. Sprinkle the raspberries with a couple tablespoons of sugar and *framboise*. Let stand for one hour and then add the peaches and serve.

Smallmouth Bass Tempura
White Rice
Sake and Tea
Fortune Cookies

Serves four

You know how to make the rice, and you can serve sushi as a first course if you are so inclined.

Choice of vegetables varies with the season.

SPRING LIST: FALL LIST:
asparagus   sweet potato
zucchini   zucchini
carrots   carrots
broccoli   broccoli

SMALLMOUTH BASS TEMPURA

> Vegetables
> 1 bottle of vegetable oil
> 2 egg yolks
> 1⅔ cups ice water
> 1⅔ cups sifted flour, plus extra for dusting
> 3 to 4 lbs. bass, in bite-size pieces
> Dipping sauces

Cut all the vegetables into pieces ½-inch-by-⅛-inch-by-2-inch. Soak potatoes first in cold water for 15 minutes. Drain, dry, and then use. Preheat oil to medium frying temperature, about 340°. Prepare batter. Lightly beat egg yolks. With the ice water in a large bowl, dump the flour in all at once. Stir a few times only. The batter should be gloppy and have the appearance of being only half-mixed. Dip vegetables and fish in flour first. Shake off excess and then mix gently in the batter only to cover and only a few at a time. Fry only a few at a time. Raise temperature slightly for cooking the fish. Let drain on paper towels; serve at once with dipping sauces. A variety of these sauces can be found at many gourmet shops and fancy supermarkets. You will want a soy sauce of some sort; keep to the Japanese types if you can. Mix a little grated ginger with the soy if you like. "Ponzu" is a good soy-type sauce with citrus juices, rice vinegar, malt, and wheat.

Sunfish on a Stick
Chocolate Chip Cookies

Serves four

This is a nice menu for your son to have in his pocket when he goes on his first solo fishing trip.

SUNFISH ON A STICK

4 little sunfish, pumpkinseeds,
    or crappies, cleaned
Salt and pepper
½ cup cornmeal
4 tbsp. hot bacon fat, or 2 tbsp.
    fat and 2 tbsp. unsalted butter

Sprinkle the cleaned fish with salt and pepper. Dip each fish in cornmeal and baste with hot bacon fat. Cook on a stick over the fire until the fish are crispy. If those who volunteered to be stick holders have returned to the fishing hole, you may also pan-fry these fish. After dipping the fish in cornmeal, melt 2 tablespoons bacon fat and 2 tablespoons unsalted butter in a pan and fry, skin and all.

CHOCOLATE CHIP COOKIES

Use the Nestlé's tollhouse cookie recipe and add an additional 2 tablespoons of white sugar (for the 6-oz.-size bag of chocolate morsels) and omit nuts. The result is a thin cookie that is crunchy and just a bit chewy.

Game Care

E d brought home the first deer of our life together—to a Boston apartment. Our small daughter in my arms, we stood on the curb of the city
street marveling over the beautiful animal lying across the top of the station
wagon. Musing slightly over the incongruity of the situation, I watched as
the car disappeared down the dark street bound for the suburban home
where it was to be "hung." And the slow realization came over me: "What
now?"

At that point I knew only to worry about the obvious mechanics of how
to get a whole carcass into the form of cut-up pieces of meat. What I was to
learn subsequently was that what had come before the car-top journey and
butchering was actually of equal significance and consequence. And worry is
what I would have done had I any game care experience. That deer had been
through a lot by the time he got to Boston.

He was a particularly large whitetail, about 210 pounds field-dressed,
and Ed had shot him in a very remote area. Ed and Larry had worked the
better part of a day just to drag the deer back to camp. And then, of course,
there was getting it across the stream and onto the roof of the car. The frail
rope footbridge that dangled above the stream did not seem the way to go.
On the other hand, forging the waist-deep stream with the 210 pounds
seemed, at best, un-fun. Weighing the options carefully, the men struck on a
somewhat modified rope and pulley system, or the old wrap around the tree
trick, for accomplishing their task.

With Larry on one side of the stream fixing a rope to the deer's antlers,
Ed walked the footbridge with the other end of the rope to wrap around a
big tree on the opposite side of the stream. The rope could have been fastened securely there, Larry could have gone to Ed's side of the river, and the
two men could have hauled the beast together or even enlisted the muscle of
the car. That could have been the way it worked. It was not. In eager anticipation of Ed's end of the rope being fastened, Larry had dragged the deer

273

close to the stream's edge. And the current's force caused the premature launching of the deer. Gone! Save for those antlers, gone forever downstream. The antlers getting hung up on a semi-submerged log proved one more good reason for saving your shots for the trophy rack. A mid-stream wrestling match between Ed, the antlers, and the submerged log followed next. Then there was trying to get the deer on top of the car and driving it eight hours to Boston. A lot had happened to this deer. Fortunately, I didn't know enough to care while standing curb-side in that city street so long ago.

Today I would question every detail of that carcass' history.

What would the day of being pulled through the woods have done to the meat? Did the stream-side bath help or hinder? How did the cold, cold of the water then the warmer air affect the deer? These questions would be coupled with the usual—was it a lung shot, what had the terrain been like, what was the deer's probable diet and age? And every bite of that deer's meat would have been scrutinized and some conclusion drawn about the taste and tenderness attributable to the deer's history. What a general pain in the neck I would have made of myself. But all those elements can, in fact, or according to folk lore anyway, affect the meat.

What is fact and what is myth? Much has been written in game cookbooks and in the outdoor literature about how different elements and field and kitchen affect the taste of what you are eating. It always has been very hard for me to discern what is simply the opinion of the writer (or is included more for the sake of tradition) and what is reason. I wanted scientific reasons for why venison must be hung and for how long, head up or down, etc. Fortunately, coming from a family of meat-packers and food technologists, I have had some sources to question.

My father is a chemical engineer who has spent thirty-five years in the food industry specializing in food processing and meat packing in scores of countries around the world. Here is restated some of the information he has provided me about the care and treatment of meat:

About freezing: Of course, the first consequence of freezing is that it cuts down on bacteria growth and allows us to keep the meat for a long time. At the same time it has several other consequences. Meat has a very high water content—over 65 percent. Freezing causes the globules of water cells to crystallize. The size of the crystals is in inverse proportion to the speed of freezing. If the freezing occurs quickly, the crystals will be quite small. If the freezing happens slowly, the crystals will be quite large and cause any yet-unfrozen water to exude out of the meat. In addition, water expands as it freezes, and may cause a bursting of the cells if done slowly. Consequently, slow freezing can cause the meat to lose moisture and also become mushy. Slow thawing, as in a refrigerator, may have a similar effect. As the temperature in the refrigerator varies, the cells may crystallize and then liquefy, causing the same bursting and exuding of moisture. The blowers inside frost-free freezers, or any air movement, can cause freezer burn—a desiccation of the meat.

274

All that this suggests is that if meat is going to be frozen it should be done as quickly as possible; it should be well wrapped and then thawed quickly (or at least at a consistently warm temperature). The suggested wrap for frozen meat is a first layer of aluminum foil to obtain rapid heat transfer and protection from air and then twelve hours later a second wrap of a plastic bag to protect further against air movement. Added tips are to press the foil tightly around the meat. Remember to label, date, and grade the piece, and when the bag goes over it, suck the air out before the twist-tie goes on. The labeling, of course, helps you know what you're cooking before you've thawed it. Nothing worse than to plan an *ooh-la-la* dinner and then discover you've thawed that shot-up shoveler that's been in the freezer a year (almost all meat has significantly deteriorated after a year of the freezer).

About smoking meat: A hot smoking of meat, like freezing, has the effect of cutting down on the bacteria growth, allowing the meat to be kept longer. Smoking does three things to meat: it heats it, dries it, and adds flavor to it. The long, slow heating process of smoking brings the temperature of the meat to above 127 degrees or the "denaturing point." This changes the color of the meat from blood red and kills some, but not all, of the bacteria. The meat also becomes firmer. The drying cuts the moisture content and makes the meat less hospitable to bacteria, while the addition of the smoked flavor adds some acidity, making it even more difficult for certain bacteria to grow. The amount of time a piece of smoked meat can be kept depends largely on the effectiveness of the heating, drying, and flavoring process. This may be difficult to determine. Often we don't know much about how well a piece of meat has been smoked or how long it's been hanging around since the smoking. The guidelines are perhaps to be found in the two extremes. A Smithfield ham can be kept for months, even years, unrefrigerated; something you smoke yourself in the backyard can probably go as long as a month in the refrigerator and probably six months to a year in the freezer. Fortunately, meat is quite forgiving. And, as my father would say, it will let you know when it's had it.

About hanging meat: Hanging meat, or aging it, tenderizes it. The aging process begins after rigor mortis has peaked. Rigor mortis begins a few hours after the animal has been shot and increases very rapidly, peaking at about ten to twenty-four hours. It then will decline, with the curve flattening at about forty-eight hours and continuing to decline for two weeks. The meat will be at its toughest stage during rigor mortis and then it will become increasingly more tender. The amount of time for aging to occur is significantly affected by temperature. This is why the location of your hunt has a great deal to do with how long the meat should be hung and how it should be handled right after shooting it. In general, the higher the temperature the faster the aging process and the softer the meat. Of course, if the temperature is too high, growth of bacteria is promoted, too. Consequently, how long an animal should be hung has to do with your own taste buds and the temperature control over the period of aging (a good regulated temperature of 45 to 50 degrees is optimum).

Taste being the key, it is difficult to advise in such matters. But since much of what is found acceptable is based on what Americans are used to, the guideline might start at what is desirable for beef, and in this country all beef is aged about two weeks.

We age our venison anywhere from a week to two, depending on the weather and how long the temperatures have held steady. This, of course, is the bottom line for us. If you are not rigged with a cooler, the length of time for aging becomes somewhat a function of what the weatherman dictates and has not much to do with what has been advised or found to be most desirable.

About cleaning the meat: In our culture the taste of blood is generally not well received, and some lengths should be gone to to clean the animal properly if you wish to comply with cultural norms. Of course, the hunter can always help by trying for a lung shot on the bigger animals such as deer. The lung shot will guarantee the least amount of damage, blood or otherwise, to the meat and also kill the animal quickly. Hanging the animal for aging or butchering with the head to the ground is suggested for the sake of cleanliness. A spraying with hot water before freezing or refrigeration is also advisable for meat in order to keep down the bacteria count. Use paper towels to pat the meat dry rather than the kitchen dish towel (no need to add the bacteria from the towel back into the meat).

Other things which can affect the flavor of the meat: Age, size, and even sex of the animal can affect the taste of the glandular meat (neck and shoulder meat). An old, big female is likely to have tougher, stronger flavored neck meat than the saddle from a young, small buck.

Fat contains the flavor of what the animal has been eating and will flavor the meat if left on while cooking.

To soak meat in water, salted water, or milk causes some exuding of flavor from the meat. Then, after the exuding, the flavor of the salt and milk will mask what the animal has been feeding on.

The effect of cooking: The purpose of cooking a piece of meat is to render it more digestible and to eliminate any diseases. The specifics of how something is cooked get into a matter of taste, of course, but certain generalizations can be made. The longer and slower meat is cooked, the more tender and easily digestible it becomes (it also loses more of the vitamins). The higher and shorter the heat, the juicier the meat and the crisper the skin. Finally, to cook a bird "in the round" probably does nothing to the taste of the meat. It probably does make the innards more convenient to eat if you like them. One word of caution, however, on this. Innards, particularly the liver, are the body's depository for several types of chemicals that animals consume. In this insecticide-laden society that is worth remembering.

So how to know the taste. You can't. You can know that a neck roast from a big, old, bark-eating female deer with blood and fat all over it and cooked ten hours after it was shot or a year after being in the freezer, unwrapped, then cooked on a high heat for a long time won't taste very good. But you knew that before you read this. Every time an element is altered, the taste is altered. And what must be kept in perspective are those elements that you have some control over. I hope that the generalized facts listed above that determine flavor and texture will help you determine what things you are going to strive to control. It is possible to control the temperature for hanging by purchasing your very own $10,000 meat locker. It is possible to break the law and shoot a springtime buck. It is possible to eat only the saddle roast from a deer dead one hour. All these things are possible, but often impractical or illegal or un-fun. Focus on what suits you to control and beware of the risks when you do cut corners. Certainly the height of control is to make the meat into what we eat every day: created, maintained, slaughtered, and packaged meat with a predictable flavor. I hope that the adventurous spirit in you is willing to try to eat and cook what the hunter presents. Be smart and energetic when preserving and cooking game but also willing to improvise when a lack of ideal circumstances or utensils dictates it.

Lastly, remember that in the final analysis what often constitutes proper game care is usually linked to what makes the meat taste "good." And what constitutes "good" in taste is not always agreed upon.

A Few Suggestions
for Cooking Game

W hen I first started to cook game, and to read game cookbooks, I automatically skipped over this type of chapter. After all, I knew how to cook, and I could see on their list of necessary utensils such items as "pepper grinder." What an insult! Of course, a few game dinner failures would send me lurking into the bathroom, four game cookbooks at a time, to surreptitiously read every "tips" section I could lay my hands on.

Certainly much of what has been said in this book is not new or edifying. Just as many of the recipes are not "new." Many of the suggestions and non-game recipes are reiterated in some other place in the book. This is not because I think you didn't get it or perhaps that you didn't even know it before, it is because I believe people read cookbooks differently. If you are like me you have used recipes, maybe a whole menu here and there, long before reading any of the long text chapters. So for the reader like myself there are the suggestions woven around the edges of each menu. For the Cintra types (who actually read a cookbook while standing on one leg in the bookstore) or for those insecure moments when you panic and will read anything with the word "game" in it, there is this chapter. We've tried to present the information in such a way as to please and ease your brain and eye, as well as your palate, no matter what kind of cookbook reader you are.

There is another reason for the repetition. What we want to impart to you is not simply a series of recipes but rather a series of techniques, an attitude about cooking game which will spark you and provide a reliable base for you to build your own creations. But of course the techniques must be known by rote for the creations to have a hope of being successful. And repetition is the handmaiden to rote learning.

For more years than I care to admit to, I was afraid to go hunting by myself. Without my husband to direct me around the marsh in the dark or handle the dog, I was convinced I was incapable of survival afield. But as the impracticality of always hunting together (who can find a babysitter other than a husband at 4:30 in the morning) became more apparent, I knew I must learn to venture out alone. Donning hunting attire laid out the night before to prevent dark-room fumble, I was releasing the dog from his pen not more than ten-minutes after the alarm had gone off. With six checks to my breast pocket for my license, another reexamination of the shells in each side pocket (duck loads in the right side, goose loads in the left), I was happy I had not spent the time to stop for coffee—I certainly didn't need the extra buzz. There was a half-hour's drive to the marsh and then a ten-minute marsh walk for this morning pass shoot at black ducks. There sure seemed to be more ditches in the marsh to cross than I remembered, and it did seem unusually dark. I realized that I had forgotten to borrow Ed's watch with the little light in it so I would know when the legal shooting time had arrived. I'd have to estimate how much time had transpired since my last glance at the car clock. I could do that, couldn't I? (What a Doubting Dolly I was becoming.)

I waited in my spot and heard the whistle of wings and saw the speeding dots pass before me. It must be time now. The dog was quivering next to me. I saw the perfect shot coming. I fired, and the duck tumbled and bounced on the ground—across the big creek. I sent the dog. But the dog was not trained to do his fancy retrieves, like across the big creek, for me, only for Ed. And I had to send him again and again. When the dog finally made it to the other side of the creek he couldn't find the duck. And then I began to doubt where I thought it had fallen, and then to doubt that I had even seen it fall. Maybe I'd shot at an illegal time. It was dark, and my eyes played funny, anticipatory tricks in that light and with those high expectations. What made matters worse is that I had spent so much time trying to get the dog to do the retrieving that the tide had come up to the point that the creek was now totally uncrossable in my hip-boots. Now I had to go find a boat. I spent the next hour or so borrowing a friend's boat, paddling to the other side of the creek, and scouting for my duck. It would have been so nice if my first time out alone I had come back with dinner. But it was not to be. The friend who lent me the boat did tell me sometime later that their dog had found a half disintegrated duck in that part of the marsh several days later. Maybe it was mine.

I had hunted that marsh for three years with Ed before doing it myself. Nothing could have been more mechanical. But of course nothing interesting in life is truly mechanical. The duck will fall in a difficult location to reach, the dog will balk at the directions, the phone will ring in the middle of rolling out the pastry dough, the child will demand attention when the venison is ready to serve. Practice has only made it all as good as it can be. And these menus cannot guarantee that you will reach the total nirvana of perfectly executed game dinners without still having some moments of doubt. Let this listing of suggestions at least offer you the security that basically you know what you're doing.

Game dinners cannot always be planned well in advance. When the first bird of the season has been shot and it seems sacrilege to freeze him, this is not the time to start ordering walnut oil from a catalog or searching your gourmet shops for porcini mushrooms. And certainly alongside the importance of practicing good techniques should be the stress on using good ingredients. Spending the time and money is worth it for bettering the meal and is the very least a cook can do. Remember, the hunter has probably spent three times the money and time to get the critter to the kitchen than you have by stocking good brandy.

For me the fall season becomes a time for "laying in" supplies and "putting up" homemade items to assist when preparing game. This preparation will also make the cooking of game menus very easy.

Here are some things to buy and keep around:

Fresh herbs—Buy the little plants that come in cheap plastic containers for a few dollars and use the leaves without care or worry to the health of the plant. When the leaves are gone, buy another plant.

Dried wild mushrooms—Most gourmet shops have them, and their earthy taste goes much better with the flavor of game than the rubber mushrooms found in grocery stores.

Unsalted butter—Salt was used to mask flavor. We don't want to mask flavor and don't need to add salt to the diet. So better to use unsalted butter.

Birds Eye Tiny Tender Peas—They are almost as good as the fresh ones.

Pepperidge Farm pastry sheets—This is the best store-bought pastry dough. (But still will not compare to well-made, homemade pastry.)

Good cooking oils—A good green olive oil, a walnut, or a hazelnut are good oils and can be purchased through catalogs and in gourmet shops. The walnut and hazelnut oils will go rancid if you don't use them up after five months or so. Since they are expensive, it might be worth splitting a bottle with a friend.

Sun-dried tomatoes—Cintra and I have arguments about exactly how difficult to find, and expensive, sun-dried tomatoes are. I think very and she thinks not at all. In either case they are so wonderful and have so many uses, they're worth accumulating no matter what. They can be found in gourmet shops or Italian grocery stores.

Wild rice—Wild rice is a classic with game and always a good idea to have around. I don't care for the mixed brown and wild rice, but this is a matter of taste.

Interesting liqueurs and brandy—They will turn a dull item into something very interesting and are fun to play with.

Juniper berries—These seem to be listed in every game cookbook and are among the items I think worth laying in.

Here are some things to make and keep around:

Veal stock—It is worth it; it is worth it; it is worth it. Veal stock would probably make horse meat taste good. It cannot be bought. It can be frozen.

Chicken stock—Although chicken stock can be bought, it is better homemade; it has less salt for one thing. If you must buy chicken stock, and you live in an area where College Inn brand is available, we recommend it.

Jellies—Good homemade jellies add not only an oft-needed taste but style to an otherwise flat game dinner. Two of my favorites are beach plum and rose-hip.

Breads—Having homemade herb bread around can do the same as the homemade jellies—really add class to the meal. Squishy white bread does not seem to have the same effect.

Compound butter—Several different compound butters are listed in this book and all can be kept in the freezer for at least a couple weeks. They are good for those last-minute attempts at making a dinner *ooh-la-la*. Also, provides a good vehicle for freezing some of the hard-to-get fresh herbs.

Homemade mayonnaise—This is good to have on hand to use on leftover game.

MAYONNAISE

1 tbsp. vinegar
2 tsp. prepared mustard
½ tsp. salt
¼ tsp. ground pepper
3 egg yolks
2 cups oil (olive or corn oil)

In a bowl put vinegar, mustard, salt, and pepper. Whisk to dissolve the salt. Add the egg yolks and whisk 1 minute till frothy. Add the oil very slowly, in dribbles, whisking all the while. Dribble the oil in for at least the first ½ cup. You may add it faster as the mayonnaise thickens. If the mixture is too thick, add a little hot water to thin. This will also slightly poach the eggs and keep the mayonnaise from separating. When all is combined, you have a mayonnaise which now can be seasoned to your own taste. Adjust the salt, pepper, and mustard. It is now mayonnaise, and you may consider adding lemon juice, herbs, parsley, or watercress. Be sure to combine any added herbs in warm water as they will not dissolve in all that oil.

What equipment to obtain is, I believe, truly a personal decision. In general, I don't believe in purchasing expensive equipment until the level of use warrants the cost. It irritates me when I watch professional cooks on television dictate to me how to poach a salmon when they are casually heaving around their 3½-foot long poacher. Very few people have a 3½-foot long poacher or the stove to accommodate it, much less the wherewithal to purchase such items. Better the TV cook should tell us how to poach in the dishwasher or use the turkey roaster. There are a few items, however, which are important to know about because of their particular usefulness with game. These I list below.

Good poultry shears—These are a handy item not only for cutting up cooked birds but for cleaning a bird (cuts off feet and neck).

Strawberry huller—These are nice little pinchers that are designed to pull the green tops off strawberries, but actually seem better suited to pulling the pinfeathers out of early-season ducks.

Small roasting pans—In general, meat cooks better in a pan which nicely accommodates it, not too big or small. One woodcock in a turkey roaster doesn't work well at all. Since many game birds are smaller than grocery store birds, it may be necessary to acquire an especially small roasting pan.

Good, sharp knives—A good set of very sharp knives sounds like the pepper grinder suggestion. But I cannot overstress how much more pleasant working on a piece of meat can be if done with a variety of sizes of sharp knives that are well suited to your hand. When John Hewitt comes to visit, his house present is to sharpen my knives, and no better present could there be.

Meat grinders—Many game cookbooks contain recipes for venison sausage or ground venison burger. Easy for them to talk about. I spent one whole evening till 12:30 at night trying to get venison through my handy-dandy meat grinder. I think I ended up in tears, but I learned several things. I had chosen the mediocre leg and upper neck pieces to grind, which contain a great deal of sinew. A logical choice since those cuts are not good for much else. But just as we would have a difficult time chewing that meat, so did the grinder. A big meatlocker operation has a machine which actually removes the sinew first. Using a better cut of meat, un-aged and never frozen (so it would not be tender or mushy) and fitting the grinder with sharper blades and a tighter fitting plate might have made the procedure possible. But much easier is to hand chop the meat or put it in the food processor. Or better still, con some butcher to do it for you.

Smokers—Now that I have made the statement that I don't appreciate books and professional cooks recommending cooking methods that require expensive equipment, I will make the exception. I think smokers are great fun for cooking game, and I suggest buying one even if you can't see using it very much. Yes, yes, I say don't buy until you're sure of the amount of usage the equipment will get, and we all do own twice as much stuff as we need. But smokers add an entirely new dimension to the taste of game (unlike such items as an electric plucker), can double as an outdoor grill, and can be used for meat other than game. I think you'll find it is used more than anticipated.

Two general suggestion to bear in mind about equipment:

Food processors—These handy machines should be used sparingly on starches, only an occasional zip here, zip there. They can break down starches so they are liquefied and lose any thickening capability. This is most significant to keep in mind when making a soup when rice or pasta is used specifically to thicken.

Ovens cook very differently—You, undoubtedly, have heard this before, but I have been particularly reminded of it when setting the cooking times for the recipes in this book. Cintra and I almost had a row over the cooking time for crème brûlée due (I think) to the differences in our ovens. She kept reiterating that crème brûlée is to be just barely firm, not, as some chefs suggest, pudding-like. I knew that, but my cooking time was still 10 minutes longer than she had suggested in the recipe, and I found it nearly impossible to caramelize the brown sugar on top. I've cooked in ovens that take a long time to heat up, that don't retain the heat, and that never get super hot—all these factors affect the total amount of time something cooks and underlines the necessity of preheating and perhaps even using an auxiliary thermometer.

Once the suitable ingredients and equipment are assembled, there are those happy moments in the kitchen. There are also those unhappy moments in the kitchen. I always feel particularly bad when a game dinner doesn't come out. It seems such a waste. But everyone, yes everyone, has failures. Cintra taught me early on to pretend that the "failure" was actually something you meant to do, and that with a little doctoring, it will be as good or better than the original recipe. Very sound advice—but some of my failures have been beyond all repair. To aid in the prevention of failure we make a few suggestions:

Game birds should always be trussed. They just don't have enough fat content to be cooked with an open cavity.

Game continues to cook after it has been removed from the heat. This is, of course, true of all things but particularly true of the high-in-protein/low-in-fat ratio of game.

A good rule of thumb is, the smaller the bird the higher the oven temperature.

Precisely because ovens do vary in their cooking characteristics, it is wise to learn to determine the doneness of meat by touch (springiness when pressed or looseness of a leg), smell (you know when its beginning to burn), and sight (coloring and nice oozing juices). To rely on a recipe's stated time for cooking should be for the purposes of determining an approximate length for the cocktail hour and not much more.

Salt and pepper are more effective as flavoring if added after cooking.

Simmering is the waltz, boiling the polka. You should see only an occasional bubble when simmering.

You can always cook something more, but not less.

To "butterfly" a bird is to do this:

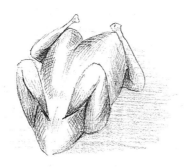

What you want to achieve here is a flattened bird with a uniform thickness. First cut out the backbone entirely, then bend the legs and wings as illustrated and insert the leg ends into two slits you have cut just below the breast meat. Press down on the entire bird to flatten. There should be no need to snap the keel bone in a smaller bird.

The purpose of butterflying is to make the cooking speedier and more even.

Stuffing a bird has the effect of putting a sponge in it. If the stuffing is dry, juices will be sucked from the bird. This may be desirable if the bird was poorly cleaned or particularly bloody. If the stuffing is very moist it can add juices. Unless the bird's cavity was immaculately clean, I suggest eating stuffing that has been cooked separately.

Many general cookbooks that contain game recipes are often referring to pen-raised game rather than wild game. The techniques and cooking times are in certain cases quite different from the pen-raised to the wild, and this should be taken into account. Ducks and geese are most noticeably different; the pen-raised varieties are fatty and often very greasy. This is not true of a properly cleaned wild duck or goose.

For some reason, game more than other meat seems to cool down very quickly, so it is particularly important to serve game on heated plates and platters.

Serving a reasonably sized portion arranged in a careful and pretty fashion on the plate is one of those signs that says you know what you're doing. Just as color photographs in food magazines have been added to create a feeling of sensuality and ambiance rather than instruction, this also is the purpose, I think, of a beautifully presented meal.

Many fine and long-time hunters never become able to create their own hunting expeditions. They are perfectly capable of hiring guides and following through the woods and pulling the trigger or simply following in the footsteps of grandfather. It is becoming a rarer commodity to find the hunter who can figure out new territory to hunt and persist in hunting there until the whereabouts of the game is consistently known. This ability takes much time for sure; I have yet to accomplish it. Certainly, too, there are many fine cooks who produce wonderful meals by simply following the recipes. But for me the greatest fun is in the new creation, the improvised and the successful experiment. It is also why the nature of game cooking—unstructured, unpredictable, and full of room to create—is so exciting to me. I only hope that my excitement is yours, too.

Cooking Fish: The Beauty of Simplicity

S ince cooking is very involved with lifestyle, this cookbook is truly a reflection of my style of life. I am a fisherman and a cook and cannot separate that, which is why this book contains only recipes for fish that are part of a fisherman's lifestyle. Nor do I wish to make a separation, for each enhances the other and perhaps dictates to the other occasionally, too. The simplicity of the recipes and menus in this book presumes this combination. I want my recipes simple enough so I can spend the day fishing. I always will prefer a grilling technique for fish; it's quick and makes the fish taste perfect. Yet I will not deny my love of cooking and so will use imagination and variation in the menu combinations or in a specific dessert or vegetable rather than on the fish.

This simplicity of lifestyle, in both cooking and fishing, seems compatible with the fashion, too. Right now the movement is away from gluttony, both in the amount you fish for and the amount you eat. Many years ago now, I can remember a foggy day on Nantucket with Mace, Ted, Knowles, and Ed. Mace and I were relegated to the house with tiny babies and the others went fishing in our new Whaler. I'll never forget the car pulling into the driveway with the boat trailered behind it and the snapper blues pouring out of the cooler and live-well and splashing onto the decks of the boat. We cleaned and foil-wrapped until two in the morning. What a lot of work! There are still many bluefish to be had, but I think Ed and Ted would now find some way to better control Knowles and themselves—I think.

I used to wonder when I was a child why I had to clean my plate because there were starving children in China. How were the Chinese children going to get what was left on my plate? This resistance to the adult's guilt trip has stood me well in later years when the fashion has gone to eating less, more simply, and staying thin. Eating fish is extremely good for you and usually has far fewer calories than meat. It is thought now that some fish even aid in preventing cancer. I have tried in this book not to erode the natural goodness or limited caloric content of fish by including a lot of heavy sauces and gooey desserts in the menus. These really aren't very compatible with fish. Fashion has complemented my lifestyle and affected this book in one other regard. Remember the days when Dad sat down to a meal and, anticipating meat, potatoes, vegetables, and dessert, would question the solvency of his marriage if he was presented with just two items on his plate? Now real men will eat just quiche and salad for Sunday's supper. I believe menus have finally gotten away from the four-item syndrome and are free to accommodate the situation and appetite.

The fisherman in me has definitely added a sense of respect for the fish in both my fishing and my cooking. I put the ones back that I do not intend to eat. I try to keep the fish cooled down from the minute he is killed till he is cooked. The sharpest knives are used and the greatest care taken in cleaning him. And the menus here presumed a certain level of concentration and respect for their preparation. It may seem in many cases that you must resemble a short-order cook to assemble these menus. Cooking everything at once and demanding that it all come to the table at the same time and remain hot requires the kind of focus on cooking that I relish. This may mean the second martini must sit untouched in the living room with the guests. But the results of such concentration in the kitchen can produce such a nice event at the table that the guests surely will forgive you your absence. It is true that advance preparation of some of the basics can make a meal with guests less hectic. Also just having some basic items in the freezer or refrigerator can make the smallmouth bass that suddenly appears for dinner that much more exciting. Making a batch of basil compound-butter and freezing it just as the basil comes into your garden or making extra homemade mayonnaise when you're throwing together a chicken salad are good habits.

Just as Mr. Fish has given you the ultimate in fishing and cooking pleasure, it is truly wonderful to be able to pass along some of that pleasure to guests or family. Spend the time and do it right. Advance preparation is one of the keys to fine cooking. To have on hand ingredients that can take an ordinary meal and make it a gourmet meal is straightforward smart. But to also spend a small amount of time and effort to prepare some basic items, such as homemade mayonnaise or vinaigrette, so they are on hand also, can begin to push you into the category of a fine cook.

When we were in Alaska last we heard about a dish that the Eskimos prepare and have on hand well in advance. It is called "stinky heads." In plastic gallon drums that had previously held the winter's supply of cooking oil, they gather the heads of all the salmon they can find, close the bucket, and bury it for a couple of weeks. They open it and eat the "stinky heads" when they really smell the fish odor permeating from the ground. This chapter is not suggesting preparation of "stinky heads." (As the Eskimo woman said, "Stinky heads make your stomach growl.") Listed below are just some nice benign things you should know how to make or have on hand.

RISOTTO

4 oz. unsalted butter or a mixture
of butter and olive oil
2 onions, chopped very fine
1½ cups Italian arborio rice
4 to 5 cups of hot fluid, either stock
(chicken or veal are both fine),
water, or a combination of both
Salt and pepper

In a heavy-bottomed, wide saucepan, heat butter. Sauté onions until translucent. Add rice. Cook, stirring until it becomes very white, shiny, and very hot to touch. Then, over medium to high heat, add only enough stock so that the rice is just covered. Holding the handle of the saucepan, firmly swish the rice around and around. Do this every 2 to 3 minutes, keeping a low simmer going in the pot in between. This is so the rice won't stick. (If you weaken and stir the rice, then you must continue to stir until done.) As soon as you can distinguish the grains of rice again, then add another ½ cup of fluid. Keep swirling the pot and adding more fluid as it becomes absorbed. Taste when you feel it is nearly finished. It should be firm to the bite, with a tender, creamy texture—not too dry and not too runny. Season with salt and pepper. If using saffron powder, dissolve in hot broth or water and add half-way through or later, depending on how strong a saffron taste you desire. The nearer to the end it is added, the stronger the taste. Parmesan and extra butter can be added at the end of the cooking.

BREADCRUMBS

You can use either fresh or dried French or Italian bread. If you need to dry the bread further, place slices on cookie sheets in a 300° oven until just hard. Break into pieces and blend in the food processor with the steel blade until fine. Then shake through a strainer. The bread crumbs that result are all of an even size and will give a better texture when cooked.

BASIC VINAIGRETTE

2 tbsp. vinegar
½ cup good olive oil
1 tsp. prepared mustard
Salt and pepper
Herbs of your choice

Combine ingredients in a blender and zip on high for a second or two.

Index